Real Estate-Backed Securities

Frank J. Fabozzi, CFA

John N. Dunlevy, CFA

Published by Frank J. Fabozzi Associates

FJF
To my beautiful wife Donna and to my children
Francesco, Patricia, and Karly

JND
To my lovely wife Dana and to my sons
Jack and Michael

© 2001 By Frank J. Fabozzi Associates
New Hope, Pennsylvania

This publication is designed to provide accurate and authoritative information in regard to the subject matter covered. It is sold with the understanding that the publisher is not engaged in rendering legal, accounting, or other professional services.

ISBN: 1-883249-96-1

Table of Contents

About the Authors

Frank J. Fabozzi is editor of the *Journal of Portfolio Management* and an Adjunct Professor of Finance at Yale University's School of Management. He is a Chartered Financial Analyst and Certified Public Accountant. Dr. Fabozzi is on the board of directors of the Guardian Life family of funds and the BlackRock complex of funds. He earned a doctorate in economics from the City University of New York in 1972 and in 1994 received an honorary doctorate of Humane Letters from Nova Southeastern University. Dr. Fabozzi is a Fellow of the International Center for Finance at Yale University.

John Dunlevy is a Senior Portfolio Manager at Beacon Hill Asset Management (Summit, NJ) where he is responsible for credit-related investments in mortgage-backed, asset-backed, and commercial mortgage-backed securities. He also serves as the firm's Director of Research. Prior to joining Beacon Hill Asset Management, Mr. Dunlevy was a Director and Senior Portfolio Manager at Hyperion Capital Management, a Director and Mortgage Sector Manager at TIAA-CREF, and an Assistant Vice President in the Capital Markets Group of Sumitomo Bank. Mr. Dunlevy has contributed chapters to several industry reference books and is an Adjunct Professor of Finance at the College of St. Elizabeth in Morristown, NJ. He has a BS degree in Accounting from Boston College, and an MBA degree from Columbia University. Mr. Dunlevy is a CFA (Chartered Financial Analyst) and a CPA (Certified Public Accountant).

Chapter 1

Why It Is Important to Understand Real Estate-Backed Securities

T he largest debt market in the United States is the mortgage market. A major innovation in the mortgage market has been the development of a wide range of residential and commercial mortgage designs from which borrowers can select. Regardless of the type of mortgage design, as a stand alone investment they typically have unattractive characteristics for both institutional and retail investors. From the perspective of investors, the major innovation in the mortgage market has been the development of securities backed by real estate mortgage loans. Since these securities use mortgages as collateral, they are referred to as *mortgage-backed securities* or, more generally, *real estate-backed securities*. Our purpose in this book is to discuss these securities.

There are two reasons why it is important to understand these securities. The first is that the creation of real estate-backed securities is the dominant force in the development of the excellent housing finance market in the United States. Understanding the innovations in the creation of real estate-backed securities provides investment bankers and U.S. policymakers with insights into future developments that will further improve the mortgage market. Policymakers in other countries will find an understanding of the development of these securities to be essential in fostering a market in their country.

As important as this understanding is to the future development of the market for residential and commercial mortgages, it is not the reason we wrote this book. We were motivated by the second reason — real estate-backed securities dominate the fixed income market. Here's the support for this view.

Consider one of the most popular fixed income indexes followed by institutional investors, the Lehman Brothers' U.S. Aggregate Index. Exhibit 1 shows the sectors of this index and the percentage of each sector in the index on December 4, 2000. *Mortgage passthrough securities* included in the index are securities guaranteed by a federally related agency[1] — the Government National Mortgage Association (Ginnie Mae) — and securities issued by two government sponsored enterprises — Federal National Mortgage Association (Fannie Mae) and the Federal Home Loan Mortgage Corporation (Freddie Mac). These securi-

---

[1] The "agency" sector shown in Exhibit 1 includes debentures issued by all government sponsored enterprises.

ties, discussed in Chapter 3, represent the largest sector of the index, constituting a little more than one-third of the index. Moreover, in the future the Treasury sector is expected to decline because of reductions in the issuance of long-term Treasury securities by the Department of the Treasury combined with buyback programs. For example, in December 1998 the Treasury sector was 38% of the index compared to 27% in December 2000. As the Treasury sector declines, the share of the mortgage passthrough sector will increase. There are some market observers who believe this sector could grow to about half the index.

Add to the mortgage passthrough sector the sector with securities backed by commercial mortgages and the real estate-backed securities component increases to 36% of the Lehman Brothers' Aggregate Index. (We will discuss commercial mortgage-backed securities in Chapter 7.)

We must add one more real estate component: asset-backed securities where the collateral is residential mortgages. In Exhibit 1 we can see that the asset-backed securities sector is 2% of the index. However, this includes asset-backed securities backed by both real estate and non-real estate loans and receivables. Exhibit 2 shows a breakdown as of early December of the sub-sectors within the asset-backed securities sector. The data in the exhibit indicate that the asset-backed securities sector is approximately 1.73% of the Lehman Aggregate index. Of this, approximately one half of 1% is backed by real estate loans — home equity loans and manufactured housing loans. (These products will be covered in Chapter 6.)

Exhibit 1: Sectors and Weight for the Lehman Brothers U.S. Aggregate Index

Sector	Percent of index
Treasury	27%
Agency	10
Mortgage Passthroughs	34
CMBS	2
ABS	2
Corporate	25
Total	100%

Source: Lehman Brothers, *Global Relative Value*, Fixed Income Research, December 4, 2000, PTF-1

Exhibit 2: Detailed Distribution of ABS Types in the Lehman Aggregate Index and the ABS Index

	Percent in Aggregate Index	Percent in ABS Index
Home Equity Loans	0.23%	13.45%
Manufactured Housing Loans	0.24	14.11
Credit Card Receivables	0.75	43.41
Auto Loans	0.27	15.78
Utility (Stranded Costs)	0.23	13.25
Total	1.73%	100.00%

Source: Data provided by Lehman Brothers.

Consequently, a fixed income portfolio manager who is seeking to build a core portfolio to match the characteristics of the Lehman Brothers' Aggregate index must understand real estate-backed securities. Moreover, in recent years we have seen the cross over of corporate buyers into the asset-backed securities market. Those investors must understand products backed by real estate loans. This can be seen in Exhibit 2 which shows the composition of the Lehman Brothers' ABS index. About 28% of the ABS index consists of securities backed by real estate loans.

In constructing a portfolio, active fixed income portfolio managers will depart from the characteristics of an index in order to enhance returns relative to the index. While there are a variety of strategies employed by active managers, one strategy is to look for securities that are not included in the index but are expected to outperform those securities in the index. There are opportunities to do this with real estate-backed securities. This can be done with securities issued by agencies that expose investors to minimal credit risk called *agency collateralized mortgage obligations*. These securities are the subject of Chapter 4. In addition, there are securities — both passthrough securities and collateralized mortgage obligations — issued by private entities that provide return enhancement opportunities for investors willing to accept credit risk. These securities, referred to as *nonagency mortgage-backed securities*, are the subject of Chapter 5.

The bottom line is that a fixed income portfolio manager seeking to build a core portfolio but who is unfamiliar with real estate-backed securities will be at a competitive disadvantage. Moreover, an active manager who is unfamiliar with real estate-backed securities may miss opportunities to enhance return in products that are not part of the index.

For a manager who is managing funds with the objective of satisfying future liabilities or seeking spread income relative to a funding source rather than managing funds against an index, real estate-backed securities are also important to understand. Products such as collateralized mortgage obligations provide an excellent opportunity to construct a portfolio with securities whose cash flows provide a better match against future liabilities.

In Chapters 3 through 7 we will discuss each type of real estate-backed security. In Chapter 2 we cover the raw material in the creation of these securities — mortgage loans. In the last chapter, Chapter 8, we explain and illustrate the state-of-the-art technology for valuing these securities and estimating their interest rate risk.

Chapter 2

Mortgages

A *mortgage loan*, or simply mortgage, is a loan secured by the collateral of some specified real estate property which obliges the borrower to make a predetermined series of payments. The mortgage gives the lender the right if the borrower defaults (i.e., fails to make the contracted payments) to "foreclose" on the loan and seize the property in order to ensure that the debt is paid off. The interest rate on the mortgage loan is called the *mortgage rate* or *contract rate*. Our focus in this book is on residential mortgage loans.

There are many types of mortgages available to borrowers. In this chapter we will describe the types of mortgages that have been used as collateral for a mortgage-backed security.

ALTERNATIVE MORTGAGE DESIGNS

There are many types of mortgage designs. By a *mortgage design* we mean the specification of the interest rate (fixed or floating), the term of the mortgage, and the manner in which the principal is repaid. We summarize the major mortgage designs below.

Fixed-Rate, Level-Payment, Fully Amortized Mortgage

The basic idea behind the design of the fixed-rate, level payment, fully amortized mortgage is that the borrower pays interest and repays principal in equal installments over an agreed-upon period of time, called the maturity or term of the mortgage. The frequency of payment is typically monthly. Each monthly mortgage payment for this mortgage design is due on the first of each month and consists of:

1. interest of $\frac{1}{12}$th of the annual interest rate times the amount of the outstanding mortgage balance at the beginning of the previous month, and
2. a repayment of a portion of the outstanding mortgage balance (principal).

The difference between the monthly mortgage payment and the portion of the payment that represents interest equals the amount that is applied to reduce the outstanding mortgage balance. The monthly mortgage payment is designed so that after the last scheduled monthly payment of the loan is made, the amount of the outstanding mortgage balance is zero (i.e., the mortgage is fully repaid or amortized).

5

Exhibit 1: Amortization Schedule for a Fixed-Rate, Level-Payment, Fully Amortized Mortgage

Mortgage loan: $100,000   Monthly payment: $742.50
Mortgage rate: 8.125%   Term of loan: 30 years (360 months)

Month	Beginning mortgage balance ($)	Monthly payment ($)	Monthly interest ($)	Scheduled principal repayment ($)	Ending mortgage balance ($)
1	100,000.00	742.50	677.08	65.42	99,934.58
2	99,934.58	742.50	676.64	65.86	99,868.72
3	99,868.72	742.50	676.19	66.31	99,802.41
25	98,301.53	742.50	665.58	76.91	98,224.62
26	98,224.62	742.50	665.06	77.43	98,147.19
27	98,147.19	742.50	664.54	77.96	98,069.23
74	93,849.98	742.50	635.44	107.05	93,742.93
75	93,742.93	742.50	634.72	107.78	93,635.15
76	93,635.15	742.50	633.99	108.51	93,526.64
141	84,811.77	742.50	574.25	168.25	84,643.52
142	84,643.52	742.50	573.11	169.39	84,474.13
143	84,474.13	742.50	571.96	170.54	84,303.59
184	76,446.29	742.50	517.61	224.89	76,221.40
185	76,221.40	742.50	516.08	226.41	75,994.99
186	75,994.99	742.50	514.55	227.95	75,767.04
233	63,430.19	742.50	429.48	313.02	63,117.17
234	63,117.17	742.50	427.36	315.14	62,802.03
235	62,802.03	742.50	425.22	317.28	62,484.75
289	42,200.92	742.50	285.74	456.76	41,744.15
290	41,744.15	742.50	282.64	459.85	41,284.30
291	41,284.30	742.50	279.53	462.97	40,821.33
321	25,941.42	742.50	175.65	566.85	25,374.57
322	25,374.57	742.50	171.81	570.69	24,803.88
323	24,803.88	742.50	167.94	574.55	24,229.32
358	2,197.66	742.50	14.88	727.62	1,470.05
359	1,470.05	742.50	9.95	732.54	737.50
360	737.50	742.50	4.99	737.50	0.00

To illustrate this mortgage design, consider a 30-year (360-month) $100,000 mortgage with a mortgage rate of 8.125%. The monthly mortgage payment would be $742.50. Exhibit 1 shows for selected months how each monthly mortgage payment is divided between interest and repayment of principal. At the beginning of month 1, the mortgage balance is $100,000, the amount of the original loan. The mortgage payment for month 1 includes interest on the $100,000 borrowed for the month. Since the interest rate is 8.125%, the monthly interest rate is 0.0067708 (0.08125 divided by 12). Interest for month 1 is therefore $677.08 ($100,000 times 0.0067708). The $65.42 difference between the monthly mortgage payment of $742.50 and the interest of $677.08 is the portion of the monthly mortgage payment that represents repayment of principal. The $65.42 in month 1 reduces the mortgage balance.

The mortgage balance at the end of month 1 (beginning of month 2) is then $99,934.58 ($100,000 minus $65.42). The interest for the second monthly mortgage payment is $676.64, the monthly interest rate (0.0067708) times the mortgage balance at the beginning of month 2 ($99,934.58). The difference between the $742.50 monthly mortgage payment and the $676.64 interest is $65.86, representing the amount of the mortgage balance paid off with that monthly mortgage payment. Notice that the last mortgage payment in month 360 is sufficient to pay off the remaining mortgage balance.

As Exhibit 1 clearly shows, *the portion of the monthly mortgage payment applied to interest declines each month and the portion applied to reducing the mortgage balance increases.* The reason for this is that as the mortgage balance is reduced with each monthly mortgage payment, the interest on the mortgage balance declines. Since the monthly mortgage payment is fixed, an increasingly larger portion of the monthly payment is applied to reduce the principal in each subsequent month.

Servicing Fee and the Cash Flows
Every mortgage loan must be serviced. Servicing of a mortgage loan involves collecting monthly payments and forwarding proceeds to owners of the loan, sending payment notices to mortgagors, reminding mortgagors when payments are overdue, maintaining records of principal balances, administering an escrow balance for real estate taxes and insurance purposes, initiating foreclosure proceedings if necessary, and furnishing tax information to mortgagors when applicable.

The servicing fee is a portion of the mortgage rate. If the mortgage rate is 8.125% and the servicing fee is 50 basis points, then the investor receives interest of 7.625%. The interest rate that the investor receives is said to be the *net interest* or *net coupon.* The servicing fee is commonly called the *servicing spread.*

The dollar amount of the servicing fee declines over time as the mortgage amortizes. This is true for not only the mortgage design that we have just described, but for all mortgage designs.

Prepayments and Cash Flow Uncertainty
Our illustration of the cash flows from a fixed-rate, level-payment, fully amortized mortgage assumes that the homeowner does not pay off any portion of the mortgage balance prior to the scheduled due date. But homeowners do pay off all or part of their mortgage balance prior to the maturity date. Payments made in excess of the scheduled principal repayments are called *prepayments.* We'll look more closely at the factors that affect prepayment behavior in Chapter 3.

The effect of prepayments is that the amount and timing of the cash flows from a mortgage are not known with certainty. This risk is referred to as *prepayment risk*. For example, all that the investor in a $100,000, 8.125% 30-year FHA-insured mortgage knows is that as long as the loan is outstanding, interest will be received and the principal will be repaid at the scheduled date each month; then at the end of the 30 years, the investor would have received $100,000 in principal payments. What the investor does not know — the uncertainty — is for how long the loan will be outstanding, and therefore what the timing of the principal payments will be. This is true for all mortgage loans, not just fixed-rate, level-payment, fully amortized mortgages.

Adjustable-Rate Mortgages

While most mortgage-backed securities are backed by fixed-rate mortgages, adjustable-rate mortgages (ARMs) have become more and more popular among home buyers. The popularity of ARMs in the 1990s can be attributed to the historically steep yield curve in the early part of the decade. Many first time home buyers find an ARM to be more affordable in the mortgage's early years and are willing to take on the risk of higher rates in the future. ARMs have also gained popularity in the investment community since the early 1990s. Depository institutions found ARMs provided a better match against their liabilities. In 1988, there was only one mutual fund which would invest the majority of its assets in securities backed by ARMs and it had about $20 million in assets. By the early 1990s, there were at least 25 ARM mutual funds with total assets in excess of $20 billion.

The Basic Structure

As the name implies, an ARM has an adjustable or floating coupon instead of a fixed one. The coupon adjusts periodically — monthly, semiannually, or annually. Some ARMs even have coupons that adjust every three years or five years. The coupon formula for an ARM is specified in terms of an index level plus a margin. We'll discuss the common indices that are used below. The margin is typically 2% to 3%.

At origination, the mortgage usually has an initial rate for an initial period (*teaser period*) which is slightly below the rate specified by the coupon formula. This is called a *teaser rate* and makes it easier for first time home buyers to qualify for the loan. At the end of the teaser period, the loan rate is reset based on the coupon formula. Once the loan comes out of its teaser period and resets based on the coupon formula, it is said to be *fully indexed*.

To protect the homeowner from interest rate shock, there are caps or ceilings imposed on the coupon adjustment level. There are periodic caps and lifetime caps. The *periodic cap* limits the amount of coupon reset upward or downward from one period to another. The *lifetime cap* is the maximum absolute level for the coupon rate that the loan can reset to for the life of the mortgage.

Since the borrower prefers to be warned in advance of any interest rate adjustment, the coupon determination actually has to take place prior to the coupon reset. This is called the *lookback period*. A typical lookback period for CMT ARMs is 45 days, meaning that the CMT rate 45 days before the anniversary date is being used to reset the coupon for the next period.

There are ARMs that can be converted into fixed-rate mortgages at the option of the borrower. These ARMS, called *convertible ARMs,* reduce the cost of refinancing. When converted, the new loan rate may be either (1) a rate determined by the lender or (2) a market-determined rate. A borrower can typically convert at any time between the first and fifth anniversary dates from the origination date.

Due to the caps and conversion feature, the value of an ARM and securities backed by ARMs must be determined using the methodology described in Chapter 8. This is because the methodology described, option-adjusted spread, considers the potential path of interest rates over the life of the ARM and how that path affects the coupon rate after adjusting for periodic and lifetime caps and whether the borrower will exercise the conversion option.

Indices Used

Two categories of indices have been used in ARMs: (1) market determined rates and (2) calculated cost of funds for thrifts. The index will have an important impact on the performance of an ARM and its value. The most common market determined rates used are the 1-year, 3-year, or 5-year Constant Maturity Treasury (CMT) and 3-month or 6-month London Interbank Offered Rate (LIBOR).

The cost of funds index for thrifts is calculated based on the monthly weighted average interest cost for liabilities of thrifts. The most popular is the Eleventh Federal Home Loan Bank Board District Cost of Funds Index (COFI). About 25% of ARMs are indexed to this reference rate. The Eleventh District includes the states of California, Arizona, and Nevada. The cost of funds is calculated by first computing the monthly interest expenses for all thrifts included in the Eleventh District. The interest expenses are summed and then divided by the average of the beginning and ending monthly balance. The index value is reported with a one month lag. For example, June's Eleventh District COFI is reported in July. The mortgage rate for a mortgage based on the Eleventh District COFI is usually reset based on the previous month's reported index rate. For example, if the reset date is August, the index rate reported in July will be used to set the mortgage rate. Consequently, there is a two month lag by the time the average cost of funds is reflected in the mortgage rate. This obviously is an advantage to the borrower when interest rates are rising and a disadvantage to the investor. The opposite is true when interest rates are falling.

Describing ARMs

The attributes needed to describe an ARM are the teaser rate, teaser period, index, margin, reset frequency, periodic cap, and lifetime cap. Of course, maturity is important too, but almost all ARMs are 30-year loans, unlike 5-year, 7-year, 15-year, and 20-year fixed-rate loans.

For example, a "6% 1-year CMT + 3% ARM with 2/12 caps" means the loan has a 6% coupon for the first year. It will reset the second year coupon to the then 1-year CMT index rate plus 3% on the anniversary date subject to the 2% periodic cap and 12% lifetime cap constraints. If the prevailing CMT rate is 4.8%, the coupon will simply reset to 7.8% (4.8% + 3%). If the prevailing CMT rate is 5.5%, the coupon can only reset to 8% (the old 6% rate + the 2% periodic cap, not 8.5% — the sum of the prevailing rate plus the 3% margin) because the 2% periodic cap only allows a maximum of 2% movement (plus or minus) in the coupon rate from one period to another. The 12% lifetime cap limits the coupon to 12% during the life of the loan.

Agency ARM Programs

In the next chapter we will discuss mortgage passthrough securities issued by three agencies — Ginnie Mae, Fannie Mae, and Freddie Mac, These agencies have several standardized ARM programs to promote uniformity and liquidity in TBA trading of passthrough securities backed by a pool of ARMs (although ARMs also trade on a specified pool basis). The three most common programs are summarized in Exhibit 2.

While the programs in Exhibit 2 are the most common standardized ARM programs sponsored by the agencies, there are many variations. For instance, there are 3-year CMT ARMs that reset every three years off the 3-year CMT index and 5-year CMT ARMs that reset every five years off the 5-year CMT index. There are also 6-month Treasury bill ARMs that reset off the 6-month Treasury bill rate semiannually with a 1% periodic cap. There are semiannual and annual COFI ARMs that work exactly like CMT ARMs. There are also quarterly reset LIBOR ARMs that reset off the 3-month moving average LIBOR.

There exists another group of hybrid fixed/ARM loans that look like both fixed- and adjustable-rate mortgages. For instance, a "10/1 loan" has a fixed coupon for ten years, then it will convert to a 1-year CMT ARM starting the 11th year. A "7/23 loan" is a fixed rate loan that will reset only once for the life of the loan at the end of the 7th year to the prevailing market rate which will then be fixed for the remaining 23 years.

Exhibit 2: Agency ARM Programs

	PROGRAMS			
	Ginnie ARM	CMT ARM	COFI ARM	LIBOR ARM
Agency	GNMA	FNMA FHLMC	FNMA FHLMC	FNMA FHLMC
Teaser Period	1 year	1 year	6 months	6 months
Reset Frequency	annually	annually	monthly	semi-annually
Index	1-year CMT	1-year CMT	11th COFI	6-month LIBOR
Margin	2%	2% to 4%	2% to 4%	2% to 4%
Periodic Cap	1%	2%	none	1%
Lifetime Cap	teaser rate +5%	teaser rate +6%	teaser rate +6%	teaser rate +6%
Lookback	45 days	45 days	3 months	45 days
Convertability	No	Yes/No	No	Yes/No

Balloon Mortgages

In a *balloon mortgage*, the borrower is given long-term financing by the lender, but at specified future dates the contract rate is renegotiated. Thus, the lender is providing long-term funds for what is effectively a short-term borrowing, how short depending on the frequency of the renegotiation period. Effectively it is a short-term balloon loan in which the lender agrees to provide financing for the remainder of the term of the mortgage. The balloon payment is the original amount borrowed less the amount amortized. Thus, in a balloon mortgage, the actual maturity is shorter than the stated maturity.

Two-Step Mortgages

Akin to the idea of a balloon loan with a refinancing option for the borrower is a fixed-rate mortgage with a single rate reset at some point prior to maturity. Unlike a refinancing option, this rate reset occurs without specific action on the part of the borrower.

Unlike in balloon mortgages, the rate reset on the two-step mortgage does not consist of a repayment of the initial loan and the origination of a new one; thus, a 30-year two-step mortgage has a 30-year final maturity, rather than the shorter final maturity of a balloon mortgage. Essentially, then, the two-step mortgage is an adjustable-rate mortgage with a single reset.

Growing Equity Mortgages

A *growing equity mortgage* (GEM) is a fixed-rate mortgage whose monthly mortgage payments increase over time. The initial monthly mortgage payment is the same as for a level payment mortgage. The higher monthly mortgage payments are applied to paying off the principal. As a result, the principal of a GEM is repaid faster. For example, a 30-year $100,000 GEM loan with a contract rate of 8.125% might call for an initial monthly payment of $742.50 (the same as a level-payment 8.125% 30-year mortgage loan). However, the GEM payment would gradually increase, and the GEM might be fully paid in only 15 years.

Tiered Payment Mortgages

Another mortgage design with a fixed rate and a monthly payment that graduates over time is the *tiered payment mortgage* (TPM). The initial monthly mortgage payments are below those of a traditional mortgage. There is no negative amortization because withdrawals are made from a buydown account to supplement the initial monthly payments to cover the shortfall of interest. The buydown account is established at the time the loan is originated by the borrower, lender, or a third party such as a relative or business associate.

CONVENTIONAL VERSUS INSURED MORTGAGES

When the lender makes the loan based on the credit of the borrower and on the collateral for the mortgage, the mortgage is said to be a *conventional mortgage*. The lender may require the borrower to obtain mortgage insurance to insure against default by the borrower. It is usually required by lenders on loans with a loan-to-value (LTV) ratio greater than 80%.The amount of insurance is based on the original LTV and the borrower's credit. The amount insured may decline as the LTV ratio declines. The cost of the insurance can be paid by the borrower upfront or on a monthly basis.

There are two forms of this insurance: insurance provided a government agency and private mortgage insurance. The federal agencies that provide this insurance to qualified borrowers are the Federal Housing Administration (FHA), the Veterans Administration (VA), and the Rural Development Administration (RDA). Private mortgage insurance can be obtained from a mortgage insurance company.

Another form of insurance may be required for mortgages on properties that are located in geographical areas where the occurrence of natural disasters such as floods and earthquakes is higher than usual. This type of insurance is called *hazard insurance*.

CONFORMING VERSUS NONCONFORMING MORTGAGES

In the next three chapters we will discuss mortgage-backed securities issued by agencies of the U.S. government and private entities. In order for a loan to be included in a pool of loans backing an agency security, it must meet specified underwriting standards. These standards set forth the maximum size of the loan, the loan documentation required, the maximum loan-to-value ratio, and whether or not insurance is required.

If a loan satisfies the underwriting standards for inclusion as collateral for an agency mortgage-backed security, it is called a *conforming mortgage*. If a loan fails to satisfy the underwriting standards, it is called a *nonconforming mortgage*. Loans that fail to quality as a conforming mortgage because they exceed the maximum loan size are called *jumbo mortgages*. Loans that fail to qualify because of documentation are called either "no doc" or "low doc" mortgages, the former indicating that the lender did not require documentation to verify the borrower's income and the latter that there was only limited documentation to verify the borrower's income.

LOAN PURPOSE

There are also loans based on the purpose of the loan. Understanding the purpose of a loan can better help investors understand the potential prepayment behavior of borrowers with such loans that back a security.

Here are some examples. A loan taken out to finance the purchase of a new home is called a *purchase loan*. This type of loan is a steady source of supply during periods of prepayment uncertainty. That is, these loans represent the typical mobility component of housing pools. Purchase loans often result from housing turnover resulting from new household formation, homeowners, trading-up or down, divorce, death, retirement, etc. A loan to refinance an existing mortgage is called a *refinancing loan* or *refi loan*. When the loan is used to allow the borrower to withdraw equity from a home that has appreciated, it is called an *equity take-out loan*.

A loan used for financing a home purchased because the borrower was relocated by a corporation is called a *relocation loan* or *relo loan*. Freddie Mac, Fannie Mae, and several private originators have programs for relo loans and have securitized these loans. The loans are subsidized by corporate employers and must meet certain standards in order to qualify for an originator's relo loan program.

PREPAYMENT PENALTY MORTGAGES

The majority of mortgages outstanding do not penalize the borrower from prepaying any part or all of the outstanding mortgage balance. In recent years mortgage originators have begun originating *prepayment penalty mortgages* (PPMs).

The laws and regulations governing the imposition of prepayment penalties are established at the federal and state levels.[1] Usually, the applicable laws for fixed-rate mortgages are specified at the state level. There are states that do not permit prepayment penalties on fixed-rate mortgages with a first lien. There are states that do permit prepayment penalties but restrict the type of penalty. For some mortgage designs such as adjustable-rate and balloon mortgages, there are federal laws that override state laws.

The basic structure of a PPM is as follows. There is a specified time period where prepayments are not permitted. This time period is called the *lockout period*. Typically this period is either three years or five years. Depending on the structure, a certain amount of prepayments may be made during the lockout period without the imposition of a prepayment penalty. The common prepayment penalty structure is one that allows partial prepayments up to 20% of the original loan amount in any consecutive 12-month period without a prepayment penalty. When a prepayment penalty is imposed, it is typically as follows:[2]

- If there is a 3-year lockout period, the prepayment penalty is the lesser of 2% of any prepayment amount within three years that is greater than 20%

---

[1] For a discussion of these laws and regulations, see Anand K. Bhattacharya and Paul C. Wang, "Prepayment Penalty MBS," Chapter 4 in Frank J. Fabozzi (ed.), *The Handbook of Mortgage-Backed Securities: Fifth Edition* (New York, NY: McGraw Hill Publishing Company, 2001). The information in this section draws from that chapter.

[2] The prepayment penalty structures are explained in Bhattacharya and Wang, "Prepayment Penalty MBS."

of the original mortgage, or six months of interest on the portion of the pre-payment amount that exceeds 20% of the original principal balance.

• If there is a 5-year lockout period, the prepayment penalty is six months interest on any prepayment amount in the first five years that is greater than 20% of the original principal balance.

For example, suppose that a borrower with a PPM with a mortgage rate of 8.5%, original principal balance of $150,000, and a lockout period of five years refinances within the first five and prepays the entire balance. The prepayment penalty will be six months of interest on the amount prepaid in excess of the 20% of the original principal balance. Since 80% of the original principal balance of $150,000 is $120,000 and interest for one year at 8.5% is $10,200 (8.5% times $120,000). The prepayment penalty is 6-month's interest, $5,100.

The motivation for the PPM is that it reduces prepayment risk for the lender during the lockout period. It does so by effectively making it more costly for the borrower to prepay. In exchange for this reduction in prepayment risk, the lender will offer a mortgage rate that is less than that of an otherwise comparable mortgage loan without a prepayment penalty.

SUMMARY

In this chapter we surveyed the various types of mortgages that are have been pooled to create mortgage-backed securities. The various mortgage designs include (1) fixed-rate, level payment fully amortizing mortgages, (2) adjustable-rate mortgages, (3) balloon mortgages, (4) two-step mortgages, (5) growing equity mortgages, and (6) tiered payment mortgages. There are noninsured mortgages (called conventional mortgages) and insured mortgages. The latter are insured either by a government agency or a private entity. Conforming mortgages are those that satisfy the underwriting standards established by an agency for inclusion in a pool of mortgages that back a security. Nonconforming mortgages are those that fail one or more of the underwriting standards. Nonconforming mortgages include jumbo mortgages, no doc mortgages, and low doc mortgages. Mortgages are also categorized according to the purpose of the loan. Examples are refinancing loans, equity takeout loans, and relocation loans. Finally, in recent years, prepayment penalty mortgages have been originated.

Chapter 3

Agency Passthrough Securities and Mortgage Strips

M ortgage-backed securities are securities backed by a pool (collection) of mortgage loans. Any type of mortgage loans, residential or commercial, can be used as collateral for a mortgage-backed security. We defer discussion of mortgage-backed securities backed by commercial mortgage loans until Chapter 7. Residential mortgage-backed securities include the following securities: (1) mortgage passthrough securities, (2) collateralized mortgage obligations, and (3) stripped mortgage-backed securities. The latter two mortgage-backed securities are referred to as *derivative mortgage-backed securities* because they are created from mortgage passthrough securities. In this chapter we describe mortgage passthrough securities and stripped mortgage-backed securities issued by either a government agency or a government sponsored enterprise. We shall refer to such mortgage-backed securities as *agency mortgage-backed securities.*[1] In Chapters 5 and 6, we look at credit sensitive mortgage-backed securities — that is, securities not backed by an agency of the U.S. government or a government sponsored enterprise.

MORTGAGE PASSTHROUGH SECURITIES

Investing in mortgages exposes an investor to default risk and prepayment risk. A more efficient way is to invest in a *mortgage passthrough security.* This is a security created when one or more holders of mortgages form a pool (collection) of mortgages and sell shares or participation certificates in the pool. A pool may consist of several thousand or only a few mortgages. When a mortgage is included in a pool of mortgages that is used as collateral for a mortgage passthrough security, the mortgage is said to be *securitized.*

The cash flows of a mortgage passthrough security depend on the cash flows of the underlying mortgages. As we explained in the previous chapter, the cash flows consist of monthly mortgage payments representing interest, the scheduled repayment of principal, and any prepayments.

Payments are made to security holders each month. Neither the amount nor the timing, however, of the cash flows from the pool of mortgages are identical to those of the cash flows passed through to investors. The monthly cash flows

---

[1] Some market participants refer to passthrough securities issued by government sponsored enterprises as *conventional mortgage-backed securities.*

for a passthrough are less than the monthly cash flows of the underlying mortgages by an amount equal to servicing and other fees. The other fees are those charged by the issuer or guarantor of the passthrough for guaranteeing the issue. The coupon rate on a passthrough, called the *passthrough coupon rate*, is less than the mortgage rate on the underlying pool of mortgage loans by an amount equal to the servicing fee and guarantee fee.

The timing of the cash flows is also different. The monthly mortgage payment is due from each mortgagor on the first day of each month, but there is a delay in passing through the corresponding monthly cash flow to the security holders. The length of the delay varies by the type of passthrough security.

Not all of the mortgages that are included in a pool of mortgages that are securitized have the same mortgage rate and the same maturity. Consequently, when describing a passthrough security, a weighted average coupon rate and a weighted average maturity are determined. A *weighted average coupon rate*, or WAC, is found by weighting the mortgage rate of each mortgage loan in the pool by the amount of the mortgage balance outstanding. A *weighted average maturity*, or WAM, is found by weighting the remaining number of months to maturity for each mortgage loan in the pool by the amount of the mortgage balance outstanding.

For example, suppose a mortgage pool has just five loans and the outstanding mortgage balance, mortgage rate, and months remaining to maturity of each loan are as follows:

Loan	Outstanding mortgage balance	Weight in pool	Mortgage rate	Months remaining
1	$125,000	22.12%	7.50%	275
2	$85,000	15.04%	7.20%	260
3	$175,000	30.97%	7.00%	290
4	$110,000	19.47%	7.80%	285
5	$70,000	12.39%	6.90%	270
Total	$565,000	100.00%		

The WAC for this mortgage pool is:

$$0.2212\ (7.5\%) + 0.1504\ (7.2\%) + 0.3097\ (7.0\%) + 0.1947\ (7.8\%)$$
$$+ 0.1239\ (6.90\%) = 7.28\%$$

The WAM for this mortgage pool is

$$0.2212\ (275) + 0.1504\ (260) + 0.3097\ (290) + 0.1947\ (285)$$
$$+ 0.1239\ (270) = 279 \text{ months (rounded)}$$

Features of Agency Passthroughs

Features of agency passthroughs vary not only by agency but also by program offered. The key features of a passthrough will have an impact on its investment characteristics (particularly its prepayment characteristics). These general features, summarized below and discussed further when we review the various agency programs, can be classified into five groups: (1) the type of guarantee, (2) the numbers of lenders whose mortgage loans are permitted in a pool, (3) the mortgage design of the loans, (4) the characteristics of the mortgage loans in a pool, and (5) the payment procedure.

Type of Guarantee

An agency can provide two types of guarantees. One type is the timely payment of both interest and principal, meaning the interest and principal will be paid when due, even if any of the mortgagors fail to make their monthly mortgage payments. Passthroughs with this type of guarantee are referred to as *fully modified passthroughs.* The second type guarantees both interest and principal payments; however, it only guarantees the timely payment of interest. The scheduled principal is passed through as it is collected with a guarantee that the scheduled payment will be made no later than a specified date. Passthroughs with this type of guarantee are called *modified passthroughs*.

Number of Lenders Permitted in a Pool

A pool may consist of mortgages originated by a single lender or multiple lenders. A single-lender pool may have mortgage loans concentrated in one geographical area or a few states. In multiple-lender pools, the underlying mortgage loans have greater geographical diversification of borrowers.

Mortgage Design of the Loans

Earlier we described different types of mortgage designs. Agency passthroughs have pools of loans with various mortgage designs.

Characteristics of the Mortgage Loans in the Pool

Not all mortgage loans are permitted in a pool that collateralizes a passthrough. The underwriting standards established by the agency specify the permissible loans. The key underwriting standards are summarized below.

Mortgage Loans Permitted in the Pool Mortgage loans can be classified as government-insured loans and conventional loans.

Maximum Size of a Loan For agency securities, the loan limits are reset annually.

Amount of Seasoning Permitted The seasoning of a mortgage loan refers to the time which has passed since the loan was originated.

Assumability of Mortgages If a mortgage loan may be taken over by another borrower, the loan is said to be assumable.

Maturity Programs are available with mortgage loans of different maturities. For example, a pool can have a stated maturity of 30 years, even though not all of the mortgage loans in the pool have a maturity of 30 years, since seasoned loans may be included.

Servicing Spread Permitted As explained earlier, for an individual mortgage loan the servicing spread is the difference between the coupon rate paid by the homeowner and the interest rate received by the investor. A maximum servicing spread permitted in an agency passthrough is specified.

Payment Procedure
Differences in payment procedures involve payment delays and the method of payment.

Payment Delays Payment delays for passthroughs occur for two reasons. First, monthly payments made by homeowners are made in arrears. That is, the payment for the funds borrowed in, say, March are due on the first of the month of April, the normal delay when investing in mortgage loans. When the payments are received by the trustee, they must be processed and the checks mailed to passthrough investors. The actual delay for passthrough investors — that is, the number of days that payment is delayed beyond the normal delay — varies with the agency and agency program. The "stated delay" of a passthrough is the normal delay plus the actual delay. If the payment is made on the 15th of the month, then the actual delay is 14 days, since the monthly payment would have been due on the first of the month. If the stated delay for a passthrough is 44 days, then the actual delay is 14 days.

Method of Payment By method of payment, we mean how many monthly checks an investor who owns several pools of an agency will receive. There can be either one check for all pools or multiple checks.

Types of Agency Mortgage Passthrough Securities
There are three types of agency passthrough securities. Each agency has different programs.

Government National Mortgage Association MBS
Government National Mortgage Association (nicknamed "Ginnie Mae") passthroughs are guaranteed by the full faith and credit of the U.S. government. For this reason, Ginnie Mae passthroughs are viewed as risk-free in terms of default risk, just like Treasury securities. The security guaranteed by Ginnie Mae is called a *mortgage-backed security* (MBS). Ginnie Mae MBSs are issued under one of two programs: GNMA I (established in 1970) and GNMA II (established in 1983).

Type of Guarantee All Ginnie Mae MBS are fully modified passthroughs.

Number of Lenders Permitted in a Pool Only single-lender pools are permitted under the GNMA I program; both single-lender and multiple-lender pools are allowed in the GNMA II program. Single-lender pools issued under the GNMA II program are called *custom pools*; multiple-lender pools are called *jumbo pools*.

Mortgage Design of the Loans Under the two programs, passthroughs with different types of mortgage designs are issued. The large majority of GNMA MBS are backed by single-family mortgages, where a single-family mortgage is a loan for a 1-to-4 family primary residence with a fixed-rate, level-payment mortgage. A Ginnie Mae MBS of this type is referred to as a "GNMA SF MBS." Exhibit 2 in Chapter 2 describes the various programs for ARMs.

Characteristics of the Mortgage Loans in the Pool The key underwriting standards for the mortgage loans are summarized below.

1. Mortgage Loans Permitted in the Pool Only mortgage loans insured or guaranteed by either the Federal Housing Administration, the Veterans Administration, or the Rural Development Administration can be included in a mortgage pool guaranteed by Ginnie Mae.

2. Maximum Size of a Loan The maximum loan size is set by Congress, based on the maximum amount that the FHA, VA, or RHS may guarantee. The maximum for a given loan varies with the region of the country and type of residential property.

3. Amount of Seasoning Permitted In both programs, only newly originated mortgage loans may be included in a pool. These are defined as mortgage loans that have been seasoned less than 24 months.

4. Assumability of Mortgages Assumable mortgages are permitted in the pool.

5. Maturity Within the single-family MBS, there are pools that consist of 30-year or 15-year mortgages that collateralize the security. The 15-year pools are commonly referred to as "midgets."

6. Servicing Spread In the GNMA I program, the servicing spread is 50 basis points; for the GNMA II program, the servicing spread may vary from 50 to 150 basis points.

Payment Procedure The stated delays for GNMA I and II programs are 45 and 50 days, respectively. Thus, corresponding actual delays are 14 and 19 days, respectively. The method of payment also differs between the two programs. In the GNMA I program, payments are made by the individual servicers. In the

GNMA II program, payments from all pools owned by an investor are consolidated and paid in one check by the central paying agent.

Federal Home Loan Mortgage Corporation PC

The Federal Home Loan Mortgage Corporation (nicknamed "Freddie Mac") is a government sponsored enterprise that issues a passthrough security that is called a *participation certificate* (PC). Although a guarantee of Freddie Mac is not a guarantee by the U.S. government, most market participants view Freddie Mac PCs as similar, although not identical, in credit worthiness to Ginnie Mae passthroughs.

Freddie Mac has two programs from which it creates PCs: the Cash Program and the Guarantor/Swap Program. The underlying loans for both programs are conventional mortgages. In the cash program the mortgages that back the PC include individual conventional 1- to 4-family mortgage loans that Freddie Mac purchases from mortgage originators, pools, and then sells. Under the Guarantor/Swap Program, Freddie Mac allows originators to swap pooled mortgages for PCs backed by those mortgages. For example, a thrift may have $50 million of mortgages. It can swap these mortgages for a Freddie Mac PC whose underlying mortgage pool is the $50 million mortgage pool the thrift swapped for the PC. The PCs created under the first program are called *Cash PCs* or *Regular PCs*, under the second program they are called *Swap PCs*.

Type of Guarantee There are both modified passthroughs and fully modified passthroughs. Non-Gold PCs that have been issued as part of the Cash program and almost all that have been issued as part of the Guarantor/Swap program are modified passthroughs. There are a very small number of non-Gold PCs in the latter program that fully modified passthroughs. All Gold PCs issued are fully modified passthroughs. The Gold program was created in an effort to improve Freddie Mac's old PC pools, which lacked the timely payment of prinicipal guarantee contained in Fannie Mae pools. Additionally, the Freddie Mac Gold program shortened the total delay period from 75 days to 45 days. Currently the vast majority of Freddie Mac pools are Gold PCs.

For modified PCs issued by Freddie Mac, the scheduled principal is passed through as it is collected, with Freddie Mac only guaranteeing that the scheduled payment will be made no later than one year after it is due.

Number of Lenders Permitted in a Pool There are only multiple-lender pools in the Cash Program. In the Guarantor/Swap program, there are both single-lender and multiple-lender pools.

Mortgage Design of the Loans There are pools with fixed-rate, level-payment, fully amortized mortgage loans, adjustable-rate mortgage loans, and balloon mortgage loans. A wide variety of ARM PCs are issued under both the Cash and Guarantor/Swap programs. (See Exhibit 2 in Chapter 2.)

Characteristics of the Mortgage Loans in the Pool The key underwriting standards for the mortgage loans are summarized below.

1. Mortgage Loans Permitted in the Pool The majority of PCs are backed by conventional mortgage loans. There are a small portion of PCs which are backed by FHA and VA guaranteed mortgage loans.

2. Maximum Size of a Loan The maximum loan size is set each year based on the annual percentage change in the average price of conventionally financed homes as determined by the Federal Home Loan Bank Board. The maximum loan for a 1-to-4 family residence depends on the number of units.

3. Amount of Seasoning Permitted There are no limits on seasoning for either program.

4. Assumability of Mortgages No assumable mortgages are permitted in a pool.

5. Maturity There are 30-year and 15-year Freddie Mac Regular and Swap PCs. The 15-year Regular PCs are called "gnomes" and the Swap PCs are called "non-gnomes."

6. Net Interest Spread Permitted In general, the net interest spread can be 50 to 250 basis points for both programs.

Payment Procedure The stated delay and actual delay for non-Gold PCs issued as part of either program are 75 and 44 days, respectively. The Gold PCs have a shorter payment delay; the stated delay is 45 days, the actual delay is 14 days. One monthly check is received in both programs for all pools an investor owns.

Federal National Mortgage Association MBS
The passthroughs issued by the Federal National Mortgage Association (nicknamed "Fannie Mae") are called *mortgage-backed securities* (MBSs). Like a Freddie Mac PC, a Fannie Mae MBS is not the obligation of the U.S. government since Fannie Mae is a government sponsored enterprise. Fannie Mae also has a swap program similar to that of Freddie Mac, through which it issues most of its MBSs.
    There are four standard MBS programs established by Fannie Mae, which we discuss below. In addition to its regular programs, Fannie Mae issues securities known as "boutique" securities. These are securities that are issued through negotiated transactions and not backed by one of the mortgage loan types in its regular program.

Type of Guarantee All Fannie Mae MBSs are fully modified passthroughs.

Number of Lenders Permitted in a Pool There are only multiple-lender pools in the Cash program. In this program Fannie Mae purchases mortgage loans from various lenders and then creates a pool to collateralize the MBS. In Fannie Mae's Guarantor/Swap program there are both single-lender and multiple-lender pools.

Mortgage Design of the Loans Three of the four standard programs have pools backed by mortgage loans that are fixed-rate, level-payment, fully amortized mortgages. The fourth standard program is a MBS collateralized by adjustable-rate mortgage loans. Exhibit 2 of the previous chapter describes the various ARMs programs.

Characteristics of the Mortgage Loans in the Pool The key underwriting standards for the mortgage loans are summarized below.

1. Mortgage Loans Permitted in the Pool Two of the four standard programs are backed by conventional mortgages. One is backed by FHA-insured or VA-guaranteed mortgages. Securities issued from the two programs backed by conventional mortgages are called *Conventional MBSs*. The MBSs that are backed by FHA-insured or VA-guaranteed mortgages are called *Government MBSs*.

2. Maximum Size of a Loan The maximum loan size is the same as for Freddie Mac PCs.

3. Amount of Seasoning Permitted There are no limits on seasoning.

4. Assumability of Mortgages No assumable mortgages are permitted in a pool.

5. Maturity The securities issued from the two programs backed by conventional mortgages are 30-year and 15-year MBS, commonly referred to as the *Conventional Long-Term* and *Conventional Intermediate-Term MBS*, respectively. The 15-year MBSs are also known as "dwarfs." The MBSs that are backed by 30-year FHA-insured or VA-guaranteed mortgages are called *Government Long-Term MBSs*.

6. Net Interest Spread Permitted In general, the net interest spread can be 50 to 250 basis points for both programs.

7. Payment Procedure The stated delay is 55 days and the actual delay 24 days.

Prepayment Conventions and Cash Flow

In order to value a passthrough security, it is necessary to project its cash flow. The difficulty is that the cash flow is unknown because of prepayments. The only way to project a cash flow is to make some assumption about the prepayment rate over the life of the underlying mortgage pool.

Estimating the cash flow from a passthrough requires making an assumption about future prepayments. Two conventions have been used as a benchmark for prepayment rates — conditional prepayment rate and Public Securities Association prepayment benchmark.

Conditional Prepayment Rate

One convention for projecting prepayments and the cash flow of a passthrough assumes that some fraction of the remaining principal in the pool is prepaid each month for the remaining term of the mortgage. The prepayment rate assumed for a pool, called the *conditional prepayment rate* (CPR), is based on the characteristics of the pool (including its historical prepayment experience) and the current and expected future economic environment.

The CPR is an annual prepayment rate. To estimate monthly prepayments, the CPR must be converted into a monthly prepayment rate, commonly referred to as the *single-monthly mortality rate* (SMM). The following formula is used to calculate the SMM for a given CPR:

$$SMM = 1 - (1 - CPR)^{1/12} \tag{1}$$

For example, suppose that the CPR is 6%. The corresponding SMM is:

$$SMM = 1 - (1 - 0.06)^{1/12} = 1 - (0.94)^{0.08333} = 0.005143$$

An SMM of $w\%$ means that approximately $w\%$ of the remaining mortgage balance at the beginning of the month, less the scheduled principal payment, will prepay that month. That is,

$$\text{prepayment for month } t = SMM \times (\text{beginning mortgage balance for month } t - \text{scheduled principal payment for month } t) \tag{2}$$

For example, suppose that an investor owns a passthrough in which the remaining mortgage balance at the beginning of some month is $290 million. Assuming that the SMM is 0.5143% and the scheduled principal payment is $3 million, the estimated prepayment for the month is:

$$0.005143 \times (\$290,000,000 - \$3,000,000) = \$1,476,041$$

PSA Prepayment Benchmark

The Public Securities Association (PSA) prepayment benchmark is expressed as a monthly series of CPRs.[2] The PSA benchmark assumes that prepayment rates are low for newly originated mortgages and then will speed up as the mortgages become seasoned.

The PSA benchmark assumes the following prepayment rates for 30-year mortgages:

---

[2] This benchmark is commonly referred to as a prepayment model, suggesting that it can be used to estimate prepayments. Characterization of this benchmark as a prepayment model is inappropriate. It is simply a market convention regarding the pattern of prepayments.

(1) a CPR of 0.2% for the first month, increased by 0.2% per year per month for the next 30 months when it reaches 6% per year, and
(2) a 6% CPR for the remaining years.

This benchmark, referred to as "100% PSA" or simply "100 PSA," is graphically depicted in Exhibit 1. Mathematically, 100 PSA can be expressed as follows:

if $t < 30$ then CPR = 6% $(t/30)$
if $t > 30$ then CPR = 6%

where t is the number of months since the mortgages originated.

Slower or faster speeds are then referred to as some percentage of PSA. For example, 50 PSA means one-half the CPR of the PSA prepayment benchmark CPR; 150 PSA means 1.5 times the CPR of the PSA prepayment benchmark CPR; 300 PSA means three times the CPR of the prepayment benchmark CPR. A prepayment rate of 0 PSA means that no prepayments are assumed.

The CPR is converted to an SMM using equation (1). For example, the SMM for month 5, month 20, and months 31 through 360 assuming 100 PSA are calculated as follows:

for month 5: CPR = 6% (5/30) = 1% = 0.01

$$SMM = 1 - (1 - 0.01)^{1/12} = 1 - (0.99)^{0.08333} = 0.000837$$

for month 20: CPR = 6% (20/30) = 4% = 0.04

$$SMM = 1 - (1 - 0.04)^{1/12} = 1 - (0.96)^{0.08333} = 0.003396$$

Exhibit 1: Graphical Depiction of 100 PSA

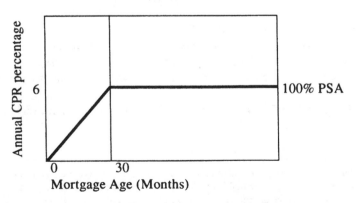

for months 31-360: CPR = 6%

$$\text{SMM} = 1 - (1 - 0.06)^{1/12} = 1 - (0.94)^{0.08333} = 0.005143$$

The SMM for month 5, month 20, and months 31 through 360 assuming 165 PSA are computed as follows:

for month 5: CPR = 6% (5/30) = 1% = 0.01

165 PSA = 1.65 (0.01) = 0.0165

$$\text{SMM} = 1 - (1 - 0.0165)^{1/12} = 1 - (0.9835)^{0.08333} = 0.001386$$

for month 20: CPR = 6% (20/30) = 4% = 0.04

165 PSA = 1.65 (0.04) = 0.066

$$\text{SMM} = 1 - (1 - 0.066)^{1/12} = 1 - (0.934)^{0.08333} = 0.005674$$

for months 31-360: CPR = 6%

165 PSA = 1.65 (0.06) = 0.099

$$\text{SMM} = 1 - (1 - 0.099)^{1/12} = 1 - (0.901)^{0.08333} = 0.007828$$

Notice that the SMM assuming 165 PSA is not just 1.65 times the SMM assuming 100 PSA. It is the CPR that is a multiple of the CPR assuming 100 PSA.

Illustration of Monthly Cash Flow Construction

We now show how to construct a monthly cash flow for a hypothetical passthrough given a PSA assumption. For the purpose of this illustration, the underlying mortgages for this hypothetical passthrough are assumed to be fixed-rate, level-payment, fully amortized mortgages with a weighted average coupon (WAC) rate of 8.125%. It will be assumed that the passthrough rate is 7.5% with a weighted average maturity (WAM) of 357 months.

Exhibit 2 shows the cash flow for selected months assuming 100 PSA. The cash flow is broken down into three components: (1) interest (based on the passthrough rate), (2) the regularly scheduled principal repayment, and (3) pre-payments based on 100 PSA.

Let's walk through Exhibit 2 column by column.

Column 1: This is the month.

Column 2: This column gives the outstanding mortgage balance at the beginning of the month. It is equal to the outstanding balance at the beginning of the previous month reduced by the total principal payment in the previous month.

Exhibit 2: Monthly Cash Flow for a $400 Million Passthrough with a 7.5% Passthrough Rate, a WAC of 8.125%, and a WAM of 357 Months Assuming 100 PSA

(1)	(2)	(3)	(4)	(5)	(6)	(7)	(8)	(9)
Month	Outstanding Balance	SMM	Mortgage Payment	Net Interest	Scheduled Principal	Prepayment	Total Principal	Cash Flow
1	$400,000,000	$0.00067	$2,975,868	$2,500,000	$267,535	$267,470	$535,005	$3,035,005
2	399,464,995	0.00084	2,973,877	2,496,636	269,166	334,198	603,364	3,100,020
3	398,861,631	0.00101	2,971,387	2,492,885	270,762	400,800	671,562	3,164,447
4	398,190,069	0.00117	2,968,399	2,488,688	272,321	467,243	739,564	3,228,252
5	397,450,505	0.00134	2,964,914	2,484,066	273,843	533,493	807,335	3,291,401
6	396,643,170	0.00151	2,960,931	2,476,020	275,327	599,514	874,841	3,353,860
7	395,768,329	0.00168	2,956,453	2,473,552	276,772	665,273	942,045	3,415,597
8	394,826,284	0.00185	2,951,480	2,467,664	278,177	730,736	1,008,913	3,476,577
9	393,817,371	0.00202	2,946,013	2,461,359	279,542	795,869	1,075,410	3,536,769
10	392,741,961	0.00219	2,940,056	2,454,637	280,865	860,637	1,141,502	3,596,140
11	391,600,459	0.00236	2,933,608	2,447,503	282,147	925,008	1,207,155	3,654,658
27	364,808,016	0.00514*	2,766,461	2,280,050	296,406	1,874,688	2,171,094	4,451,144
28	362,636,921	0.00514	2,752,233	2,266,481	296,879	1,863,519	2,160,398	4,426,879
29	360,476,523	0.00514	2,738,078	2,252,978	297,351	1,852,406	2,149,758	4,402,736
30	358,326,766	0.00514	2,723,996	2,239,542	297,825	1,841,347	2,139,173	4,378,715
100	231,249,776	0.00514	1,898,682	1,445,311	332,928	1,187,608	1,520,537	2,965,848
101	229,729,239	0.00514	1,888,917	1,435,808	333,459	1,179,785	1,513,244	2,949,052
102	228,215,995	0.00514	1,879,202	1,426,350	333,990	1,172,000	1,505,990	2,932,340
103	226,710,004	0.00514	1,869,538	1,416,938	334,522	1,164,252	1,498,774	2,915,712
104	225,211,230	0.00514	1,859,923	1,407,570	335,055	1,156,541	1,491,596	2,899,166
105	223,719,634	0.00514	1,850,357	1,398,248	335,589	1,148,867	1,484,456	2,882,703
200	109,791,339	0.00514	1,133,751	686,196	390,372	562,651	953,023	1,639,219
201	108,838,316	0.00514	1,127,920	680,239	390,994	557,746	948,740	1,628,980
202	107,889,576	0.00514	1,122,119	674,310	391,617	552,863	944,480	1,618,790
203	106,945,096	0.00514	1,116,348	668,407	392,241	548,003	940,243	1,608,650
300	32,383,611	0.00514	676,991	202,398	457,727	164,195	621,923	824,320
301	31,761,689	0.00514	673,510	198,511	458,457	160,993	619,449	817,960
302	31,142,239	0.00514	670,046	194,639	459,187	157,803	616,990	811,629
303	30,525,249	0.00514	666,600	190,783	459,918	154,626	614,545	805,328
352	3,034,311	0.00514	517,770	18,964	497,226	13,048	510,274	529,238
353	2,524,037	0.00514	515,107	15,775	498,018	10,420	508,437	524,213
354	2,015,600	0.00514	512,458	12,597	498,811	7,801	506,612	519,209
355	1,508,988	0.00514	509,823	9,431	499,606	5,191	504,797	514,228
356	1,004,191	0.00514	507,201	6,276	500,401	2,591	502,992	509,269
357	501,199	0.00514	504,592	3,132	501,199	0	501,199	504,331

*Since the WAM is 357 months, the underlying mortgage pool is seasoned an average of three months. Therefore, the CPR for month 27 is 6%.

Column 3: This column shows the SMM for 100 PSA. Two things should be noted in this column. First, for month 1, the SMM is for a passthrough that has been seasoned three months. That is, the CPR is 0.8%. This is because the WAM is 357. Second, from month 27 on, the SMM is 0.00514 which corresponds to a CPR of 6%.

Column 4: The total monthly mortgage payment is shown in this column. Notice that the total monthly mortgage payment declines over time as prepayments reduce the mortgage balance outstanding. There is a formula to determine what the monthly mortgage balance will be for each month given prepayments.[3]

Column 5: The monthly interest paid to the passthrough investor is found in this column. This value is determined by multiplying the outstanding mortgage balance at the beginning of the month by the passthrough rate of 7.5% and then dividing by 12.

Column 6: This column gives the regularly scheduled principal repayment. This is the difference between the total monthly mortgage payment [the amount shown in column (4)] and the gross coupon interest for the month. The gross coupon interest is found by multiplying 8.125% by the outstanding mortgage balance at the beginning of the month and then dividing by 12.

Column 7: The prepayment for the month is reported in this column. The prepayment is found by using equation (2). For example, in month 100 the beginning mortgage balance is $231,249,776, the scheduled principal payment is $332,928, and the SMM at 100 PSA is 0.00514301 (only 0.00514 is shown in the exhibit to save space), so the prepayment is:

$$0.00514301 \times (\$231,249,776 - \$332,928) = \$1,187,608$$

Column 8: The total principal payment, which is the sum of columns (6) and (7), is shown in this column.

Column 9: The projected monthly cash flow for this passthrough is shown in this last column. The monthly cash flow is the sum of the interest paid to the passthrough investor [column (5)] and the total principal payments for the month [column (8)].

Exhibit 3 shows selected monthly cash flows for the same passthrough assuming 165 PSA.

---

[3] The formula is presented in Frank J. Fabozzi and Steven V. Mann, *Introduction to Fixed Income Analytics* (New Hope, PA: Frank J. Fabozzi Associates, 2001).

Exhibit 3: Monthly Cash Flow for a $400 Million Passthrough with a 7.5% Passthrough Rate, a WAC of 8.125%, and a WAM of 357 Months Assuming 165 PSA

(1)	(2)	(3)	(4)	(5)	(6)	(7)	(8)	(9)
Month	Outstanding Balance	SMM	Mortgage Payment	Net Interest	Scheduled Principal	Prepayment	Total Principal	Cash Flow
1	$400,000,000	$0.00111	$2,975,868	$2,500,000	$267,535	$442,389	$709,923	$3,209,923
2	399,290,077	0.00139	2,972,575	2,495,563	269,048	552,847	821,896	3,317,459
3	398,468,181	0.00167	2,968,456	2,490,426	270,495	663,065	933,560	3,423,986
4	397,534,624	0.00195	2,963,513	2,484,591	271,873	772,949	1,044,822	3,529,413
5	396,489,799	0.00223	2,957,747	2,478,061	273,181	882,405	1,155,586	3,633,647
6	395,334,213	0.00251	2,951,160	2,470,839	274,418	991,341	1,265,759	3,736,598
7	394,068,451	0.00279	2,943,755	2,462,928	275,583	1,099,664	1,375,246	3,838,174
8	392,693,208	0.00308	2,935,534	2,454,333	276,674	1,207,280	1,483,954	3,938,287
9	391,209,254	0.00336	2,926,503	2,445,058	277,690	1,314,099	1,591,789	4,036,847
10	389,617,464	0.00365	2,916,666	2,435,109	278,631	1,420,029	1,698,659	4,133,769
11	387,918,805	0.00393	2,906,028	2,424,493	279,494	1,524,979	1,804,473	4,228,965
27	347,334,116	0.00865*	2,633,950	2,170,838	282,209	3,001,955	3,284,164	5,455,002
28	344,049,952	0.00865	2,611,167	2,150,312	281,662	2,973,553	3,255,215	5,405,527
29	340,794,737	0.00865	2,588,581	2,129,967	281,116	2,945,400	3,226,516	5,356,483
30	337,568,221	0.00865	2,566,190	2,109,801	280,572	2,917,496	3,198,067	5,307,869
100	170,142,350	0.00865	1,396,958	1,063,390	244,953	1,469,591	1,714,544	2,777,933
101	168,427,806	0.00865	1,384,875	1,052,674	244,478	1,454,765	1,699,243	2,751,916
102	166,728,563	0.00865	1,372,896	1,042,054	244,004	1,440,071	1,684,075	2,726,128
103	165,044,489	0.00865	1,361,020	1,031,528	243,531	1,425,508	1,669,039	2,700,567
104	163,375,450	0.00865	1,349,248	1,021,097	243,060	1,411,075	1,654,134	2,675,231
105	161,721,315	0.00865	1,337,577	1,010,758	242,589	1,396,771	1,639,359	2,650,118
200	56,746,664	0.00865	585,990	354,667	201,767	489,106	690,874	1,045,540
201	56,055,790	0.00865	580,921	350,349	201,377	483,134	684,510	1,034,859
202	55,371,280	0.00865	575,896	346,070	200,986	477,216	678,202	1,024,273
203	54,693,077	0.00865	570,915	341,832	200,597	471,353	671,950	1,013,782
300	11,758,141	0.00865	245,808	73,488	166,196	100,269	266,465	339,953
301	11,491,677	0.00865	243,682	71,823	165,874	97,967	263,841	335,664
302	11,227,836	0.00865	241,574	70,174	165,552	95,687	261,240	331,414
303	10,966,596	0.00865	239,485	68,541	165,232	93,430	258,662	327,203
352	916,910	0.00865	156,460	5,731	150,252	6,631	156,883	162,614
353	760,027	0.00865	155,107	4,750	149,961	5,277	155,238	159,988
354	604,789	0.00865	153,765	3,780	149,670	3,937	153,607	157,387
355	451,182	0.00865	152,435	2,820	149,380	2,611	151,991	154,811
356	299,191	0.00865	151,117	1,870	149,091	1,298	150,389	152,259
357	148,802	0.00865	149,809	930	148,802	0	148,802	149,732

* Since the WAM is 357 months, Therefore the CPR for month 27 is 1.65 × 6% the underlying mortgage pool is seasoned an average of three months

For mortgage derivative products, the monthly cash flows in Exhibits 2 and 3 are allocated to different bond classes. Specifically, for stripped mortgage-backed securities, discussed later in this chapter, there is typically an interest only class and a principal only class. For the interest only class, Column (5) of Exhibit 2 would be the expected cash flow assuming 100 PSA and Column (5) of Exhibit 3 would be the expected cash flow assuming 165 PSA. For the principal only class, Column (8) of Exhibit 2 would be the expected cash flow assuming 100 PSA and Column (8) of Exhibit 3 would be the expected cash flow assuming 165 PSA. In the next chapter where we discuss agency collateralized mortgage obligations, we will explain that there are different classes of bondholders (called tranches) and there are rules for distributing the interest and rules for distributing the principal among the bond classes. When nonagency mortgage-backed securities are covered in Chapter 5, we will see that there are rules for distributing the interest, scheduled principal payments, and prepayments among the bond classes in the structure. Note that for agency collateralized mortgage obligations no distinction is made between prepayments and regularly scheduled principal payments, but for nonagency securities there are rules for allocating each among the bond classes in the structure. While we have not shown the servicing fee in Exhibits 2 and 3, it is noteworthy that an entity considering the acquisition of the right to service the mortgage pool would be focusing on that component of the cash flow based on some prepayment assumption.

Factors Affecting Prepayment Behavior

The factors that affect prepayment behavior are: (1) prevailing mortgage rate, (2) characteristics of the underlying mortgage pool, (3) seasonal factors, and (4) general economic activity.

Prevailing Mortgage Rate

The current mortgage rate affects prepayments in three ways. First, the spread between the prevailing mortgage rate in the market and the rate paid by the homeowner affects the incentive to refinance. Second, the path of mortgage rates since the loan was originated affects prepayments through a phenomenon referred to as *refinancing burnout*. Both the spread and path of mortgage rates affect prepayments that are the product of refinancing. The third way in which the prevailing mortgage rate affects prepayments is through its effect on the affordability of housing and housing turnover. The level of mortgage rates affects housing turnover to the extent that a lower rate increases the affordability of homes.

The single most important factor affecting prepayments because of refinancing is the current level of mortgage rates relative to the borrower's contract rate. The greater the difference between the two, the greater the incentive to refinance the mortgage loan. For refinancing to make economic sense, the interest savings must be greater than the costs associated with refinancing the mortgage. These costs include legal expenses, origination fees, title insurance, and the value of the time associated with obtaining another mortgage loan. Some of these costs — such as title insurance and origination points — will vary proportionately with the amount to be financed. Other costs such as the application fee and legal expenses are typically fixed.

Historically, it has been observed that when mortgage rates fall to more than 200 basis points below the contract rate, prepayment rates increase. However, the creativity of mortgage originators in designing mortgage loans such that the refinancing costs are folded into the amount borrowed has changed the view that mortgage rates must drop dramatically below the contract rate to make refinancing economic. Moreover, mortgage originators now do an effective job of advertising to make homeowners cognizant of the economic benefits of refinancing.

The historical pattern of prepayments and economic theory suggests that it is not only the level of mortgage rates that affects prepayment behavior, but also the path that mortgage rates take to get to the current level. To illustrate why, suppose the underlying contract rate for a pool of mortgage loans is 11% and that three years after origination, the prevailing mortgage rate declines to 8%. Let's consider two possible paths of the mortgage rate in getting to the 8% level. In the first path, the mortgage rate declines to 8% at the end of the first year, then rises to 13% at the end of the second year, and then falls to 8% at the end of the third year. In the second path, the mortgage rate rises to 12% at the end of the first year, continues its rise to 13% at the end of the second year, and then falls to 8% at the end of the third year.

If the mortgage rate follows the first path, those who can benefit from refinancing will more than likely take advantage of this opportunity when the mortgage rate drops to 8% in the first year. When the mortgage rate drops again to 8% at the end of the third year, the likelihood is that prepayments because of refinancing will not surge; those who can benefit by taking advantage of the refinancing opportunity will have done so already when the mortgage rate declined for the first time. This is the prepayment behavior referred to as the refinancing burnout (or simply, burnout) phenomenon.

In contrast, the expected prepayment behavior when the mortgage rate follows the second path is quite different. Prepayment rates are expected to be low in the first two years. When the mortgage rate declines to 8% in the third year, refinancing activity, and therefore prepayments, are expected to surge. Consequently, the burnout phenomenon is related to the path of mortgage rates.

Characteristics of the Underlying Mortgage Loans

The following characteristics of the underlying mortgage loans affect prepayments: (1) the contract rate, (2) whether the loans are FHA/VA/RHS-guaranteed or conventional, (3) the amount of seasoning, (4) the type of loan (e.g., a 30-year level payment mortgage, 5-year balloon mortgage, etc.), and (4) the geographical location of the underlying properties.

Seasonal Factors

There is a well-documented seasonal pattern in prepayments. This pattern is related to activity in the primary housing market, with home buying activity increasing in the spring, and gradually reaching a peak in the late summer. Home buying activity declines in the fall and winter. Mirroring this activity are the prepayments that result from the turnover of housing as home buyers sell their existing homes and purchase new ones. Prepayments are low in the winter months and begin to rise in the spring, reaching a peak in the summer months. However, probably because of delays in passing through prepayments, the peak may not be observed until early fall.

General Economic Activity

Economic theory would suggest that general economic activity affects prepayment behavior through its effect on housing turnover. The link is as follows: a growing economy results in a rise in personal income and in opportunities for worker migration; this increases family mobility and as a result increases housing turnover. The opposite holds for a weak economy. Some researchers suggest that prepayments can be projected by identifying and forecasting the turnover rate of the single-family housing stock.[4]

Although some modelers of prepayment behavior may incorporate macroeconomic measures of economic activity such as gross disposable product, industrial production, or housing starts, the trend has been to ignore them or limit their use to specific applications. There are two reasons why macroeconomic measures have been ignored by some modelers. First, empirical tests suggest that the inclusion of macroeconomic measures does not significantly improve the forecasting ability of a prepayment model.[5] Second, as explained later, prepayment models are based on a projection of a path for future mortgage rates. The inclusion of macroeconomic variables in a prepayment model would require the forecasting of the values of these variables over long time periods.

Macroeconomic variables, however, have been used by some researchers in prepayment models to capture the effect of housing turnover on prepayments by specifying a relationship between interest rates and housing turnover. This is the approach used in the Prudential Securities Model.[6]

Prepayment Models

A prepayment model is a statistical model that is used to forecast prepayments. It begins by modeling the statistical relationships among the factors that are

---

[4] See, for example, Joseph C. Hu, "An Alternative Prepayment Projection Based on Housing Activity," in Frank J. Fabozzi (ed.), *The Handbook of Mortgage-Backed Securities* (Chicago: Probus Publishing, 1988), pp. 639-648.

[5] Scott F. Richard and Richard Roll, "Prepayments on Fixed-Rate Mortgage-Backed Securities," *Journal of Portfolio Management* (Spring 1989), pp. 73-79.

[6] Lakbhir S. Hayre, Kenneth Lauterbach, and Cyrus Mohebbi, "Prepayment Models and Methodologies," in Frank J. Fabozzi (ed.), *Advances and Innovations in the Bond and Mortgage Markets* (Chicago, IL: Probus Publishing, 1989), p. 338.

expected to affect prepayments. One study suggests that refinancing incentives, burnout, seasoning, and seasonality explain about 95% of the variation in prepayment rates.[7] These factors are then combined into one model. For example, in the Goldman, Sachs prepayment model the effects interact proportionally through the following multiplicative function, which is used to project prepayments:

monthly prepayment rate = (refinancing incentive)
× (seasoning multiplier) × (month multiplier) × (burnout multiplier)

where the various multipliers are adjustments for the effects we discussed earlier.

The product of a prepayment forecast is not one prepayment rate but a set of prepayment rates for each month of the remaining term of a mortgage pool. The set of monthly prepayment rates, however, is not reported by Wall Street firms or vendors. Instead, a single prepayment rate is reported. One way to convert a set of monthly prepayment rates into a single prepayment rate is to calculate a simple average of the prepayment rates. The obvious drawback to this approach is that it does not take into consideration the outstanding balance each month. An alternative approach is to use some type of weighted average, selecting the weights to reflect the amount of the monthly cash flow corresponding to a monthly prepayment rate. This is done by first computing the yield for a passthrough given its market price and the set of monthly prepayment rates. Then a single prepayment rate (CPR or PSA multiple) that gives the same yield is found.

Trading and Settlement Procedures

Agency passthroughs are identified by a pool prefix and pool number provided by the agency. The prefix indicates the type of passthrough. For example, a pool prefix of 20 for a Freddie Mac PC means that the underlying pool consists of conventional mortgages with an original maturity of 15 years. A pool prefix of AR for a Ginnie Mae MBS means that the underlying pool consists of adjustable-rate mortgages. The pool number indicates the specific mortgages underlying the passthrough and the issuer of the passthrough.

There are specific rules established by the Public Securities Association for the trading and settlement of mortgage-backed securities. Our discussion here is limited to agency passthrough securities.

Many trades occur while a pool is still unspecified, and therefore no pool information is known at the time of the trade. This kind of trade is known as a "TBA" (to be announced) trade. In a TBA trade the two parties agree on the agency type, the agency program, the coupon rate, the face value, the price, and the settlement date. The actual pools underlying the agency passthrough are not specified in a TBA trade. However, this information is provided by the seller to the buyer before delivery, as explained below. There are trades where more spe-

---

[7] Scott F. Richard, "Relative Prepayment Rates on Thirty-Year FNMA, FHLMC and GNMA Fixed Rate Mortgage-Backed Securities," *Advances and Innovations in the Bond and Mortgage Markets*, pp. 351-369.

cific requirements are established for the securities to be delivered (for example, a Freddie Mac Gold with a coupon rate of 8.5% and a WAC between 9.0% and 9.2%). There are also *specified pool trades* wherein the actual pool numbers to be delivered are specified.

Passthroughs are quoted in the same manner as U.S. Treasury coupon securities. A quote of 94-05 means 94 and 5/32nds of par value, or 94.15625% of par value. The price that the buyer pays the seller is the agreed upon sale price plus accrued interest. Given the par value, the dollar price (excluding accrued interest) is affected by the amount of the pool mortgage balance outstanding. The *pool factor* indicates the percentage of the initial mortgage balance still outstanding. So, a pool factor of 90 means that 90% of the original mortgage pool balance is outstanding. The pool factor is reported by the agency each month.

The dollar price paid for just the principal is found as follows given the agreed upon price, par value, and the month's pool factor provided by the agency:

price × par value × pool factor

For example, if the parties agree to a price of 92 for $1 million par value for a passthrough with a pool factor of 85, then the dollar price paid by the buyer in addition to accrued interest is:

$$0.92 \times \$1,000,000 \times 0.85 = \$782,000$$

Trades settle according to a delivery schedule established by the PSA. This schedule is published quarterly by the PSA with information regarding delivery for the next six months. Each agency and program settles on a different day of the delivery month. There is also a distinction made in the delivery schedule by coupon rate.

By 3 p.m. eastern standard time two business days before the settlement date, the seller must furnish information to the buyer about pools that will be delivered. This is called the *48-hour rule*. The date that this information must be given is called the *notification date* or *call-out date*. Two parties can agree to depart from PSA guidelines and settle at any time.

When an investor purchases, say, $1 million GNMA 8s on a TBA basis, the investor can receive up to three pools. Three pools can be delivered because the PSA has established guidelines for standards of delivery and settlement of mortgage-backed securities,[8] under which our hypothetical TBA trade permits three possible pools to be delivered. The option of what pools to deliver is left to the seller, as long as selection and delivery satisfy the PSA guidelines.

There are many seasoned issues of the same agency with the same coupon rate outstanding at a given point in time. For example, there are more than

---

[8] Public Securities Association, *Uniform Practices for the Clearance and Settlement of Mortgage-Backed Securities.* More specifically, the requirement for good delivery permits a maximum of three pools per $1 million traded, or a maximum of four pools per $1 million for coupons of 12% or more.

30,000 pools of 30-year Ginnie Mae MBSs outstanding with a coupon rate of 9%. One passthrough may be backed by a pool of mortgage loans in which all the properties are located in California, while another may be backed by a pool of mortgage loans in which all the properties are in Minnesota. Yet another may be backed by a pool of mortgage loans in which the properties are from several regions of the country. So which pool are dealers referring to when they talk about Ginnie Mae 9s? They are not referring to any specific pool but instead to a generic security, despite the fact that the prepayment characteristics of passthroughs with underlying pools from different parts of the country are different. Thus, the projected prepayment rates for passthroughs reported by dealer firms are for generic passthroughs. A particular pool purchased may have a materially different prepayment speed from the generic. Moreover, when an investor purchases a passthrough without specifying a pool number, the seller can deliver the worst-paying pools as long as the pools delivered satisfy good delivery requirements.

Extension Risk and Contraction Risk

An investor who owns passthrough securities does not know what the cash flow will be because that depends on actual prepayments. As we noted earlier, this risk is called prepayment risk.

To understand the significance of prepayment risk, suppose an investor buys a 10% coupon Ginnie Mae at a time when mortgage rates are 10%. Let's consider what will happen to prepayments if mortgage rates decline to, say, 6%. There will be two adverse consequences. First, a basic property of fixed income securities is that the price of an option-free bond will rise. But in the case of a passthrough security, the increase in price will not be as large as that of an option-free bond because a fall in interest rates will give the borrower an incentive to prepay the loan and refinance the debt at a lower rate. This results in the same adverse consequence faced by holders of callable bonds. As in the case of those instruments, the upside price potential of a passthrough security is truncated because of prepayments. The second adverse consequence is that the cash flow must be reinvested at a lower rate. These two adverse consequences when mortgage rates decline are referred to as *contraction risk*.

Now let's look at what happens if mortgage rates rise to 15%. The price of the passthrough, like the price of any bond, will decline. But again it will decline more because the higher rates will tend to slow down the rate of prepayment, in effect increasing the amount invested at the coupon rate, which is lower than the market rate. Prepayments will slow down, because homeowners will not refinance or partially prepay their mortgages when mortgage rates are higher than the contract rate of 10%. Of course this is just the time when investors want prepayments to speed up so that they can reinvest the prepayments at the higher market interest rate. This adverse consequence of rising mortgage rates is called *extension risk*.

Therefore, prepayment risk encompasses contraction risk and extension risk. Prepayment risk makes passthrough securities unattractive for certain financial institutions to hold from an asset/liability perspective. Let's look at why particular institutional investors may find passthroughs unattractive:

1. Thrifts and commercial banks want to lock in a spread over their cost of funds. Funds are raised on a short-term basis. If they invest in fixed-rate passthrough securities, they will be mismatched because a passthrough is a longer-term security. In particular, depository institutions are exposed to extension risk when they invest in passthrough securities.

2. To satisfy certain obligations of insurance companies, passthrough securities may be unattractive. More specifically, consider a life insurance company that has issued a 4-year guaranteed investment contract (GIC). The uncertainty about the cash flow from a passthrough security and the likelihood that slow prepayments will result in the instrument being long-term make it an unappealing investment vehicle for such accounts. In such instances, a passthrough security exposes the insurance company to extension risk.

3. Consider a pension fund that wants to fund a 15-year liability. Buying a passthrough security exposes the pension fund to the risk that prepayments will speed up and the maturity of the investment will shorten to considerably less than 15 years. Prepayments will speed up when interest rates decline, thereby forcing reinvestment of prepayments at a lower interest rate. In this case, the pension fund is exposed to contraction risk.

We can see that some institutional investors are concerned with extension risk and others with contraction risk when they purchase a passthrough security. Is it possible to alter the cash flow of a passthrough so as to reduce the contraction risk and extension risk for institutional investors? This can be done, as we shall see later in this chapter.

Comparison to Treasuries

Mortgage passthroughs are often compared to Treasury securities. When we speak of comparing a mortgage passthrough security to a comparable Treasury, what does "comparable" mean? The stated maturity of a mortgage passthrough security is an inappropriate measure because of prepayments. Instead, market participants have used two measures: Macaulay duration and average life. As we explain in Chapter 8, Macaulay duration is a weighted-average term to maturity where the weights are the present value of the cash flows. The more commonly used measure is the average life.

The *average life* of a mortgage-backed security is the weighted average time to receipt of principal payments (scheduled principal payments and projected prepayments). Mathematically, the average life is expressed as follows:

$$\text{average life} = \sum_{t=1}^{T} \frac{t \times \text{projected principal received at time } t}{12 \times \text{total principal}}$$

where T is the number of months.

The average life of a passthrough depends on the PSA prepayment assumption. To see this, the average life is shown below for different prepayment speeds for the passthrough we used to illustrate the cash flow for 100 PSA and 165 PSA in Exhibits 2 and 3:

PSA Speed	50	100	165	200	300	400	500	600	700
Average life	15.11	11.66	8.76	7.68	5.63	4.44	3.68	3.16	2.78

STRIPPED MORTGAGE-BACKED SECURITIES

A mortgage passthrough security divides the cash flow from the underlying pool of mortgages on a pro rata basis to the securityholders. A *stripped mortgage-backed security* is created by altering that distribution of principal and interest from a pro rata distribution to an unequal distribution. The result is that the securities created will have a price/yield relationship that is different from the price/yield relationship of the underlying passthrough security.

In the most common type of stripped mortgage-backed securities all the interest is allocated to one class (called the *interest only* or *IO class*) and all the principal to the other class (called the *principal only* or *PO class*). The IO class receives no principal payments.

Principal-Only Securities

The PO security is purchased at a substantial discount from par value. The return an investor realizes depends on the speed at which prepayments are made. The faster the prepayments, the higher the investor's return. For example, suppose there is a mortgage pool consisting only of 30-year mortgages, with $400 million in principal, and that investors can purchase POs backed by this mortgage pool for $175 million. The dollar return on this investment will be $225 million. How quickly that dollar return is recovered by PO investors determines the actual return that will be realized. In the extreme case, if all homeowners in the underlying mortgage pool decide to prepay their mortgage loans immediately, PO investors will realize the $225 million immediately. At the other extreme, if all homeowners decide to remain in their homes for 30 years and make no prepayments, the $225 million will be spread out over 30 years, which would result in a lower return for PO investors.

Let's look at how the price of the PO would be expected to change as mortgage rates in the market change. When mortgage rates decline below the contract rate, prepayments are expected to speed up, accelerating payments to the PO holder. Thus, the cash flow of a PO improves (in the sense that principal repayments are received earlier). The cash flow will be discounted at a lower interest rate because the mortgage rate in the market has declined. The result is that the PO price will increase when mortgage rates decline. When mortgage rates rise above the contract rate, prepayments are expected to slow down. The cash flow deteriorates (in the sense that it takes longer to recover principal repayments). Couple this with a higher discount rate, and the price of a PO will fall when mortgage rates rise.

Interest-Only Securities

An IO has no par value. In contrast to the PO investor, the IO investor wants prepayments to be slow. The reason is that the IO investor receives interest only on the amount of the principal outstanding. When prepayments are made, less dollar interest will be received as the outstanding principal declines. In fact, if prepayments are too fast, the IO investor may not recover the amount paid for the IO even if the security is held to maturity.

Let's look at the expected price response of an IO to changes in mortgage rates. If mortgage rates decline below the contract rate, prepayments are expected to accelerate. This would result in a deterioration of the expected cash flow for an IO. While the cash flow will be discounted at a lower rate, the net effect typically is a decline in the price of an IO. If mortgage rates rise above the contract rate, the expected cash flow improves, but the cash flow is discounted at a higher interest rate. The net effect may be either a rise or fall for the IO.

Thus, we see an interesting characteristic of an IO: its price tends to move in the same direction as the change in mortgage rates (1) when mortgage rates fall below the contract rate and (2) for some range of mortgage rates above the contract rate. Both POs and IOs exhibit substantial price volatility when mortgage rates change. The greater price volatility of the IO and PO compared to the passthrough from which they were created is due to the fact that the combined price volatility of the IO and PO must be equal to the price volatility of the passthrough.

An average life for a PO can be calculated based on some prepayment assumption. However, an IO receives no principal payments, so technically an average life cannot be computed. Instead, for an IO a "cash flow average life" is computed, using the projected interest payments in the average life formula instead of principal.

Trading and Settlement Procedures

The trading and settlement procedures for stripped mortgage-backed securities are similar to those set by the Public Securities Association for agency passthroughs described in the previous section. The specifications are in the types of trades (TBA versus specified pool), calculations of the proceeds, and the settlement dates.

IOs and POs are extreme premium and discount securities and consequently are very sensitive to prepayments, which are driven by the specific characteristics (WAC, WAM, geographic concentration, average loan size) of the underlying loans. The TBA delivery option on IOs and POs is of too great an economic value and this value is hard to quantify. Therefore, almost all secondary trades in IOs and POs are on a specified pool basis rather than on a TBA basis.

All IOs and POs are given a trust number. Since the transactions are on a specified trust basis, they are also done based on the original face amount. For example, suppose a portfolio manager agrees to buy $10 million original face of Trust 23 PO for August settlement. At the time of the transaction, the August factor need not be known; however, there is no ambiguity in the amount to be delivered because the seller does not have any delivery option. The seller has to deliver $3 million current face amount if the August factor turns out to be 0.30 and the seller needs to deliver $2.5 million current face amount if the August factor turns out to be 0.25.

The total proceeds of a PO trade are calculated the same way as with a passthrough trade except that there is no accrued interest. For example, suppose a buyer and a seller agree to trade $10 million original face of Trust 23 PO at 75-08 ($= 75^8/_{32} = 75.25$) for settlement on August 25. The proceeds for the trade are calculated as follows assuming an August trust factor of 0.25:

$$
\underset{\text{price}}{0.7525} \times \underset{\text{original face value}}{\$10,000,000} \times \underset{\text{pool factor}}{0.25} = \underset{\text{proceeds}}{\$1,881,250}
$$

The market trades IOs based on notional principal. The proceeds include the price on the notional amount and the accrued interest. For example, suppose a buyer and a seller agree to trade $10 million original notional face of Trust 23 IO at 33-20 ($= 33^{20}/_{32} = 33.625$) for settlement on August 25. The proceeds for the trade are calculated as follows assuming an August factor of 0.25:

$$
\underset{\text{price}}{(0.33625} + \underset{\text{coupon}}{0.10} \times \underset{\text{days accrued interest}}{24 \text{ days}/360 \text{ days})} \times \underset{\text{orig. notional}}{\$10,000,000} \times \underset{\text{factor}}{0.25} = \underset{\text{proceeds}}{\$857,292}
$$

As explained earlier, agency passthrough trades settle according to a delivery schedule established by the PSA. Stripped mortgage-backed securities trades follow the same delivery schedule according to their underlying mortgages. Any other non-standard settlement dates can be agreed upon between the buyer and the seller.

SUMMARY

The basic mortgage-backed security is the mortgage passthrough security created from a pool of mortgage loans. Agency passthrough securities are those issued/guaranteed by Ginnie Mae, Fannie Mae, and Freddie Mac. A weighted average maturity and weighted average coupon can be computed for a passthrough security.

The cash flow of a passthrough includes net interest, scheduled principal repayments (i.e., scheduled amortization), and prepayments. Any amount paid in excess of the required monthly mortgage payment is a prepayment; the cash flow of a mortgage-backed security is unknown because of prepayments.

A projection of prepayments is necessary to project the cash flow of a passthrough security. The four factors that affect prepayments are (1) the prevailing mortgage rate, (2) characteristics of the underlying mortgage pool, (3) seasonal factors, and (4) general economic activity. The PSA prepayment benchmark is a series of conditional prepayment rates and is simply a market convention that describes in general the pattern of prepayments. A measure commonly used to estimate the life of a passthrough is its average life.

The prepayment risk associated with investing in mortgage passthrough securities can be decomposed into contraction risk and extension risk. Prepayment risk makes passthrough securities unattractive for certain financial institutions to hold from an asset/liability perspective.

A stripped mortgage-backed security is a derivative mortgage-backed security that is created by redistributing the interest and principal payments to two different classes. A principal-only mortgage strip (PO) benefits from declining interest rates and fast prepayments. An interest-only mortgage strip (IO) benefits from rising interest rates and a slowing of prepayments; if rates fall instead, the investor in an interest-only security may not realize the amount invested even if the security is held to maturity.

Chapter 4

Agency Collateralized Mortgage Obligations

A s explained in Chapter 3, the major drawback to investing in pools of passthroughs is the uncertainty of the cash flows. That is, depending on a pool's prepayments, the investor could have an intermediate, a short, or a long maturity investment. Collateralized mortgage obligations (CMOs) are paythrough structures that evolved to lessen that cash flow uncertainty. Additionally, by creating investment products with different average lives and durations, mortgage products could appeal to a wider audience. For example, as shown in Exhibit 1, shorter cash flow mortgage products could be targeted to address the needs of banks and thrifts. Longer mortgage products were sold to life insurance companies and pension funds.

In this chapter we will discuss CMOs. More specifically, we will discuss CMOs issued by the two government sponsored enterprises, Fannie Mae and Freddie Mac, and Ginnie Mae. We will refer to these CMOs as *agency CMOs*. We will explain how they are created, the motivation for their creation from the perspective of both the issuer and the investor, and the various types of CMO bond classes.

CREATION OF CMOS

CMOs are created by pooling, in a trust, numerous mortgage collateral pools. CMO structures allow the issuer to customize classes or tranches based on investor preferences. These preferences can be related to maturity, coupon (i.e., using discount or premium coupons creates different dollar prices), and/or degrees of prepayment risk. The CMO process is illustrated in Exhibit 2.

Exhibit 1: MBS Investor Spectrum

Average Life Range	Investor Group
0-1	Money-market funds
2-5	Banks/thrifts
5-7	Various
5-10	Total return accounts
11-20	Life insurance cos.
11-25	Pension funds

Exhibit 2: CMO Process

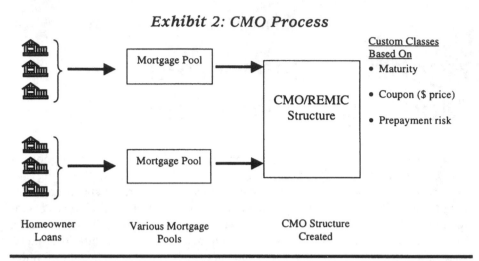

CMOs are created by dealer firms when the sum of the component classes (the CMO tranches) can be sold to investors at a level richer than where the underlying collateral can be purchased by dealer firms. Exhibit 3 shows a simple example of basic CMO arbitrage. The key factors that determine whether a CMO deal is created are:

- shape of Treasury yield curve
- CMO spreads
- collateral cost
- allocation of cash flow to classes

Each of these factors is discussed below.

First, the shape of the Treasury yield curve impacts CMO creation. Specifically, CMO arbitrage works best in a steep yield curve environment. This is because the bulk of the CMO cash flows are allocated to the shorter part of the yield curve which result in a rich execution (i.e., profitable for the dealer) versus the collateral cost — see Exhibit 3.

Second, CMO spreads or the level where the classes can be placed will determine whether the deal will be created. All things being equal, deals are more commonly printed when CMO spreads tighten and collateral prices remain unchanged. Third, given a certain set of CMO spread levels, the cost of the collateral determines whether a deal can be profitably executed.

Finally, the allocation of cash flow within the deal structure must be considered. Under normal circumstances, when the yield curve is upward sloping, current coupon or slightly premium collateral is often the collateral of choice. This is due to the fact that a faster prepayment assumption can be used for this collateral (as opposed to discount collateral) which allows more of the cash flow to be front-loaded or pushed down to the steepest (or most profitable) part of the yield curve.

Exhibit 3: Basic CMO Arbitrage

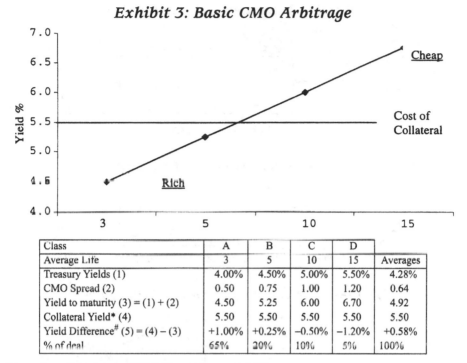

Class	A	B	C	D	
Average Life	3	5	10	15	Averages
Treasury Yields (1)	4.00%	4.50%	5.00%	5.50%	4.28%
CMO Spread (2)	0.50	0.75	1.00	1.20	0.64
Yield to maturity (3) = (1) + (2)	4.50	5.25	6.00	6.70	4.92
Collateral Yield* (4)	5.50	5.50	5.50	5.50	5.50
Yield Difference# (5) = (4) − (3)	+1.00%	+0.25%	−0.50%	−1.20%	+0.58%
% of deal	65%	20%	10%	5%	100%

* Assuming collateral cost of 5.50% (5-year Treasury + 1.00)
# Positive number reflects rich or profitable arbitrage versus collateral, negative number represent cheap or unprofitable tranche arbitrage versus collateral cost.

BASIC CMO STRUCTURES

In this section we will discuss basic CMO structures — sequential-pay CMOs, PAC bonds, and support bonds.

Sequential–Pay CMOs

The original CMO structure, which is also known as the "plain vanilla" structure, is called the *sequential-pay*. As shown in Exhibit 4, the first CMOs were simple A-B-C-D structures.

The payment rules for sequential-pay CMOs are simple. First, interest is paid to all tranches based on the principal amount outstanding at the beginning of the period. Second, principal is returned in the following manner: All principal collected, both from regularly scheduled principal and/or unscheduled principal (i.e., prepayments) is used to pay down the first class, the A class. All classes start with a beginning *factor* (the percentage of the principal still remaining) of 1.00. All principal is directed to the A class until its factor is reduced to 0. Once the A class is retired, then all principal is directed to the B class until retired, etc.

Exhibit 4: Sequential-Pay CMOs

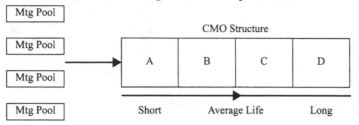

Exhibit 5: Sequential with Z Bond

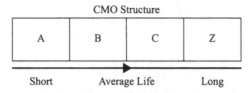

Exhibit 6: Z Bond Traditional Structure

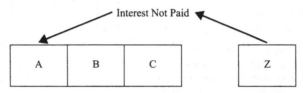

The next generation of development for the CMO was the A-B-C-Z structure shown in Exhibit 5. The Z bond was created as a way to push more of the deal's cash flow to the earlier tranches. A *Z bond* pays no current interest but defers interest until all of the deal's other classes are paid off. That is, a Z bond starts with a factor of 1.00, and unlike other bonds whose factor decreases, the factor will increase monthly by the amount of the interest deferred. Therefore, the actual cash not paid to the Z bond, in the traditional Z bond structure, is used to accelerate the pay down of the earlier classes of the sequential bond. This is illustrated in Exhibit 6.

The next variation of this structure was the formation of classes called *very accurately defined maturity* (VADM) bonds. (See Exhibit 7.) Since the exact amount of cash flow produced from deferring interest from the Z bond is known (the Z bond principal cannot pay down until all other bonds are retired), highly stable and predictable bonds can be produced. In particular, the VADM-A bond has cash flows which are almost Treasury-like with regard to their certainty. However, as the classes get longer (i.e., VADM-C), the bonds are more volatile depending on the speed of prepayments. VADMs, due to their stability, trade at tighter spreads than do sequential-pay bonds.

Exhibit 7: Z Bond with VADMs

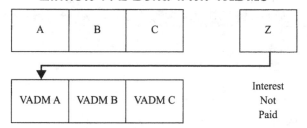

Exhibit 8: Basic PAC Structure

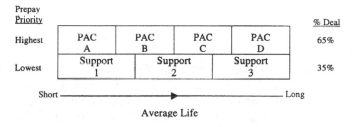

PAC Bonds

The next generation of CMO deals which came to market included the *planned amortization class* (PAC) bond structure. The PAC structure uses a mechanism which is similar to a sinking fund to determine a fixed principal schedule that will apply over a range of prepayment assumptions.

When creating a PAC bond, the CMO structure will determine how much cash flow is needed to create a desired cash flow for a bond. The deal's prepayment assumption will then be increased and decreased to determine the minimum and maximum prepayment assumptions will produce the same desired cash flows to the PAC bonds. PAC bands are then the minimum and maximum prepayment speeds which will leave the PAC bond's cash flow unchanged. PAC bands are stated as percentages of the Public Securities Association (PSA) prepayment benchmark.

The basic PAC deal structure is shown in Exhibit 8. PAC bonds get their inherent stability from the support bonds within the structure. The role of the support bond is to absorb prepayments (shorten) when prepayments are higher than expected, and to defer principal payments (extend) when prepayments are slower than expected.

Because of this increased level of cash flow certainty, PAC bonds trade at tighter (more expensive) spreads than the mortgage passthrough securities from which they are created. However, the value inherent in any particular PAC bond is a function of the following five factors:

• PAC bands
• Percentage of PACs within deal

Exhibit 9: PAC Band Drift

Prepayment Scenario	Lower Band	Upper Band	Result
Faster-than upper band	↑	↓	Narrowing of bands
Slower-than lower band	↓	↑	Widening of bands
In between bands but fast	↑	↓	Gradual narrowing
In between bands but slow	↓	↑	Gradual widening

- Collateral profile
- PAC position within deal
- PAC window

Each of these factors will be discussed briefly below.

PAC Bands
Generally, the wider the bands the better the PAC. For example, a PAC band of 100 PSA to 300 PSA is better than one of 150 PSA to 250 PSA. However, PAC bands shift over time depending on the actual prepayments. Exhibit 9 describes how PAC bands can change over time, referred to as *PAC band drift*. Investors must closely monitor not only the stated or original PAC bands but also the *effective* (or *updated*) *PAC bands*. The effective PAC bands indicate the bands for prepayments based on the remaining support bonds and the remaining schedule for the PAC bonds.

Percentage of PACs in Deal
The higher the percentage of PACs in a deal, the lower the overall stability. That is, bonds in a deal comprised of 40% PACs should perform better than those comprised of 75% PACs. This is the case because the higher the percentage of PACs in a deal the lower the percentage of support bonds (i.e., fewer shock absorbers). Investors should not be confused by PAC-2 (or PAC-II) bonds. These bonds are support bonds which have an amortization schedule (like a PAC), but their PAC bands are narrow and they are treated as support bonds when creating the bands for the traditional PACs. These bonds are also referred to as *support bonds with a schedule* or *scheduled bonds*.

Collateral Profile
PAC bands must be considered in relation to the deal's underlying collateral. For example, a wide PAC band is much more comforting when the collateral is trading as discount collateral. Likewise, seasoned collateral or collateral which has gone through at least one prepayment cycle is much more likely to experience predictable prepayments than unseasoned collateral.

PAC Position within Deal
Shorter PAC bonds generally are subject to less prepayment risk than longer PAC bonds. This is the case because shorter PACs have more support bonds outstand-

ing during their life than longer PACs. The support bonds supporting the longer PACs may have to be used to keep the shorter PACs on their amortization schedule. In a worst case scenario, the buyer of a long PAC bond may have paid-up to buy a sequential bond. That is, once all the support bonds are retired, the PAC deal will pay down like sequential-pay bonds.

PAC Window
Generally, investors prefer a narrower principal payment window. Therefore, PACs with tighter windows will trade at tighter spread levels than wider window PACs.

Support Bonds
The third major type of CMO class is the support bond. Support bonds, as previ ously mentioned, act as shock absorbers to keep the PAC bonds on schedule. Support bonds, as shown in Exhibit 10, have the highest degree of average life volatility. Because support bonds buffer the PAC bond, PAC bonds have the lowest degree of average life volatility.

Exhibit 11 illustrates the typical average life volatility for 5-year average life CMO classes by type. As shown in the exhibit, support bonds can show large swings in average life depending on the speed of prepayments. Sequential-pay bonds have a moderate average life range of 8.6 years (the change in class average life up and down 300 basis points). Finally, the average life range of PAC bonds is typically about half of that of sequential-pay bonds.

As shown in Exhibit 11, the average life volatility of support bonds can be very high. However, the factors shown in Exhibit 12 can reduce the average life volatility of support bonds.

Exhibit 10: Types of CMO Class

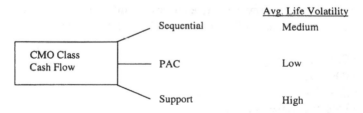

Exhibit 11: Comparison of Average Life Volatility

CMO Type	Base Case Avg Life	+300bp Avg Life	+100bp Avg Life	-300 bp Avg Life	-100bp Avg Life	300bp Avg Life Range
Sequential	5.4	9.3	6.0	0.7	1.6	8.6
PAC	5.9	5.9	5.9	1.6	3.5	4.3
Support	5.4	25.6	24.6	1.1	2.2	24.5

Exhibit 12: Factors that Can Reduce Average Life Volatility of Support Bonds

Factor	Reason
• Lower "PAC"%	• Higher Support Bond %
• Seasoned Collateral	• Lower prepayment risk
• 15-year collateral	• Lower prepayment risk
• Discount collateral	• Lower prepayment risk
• GNMA Collateral	• Small balances ⇒ Lower prepay risk

Exhibit 13: Class Coupon Shifting

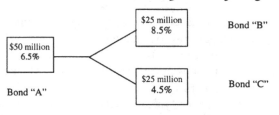

Finally, because of the higher volatility of support bonds, their cash flows are often sold in different forms. That is, these bonds are often structured into discount bonds and IOs, or floater/inverse floater combinations.

The restructuring of CMO bond classes, including floater and inverse floater combinations, will be discussed more fully in the next section.

ADVANCED CMO TOPICS

As previously mentioned, all CMO cash flows are created as sequential-pays, PAC bonds, or support bonds. However, there are several different ways to carve-up or subdivide these cash flows into different tranches. The following topics will be discussed:

- Coupon shifting
- IOs/POs
- PAC-IOs
- Floater/inverse floaters
- Two tiered index bonds
- Floater/inverse IOs

Coupon Shifting

One of the more basic ways to alter a bond's total return profile is through coupon shifting. This arbitrage is effective if the dealer can create a discount class and a premium class and sell the two classes at a combined tighter level than where the original bond tranche could have been sold. A diagram of this process is shown in Exhibit 13.

It is common to see a discounted bond class created from current coupon (or par-priced) classes. "Total return" investors will often request these discount bonds because they have a more bullish and convex profile. That is, the bond's total return performance will improve in a falling rate or a faster prepayment environment. The premium or 8.5% coupon bond will often be purchased by mutual funds that have special accounting rules for amortizing bond premiums. Additionally, these premium bonds will produce a high current cash flow necessary for dividend payments to fund shareholders.

It should be noted that the discount bond (bond B in Exhibit 13) and the premium bond (bond C) will have the same average life profile as the underlying bond from which B and C are created (bond A). Only the total return profiles will differ amongst the three bonds.

Here is an example of coupon shifting. Coupon shifting is often a function of a customer request. If, for example, a dealer starts with a $50 million 6.5% coupon class and receives an order from a customer to create a $10 million 3% coupon class, this would result in remaining class principal of $40 million with a 7.375% coupon. (See Step #1 in Exhibit 14.) However, since the remaining $40 million might be difficult to sell in its present form, suppose another order was received by the dealer from another customer for $20 million with a 5% coupon. This would be demonstrated in Step #2 in Exhibit 14. If this order were accepted, the remaining principal would be $20 million with a 9.75% coupon. If yet another order was received by the dealer to buy $10 million with a 6.5% coupon, the final $10 million in principal would have a 13% coupon. (See Step #3 in Exhibit 14.)

Exhibit 14: Coupon Shifting
Step #1

```
                              ┌──────────────┐
                              │ $10 million  │
                              │     3%       │
                              └──────────────┘
   ┌──────────────┐
   │ $50 million  │
   │    6.5%      │
   └──────────────┘
                              ┌──────────────┐
                              │ $40 million  │
                              │   7.375%     │
                              └──────────────┘
```

Step #2

```
                              ┌──────────────┐
                              │ $20 million  │
                              │     5%       │
                              └──────────────┘
   ┌──────────────┐
   │ $40 million  │
   │   7.375%     │
   └──────────────┘
                              ┌──────────────┐
                              │ $20 million  │
                              │    9.75%     │
                              └──────────────┘
```

Exhibit 14 (Continued)
Step #3

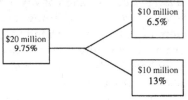

Step #4

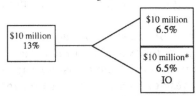

* Notional principal

Exhibit 15: Coupon Shifting Example

Before		After		
Principal	Coupon	Principal	Coupon	Reference Step in Exhibit 14
$50	6.5%	$10	3.0%	#1
		$20	5.0%	#2
		$10	6.5%	#3
		$10	6.5%	#4
		$10*	6.5%	#4
$50	6.5%	$50	6.5%	

* Notional principal

The final consideration must be the ability to place the remaining $10 million piece with a 13% super-premium coupon. Another consideration would be the ability to sell the 13% coupon as a partial IO strip. (See Step #4 in Exhibit 14.) IOs will be discussed more fully in the next section.

In summary, how a bond is ultimately carved up is a function of investor demand relative to where the bond could be placed in its pure form. (See Exhibit 15.)

IOs/POs

In Chapter 3 we discussed mortgage strips — principal only and interest only securities. When the mortgage derivative market began, these products were actually referred to as CMOs and classified as such by some mutual funds and money managers because they represented securities using a very simple rule for allocation of interest and principal between two bond classes. While we discussed IO and PO securities in Chapter 3, here we will explain in more detail how they are created and expand our discussion on their investment attributes. Then we will see how they are created within a CMO structure.

As shown in Exhibit 16, IOs and POs are created from mortgage collateral pools. In the exhibit, $25 million of 6.5% collateral can be stripped into a $25 million PO and $25 million notional balance 6.5% IO. Although the PO in this example is *not* entitled to any interest income, it will be referred to as a 6.5% PO. Also, the 6.5% IO does not have any real principal allocated to it. It is referred to as "$25 million notional" because the principal allocated to the class from which the interest cash flow is generated is $25 million.

As shown in Exhibit 17, there are three types of cash flow generated from home mortgages. The first is regular interest payments, which tend to be front loaded or larger early in the mortgage's life. All of interest cash flows are allocated to the IO class. The second type of cash flow is regular or scheduled principal. These payments tend to be back-loaded or become larger as the loan ages. The third type of cash flow is principal paid due to prepayments. Prepayments, which have become more frequent in recent years due to industry competition and "streamlined refinancing" programs, can occur at any time during a loan's life. All of the scheduled principal, as well as the prepayments, are allocated to the PO class.

Exhibit 16: Creation of IOs and POs from Mortgage Collateral Pools

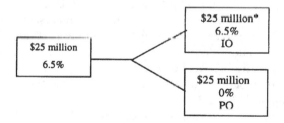

* Notional principal

Exhibit 17: Allocating Cash to IO/POs

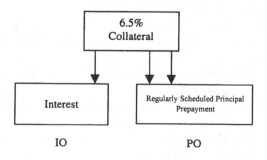

Exhibit 18: Allocation of Cash 6.5% Mortgage Passthrough Assuming No Prepayments (0% CPR)

Years	Interest	Principal	Total	% of Total Cash IO	% of Total Cash PO
1-5	$316,334	$57,685	$374,019	84.6%	15.4%
6-10	293,906	82,183	376,089	78.1	21.9
11-20	478,383	144,030	622,413	76.9	23.1
21-25	151,574	237,652	389,226	38.9	61.1
26-30	59,175	338,582	397,757	14.9%	85.5%
Total	$1,299,372	$1,000,000	$2,299,372		

Exhibit 19: Allocation of Cash 6.5% Mortgage Passthrough Assuming 20% CPR

Years	Interest	Principal	Total	% of Total Cash IO	% of Total Cash PO
1-5	$193,447	$691,125	$884,572	21.9%	78.1%
6-10	59,080	216,453	275,533	21.4	78.6
11-20	22,090	85,766	107,856	20.5	79.5
21-25	1,114	5,373	6,487	17.2	82.8
26-30	159	1,283	1,442	11.0%	89.0%
Total	$275,890	$1,000,000	$1,275,890		

Let's review the typical allocation of interest and principal produced from a $1 million 6.5% mortgage passthrough as shown in Exhibit 18. It is interesting to note that at 0% CPR nearly $1.3 million in interest cash flow is produced over the life of the mortgage. Additionally, during the first five years nearly 85% of all cash flows are allocated to interest. Conversely, it is not until years 26 to 30 that we see the situation reverse so that 85% of the cash flows are allocated to principal. Exhibit 19 shows the allocation of cash flow for the same $1 million 6.5% passthrough at 20% CPR.

Comparing the two cash flows shown in Exhibits 18 and 19, there are three interesting things to note. First, notice the total cash flows produced is $1 million less when the pool pays at 20% CPR rather than 0% CPR. Also note that the shortfall in cash flow is all allocated to the IO. Second, note that the PO's total cash flow is the same in both examples, $1 million (only the timing is different). Third, note that the total cash flows go from 85% IO during the first five years at 0% CPR to 78% PO at 20% CPR over the same period. Thus, we can see that the IO cash flows are both highly variable and uncertain depending on the timing and degree of prepayment activity within the pool. Exhibit 20 summarizes the vast differences between IOs and POs.

Finally, IOs/POs can also be created from CMO deals and/or CMO classes. However, it is much more common to create IO classes off CMO deals since IO bonds (often called *notional IOs* or *structured IOs*) are needed to create discount bonds for the short CMO bonds.

Exhibit 20: Properties of IOs/POs

Factor	IOs	POs
Initial Yield	Very high	Very low
Cash Received	Uncertain	Known
$ Invested Returned	Maybe	Yes
Duration	Negative	Positive
Value over Time	Depreciating	Appreciating
Impact of Value		
New Loans	Increase	Decrease
Higher Coupon	Decrease	Increase
Higher CPR%	Decrease	Increase

Exhibit 21: Creating CMO IO Bonds – Step #1

Class	A	B	C	D
Avg Life	3	5	10	15
Trsy Yield (1)	5.00%	5.25%	6.00%	6.50%
CMO Spread (2)	0.75	1.00	1.25	1.50
Total Yield (3)=(1)+(2)	5.75%	6.25%	7.25%	8.00%
Coll CPN% (4)	6.50%	6.50%	6.50%	6.50%
+/– Yield (5)=(4)–(3)	+0.75%	+0.25%	–0.75%	–1.50%
Premium/Discount	Premium	Premium	Discount	Discount
% Deal	65%	20%	10%	5%

Exhibit 22: Creating CMO IO – Step #2

Class	BP Strip	% Deal	BP off Collateral	% of IO
A	75	65	48.75	90.7
B	25	20	5.00	9.3
C	0	10	0.00	0.0
D	0	5	0.00	0.0
		100%	53.75	100.0%

Exhibit 21 shows how IOs are created to produce par and/or discount bonds. In the example, bond classes A and B would be stripped down to produce par bonds. In the case of bond A, 75 basis points would be stripped, whereas 25 basis points would be stripped off bond B. Bonds C and D would remain unstripped since they are already discount bonds. Therefore, the IO created will have the characteristics shown in Exhibit 22. As shown in the exhibit, the strip off bond A amounts to a 48.75 bp strip off the entire deal and represents 90.7% of the IO. On the other hand, the strip off bond B represents 5 bp off the deal and 9.3% of the IO. The bond created by the example above is very front-loaded and would be highly dependent on actual prepayment speeds.

PAC-IOs

A PAC-IO is a combination security, having properties of both a PAC bond and an IO. As the name would imply, its investment profile is still highly variable because it is an IO product created without any principal. Exhibit 23 demonstrates how a PAC-IO is created. To begin one must understand from which bonds the PAC-IO will be stripped. The first thing to notice is that PAC A is a full coupon bond and therefore not one of the PAC bonds contributing to the PAC-IO. The PAC-IO in our example is therefore created from PAC bonds B, C, and D.

Exhibit 24 demonstrates the composition of our sample PAC-IO. The bond created in the exhibit is typical in the sense that it is front-loaded and therefore at risk should the PAC bond B prepay faster than expected.

PAC-IOs are, however, rather conservative investments within the scope of IO products. Exhibit 25 summarizes the three main types of IO products — PAC-IOs, trust IOs, and inverse IOs.

PAC-IOs are priced with moderately high yield levels with modest amounts of prepayment risk. They are difficult to hedge, since a perfect hedge would require the repurchase of the underlying PAC bonds in the right percentages. Additionally, liquidity for PAC-IOs is at best, moderate.

In contrast, Trust IOs (more popularly referred to as *stripped mortgage-backed securities*, SMBS) are high yielding bonds with high degrees of prepayment risk. However, they are also the most liquid IO products and can be perfectly hedged by purchasing the companion Trust PO bonds.

Exhibit 23: Creating PAC-IOs: Step #1

% Deal

PAC A	PAC B	PAC C	PAC D	
6.5%	5.5%	6.0%	6.0%	} 65%
Support 1	Support 2		Support 3	35%

Exhibit 24: Creating PAC-IOs: Step #2

100 bp	50 bp	50bp	6.5% Coupon
			6.0
			5.5
PAC B	PAC C	PAC D	5.0
$20 million	$10 million	$10 million	4.5

Exhibit 25: Comparison of IO Products

	PAC-IOs	Trust IO	Inverse IO
Base-case yield	Moderate	High	Very high
Prepayment risk	Moderate	High	Very high
Ability to hedge	Difficult	Good	Most Difficult
Liquidity	Moderate	High	Low

Exhibit 26: Inverse Floater Creation Variables

Variable	Impact on Inverse Floater
Collateral coupon	Higher coupons ⇒ Higher leverage
Floater margin	Lower margins ⇒ Higher leverage
Floater cap	Lower cap ⇒ Higher leverage
Inverse floor	0% Floor ⇒ Maximum leverage

Exhibit 27: Creating Inverse Floaters

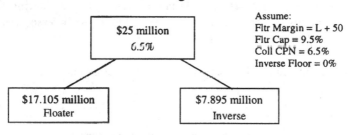

Finally, inverse IOs (which will be more fully discussed later) are very high yielding leveraged IOs. Because they are created with high leverage, they are very sensitive to actual prepayments. Additionally, they are virtually impossible to hedge and are the most illiquid of the major types of IO products.

Inverse Floaters

If all CMO classes had to be created as fixed-rate tranches, the CMO market would be substantially smaller than it is currently. The desire of many financial institutions to invest in floating-rate assets is strong because floaters are a better match for their liabilities. This is the case since many bank liabilities (such as time deposits and certificates of deposit) reset periodically based on short-term interest rates and the funding costs of other institutional investors are based on a short-term floating rate.

It is because of the strong demand for floating-rate assets, and the fixed-rate nature of the underlying collateral, that inverse floaters are created. Floaters are typically indexed to LIBOR and usually can be sold at richer levels than the underlying collateral cost, thus improving CMO arbitrage opportunities for the dealer.

Below we will walk through the process of creating an inverse floater. Exhibit 26 illustrates some important variables necessary for the creation of an inverse floater. The CMO dealer will try to maximize the arbitrage opportunity when creating a floater/inverse floater combination. As mentioned earlier, CMO floaters help the profitability of the CMO deal, therefore the dealer will try to make the floater class large relative to the inverse floater.

Exhibit 27 identifies the inverse floater creation process. The allocation of the $25 million to the floater and inverse floater bonds is determined by the use of the following formulas.

Floater principal = Total principal × Coupon/Floater cap

For our hypothetical illustration in Exhibit 27, we have:

Floater principal = 25,000,000 × 6.5%/9.5% = $17,105,000

The principal allocated to the inverse tranche is then the difference between the original $25 million and the $17.105 million floaters or $7.895 million. Next, the inverse floater formula is determined by calculating the inverse leverage and the inverse cap (sometimes referred to as the inverse intercept in the coupon formula) as shown in the next two equations:

Inverse leverage = Floater principal/Inverse principal

and

Inverse cap = Inverse leverage × Effective floater cap

For our hypothetical structure, we have the following

Inverse leverage = $17,105,000/$7,895,0003 = 2.166

Inverse cap = 2.166 × 9% = 19.5%

Putting the leverage and inverse cap together, we obtain the inverse floater's coupon formula:

Inverse formula = 19.5% − 2.166 LIBOR

Exhibit 28 shows how the monthly coupons are allocated at different LIBOR levels. As can be seen, all coupon combinations must total the coupon of the underlying cash flow (i.e., 6.5%). Note that at very high levels of interest rates, the floater bond will hit its cap and the inverse floater bond will hit its 0% floor.

Exhibit 28: Allocation of Floater/Inverse Coupons

LIBOR	Floater (%)	Inverse Floater (%)	Total (%)
4.00	4.50%	10.83	6.50
6.00	6.50%	6.50	6.50
7.00	7.50%	4.34	6.50
8.00	8.50%	2.17	6.50
10.00	9.50%	0.00	6.50
Formula	L + 50	19.5 − 2.166L	6.50%
% Class	68.42%	31.58%	100%

Exhibit 29: Typical TTIB

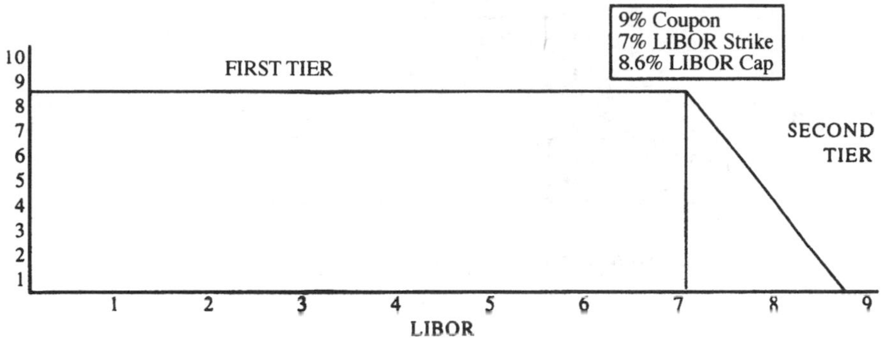

The final point about inverse floaters is that these bonds, unlike IO-type products, have full principal balances. Thus, inverse floater investors will get all their principal returned to them. Additionally, inverse floaters when monitored closely can be hedged using the swaps, Treasury, and LIBOR caps and floors markets.

Two-Tiered Index Bonds

Two-tiered index bonds (TTIBs) are a type of CMO class which combines the characteristics of a high coupon fixed-rate bond and an inverse floater. TTIB bonds are fixed-rate bonds across a wide range of interest rate scenarios. These bonds remain at a fixed coupon as long as the bond's applicable index falls below its *first tier* or *lower strike*. The TTIB's example in Exhibit 29 has a first tier or lower strike of 7% LIBOR. Suppose that the current LIBOR is 4.93%. Then the coupon in the example is at an above market rate of 9%.

The TTIB in the example, which is typical of the overall market as of this writing, maintains its 9% coupon unless LIBOR moves above 7%. If this occurs, then the bond coupon is set by the formula $48.375\% - 5.625 \times$ 1-month LIBOR. The TTIB coupon hits 0% at the *second tier*, when LIBOR hits 8.6% (called the bond's *LIBOR cap*).

A summary of the TTIB's coupon settings for the hypothetical bond in Exhibit 29 is shown below:

LIBOR Index	TTIB Coupon
<7%	9%
7% to 8.6%	$48.375 - 5.625 \times LIBOR$
>8.6%	0%

TTIBs are created in order to improve the overall execution in a CMO structure. TTIBs improve CMO execution because of the following factors:

- Allows floater to be created with higher caps
- Allows greater leverage on inverse floaters
- Allows inverse floaters to have deeper discounts

Exhibit 30: Creating TTIB - Step #1

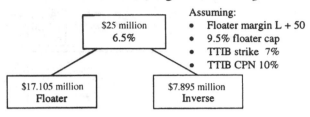

Assuming:
- Floater margin L + 50
- 9.5% floater cap
- TTIB strike 7%
- TTIB CPN 10%

Exhibit 31: Creating TTIB - Step #2

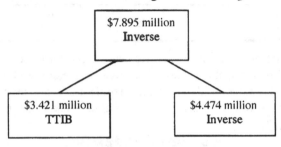

The example in Exhibit 30 illustrates the creation of a TTIB bond. TTIBs are created from the cash flows of an inverse floater. The initial step in the process, as we discussed in the previous section, is to divide a CMO class into a floater and inverse floater.

Using the formulas discussed in the previous section, we would end up with an inverse floater with the following coupon formula: $19.5\% - 2.166 \times$ LIBOR. Because of the relatively high cap on the floater and the low coupon on the collateral, a relatively low leveraged inverse is created. It is because this bond has low leverage and assuming a LIBOR level of 4.93%, a relatively low current coupon (i.e., 8.82%), that our hypothetical inverse might be difficult to sell.

Therefore, the second step is to subdivide the inverse floater into a more highly levered inverse and a TTIB as shown in Exhibit 31. The formulas for the TTIB and inverse coupon are determined by using the following equation:

$$\text{TTIB prin} = \frac{\text{Total prin} \times \text{Cpn} - \text{Floater prin(Floater margin + TTIB strike)}}{\text{TTIB Cpn}}$$

For the TTIB in Exhibit 31, the principal is

$$\text{TTIB prin} = \frac{\$25,000,000 \times 6.5\% - \$17,105,000(0.5\% + 7.0\%)}{0.10}$$

$$= \$3,421,000$$

Next we need to calculate the TTIB formula. Therefore, we must calculate both the TTIB inverse cap (intercept) and the TTIB leverage as follows:

TTIB leverage = Floater prin/TTIB prin

and

TTIB cap = TTIB leverage × (Floater cap − Floater Margin) × 100
For our hypothetical TTIB:

TTIB leverage = $17,105,000/$3,421,000 = 5

and

TTIB cap = 5 × (9.5% − 0.5%) = 45

The TTIB coupon formula is then:

TTIB coupon = 45 − 5 × LIBOR

The next step is to then determine the inverse formula for the newly created more levered inverse floater. First, the size of the new inverse is determined by subtracting the TTIB principal from the principal size of the original inverse created in Step #1 (i.e., $7.895 million − $3.421 million = $4.474 million). This means that the new inverse leverage is 3.82 ($17.105 million floaters/$4.474 million inverse). We can next calculate the new inverse cap using the following equation:

Inverse cap = Inverse leverage × TTIB lower strike × 100

For our hypothetical TTIB, the inverse cap is:

Inverse cap = 3.82 × 7% × 100 = 26.76

Therefore, the inverse floater coupon formula becomes:

Inverse coupon = 26.76 − 3.82 × LIBOR

The inclusion of the TTIB in the sample CMO deal structure had the following effect on the deal.

- Creation of a smaller inverse (17.9% of structure with TTIB versus 31.56% originally)
- Higher inverse leverage (3.82 with TTIB versus 2.166 originally)
- Inverse with more bullish profile

As previously mentioned, CMO classes get created if they can be sold at tighter executions than in their pure form. Exhibit 32 shows five scenarios and their respective impacts on inverse floater leverage.

There are several interesting things to note regarding the results reported in Exhibit 32. First, in all scenarios the inclusion of the TTIB in the CMO structure allows for a more highly leveraged inverse floater. Second, the use of higher coupon collateral allows for a more leveraged inverse floater (see Scenario 3). Third, the use of a higher cap on the floating-rate bond results in lower inverse leverage (see Scenario 2). Fourth, lowering the TTIB coupon increases inverse floater leverage (see Scenario 4). Finally, lowering the strike level on the TTIB also increases inverse leverage (see Scenario 5).

Finally, Exhibit 33 shows how the class coupons are allocated to the various bonds under different interest rate scenarios.

Inverse IOs

Inverse IOs are the most complex securities currently trading within the CMO market. This is the case because these are hybrid bonds which have to be created using a multi-step process. Inverse IOs are part premium bond, part inverse floater, and part IO. Also because these bonds are IOs, the return of the buyer's investment dollars remain at risk.

An inverse IO is created from a fixed-rate bond through the issuance of a floater which uses the entire principal of the fixed-rate class. The floater will typically have to be capped at the coupon rate of the underlying fixed-rate bond since the inverse IO is not allocated any principal. Since this cap is almost always higher than the current coupon level, the underlying fixed-rate bond is usually a premium bond.

Exhibit 32: Inverse Floater Leverage Worksheet

Scenario	Coll Cpn (%)	Fltr Cap (%)	Fltr %	TTIB Cpn (%)	TTI B Strike (%)	No TTIB Inverse Leverage	With TTIB Inverse Leverage
Base 1	6.5	9.5	68.42	10.0	7.0	2.17	3.82
2	6.5	10.0	65.00	10.0	7.0	1.86	3.47
3	7.0	9.5	73.68	10.0	7.0	2.80	6.36
4	6.5	9.5	68.42	9.0	7.0	2.17	4.18
5	6.5	9.5	68.42	10.0	6.5	2.17	4.73

Exhibit 33: Allocation of Bond Class Coupon

LIBOR	No TTIBS			With TTIB			
	Floater Coupon	Inverse Floater Coupon	Wgt Avg. Coupon	Floater Coupon	TTIB Coupon	Inverse Floater Coupon	Wtg Avg. Coupon
4%	4.50%	10.84%	6.5%	4.50%	10.00%	11.48%	6.5%
6%	6.50	6.50	6.5	6.50	10.00	3.84	6.5
8%	8.50	2.17	6.5	8.50	5.00	0.00	6.5
10%	9.50	0.00	6.5	9.50	0.00	0.00	6.5
Formula	L + 50	19.5-2.166L	6.5%	L + 50	45-5L	26.76-3.82L	6.5%
% Class	68.42%	31.58%	100.0%	68.42%	13.68%	17.90%	100.0%

Exhibit 34: Creating an Inverse IO: Step #1

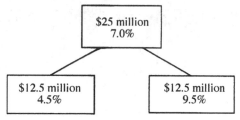

Exhibit 35: Creating an Inverse IO: Step #2

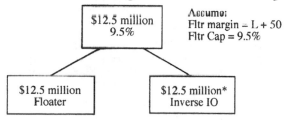

* Notional principal balance

Exhibit 36: Inverse IO Investment Characteristics

	(A)	–	(B)	=	(A) – (B)
Characteristics	Premium Fixed Rate		Floater		Inverse IO
Duration	Positive		Short		Very long
Convexity	Negative		Neutral		Very negative
Yield	Moderate		Low		Very high
Leverage	None		Low		Very high

Therefore, as stated above, the first step in the creation of an inverse IO is the creation of a premium bond class. This first step is illustrated in Exhibit 34. The next step is to take the premium tranche and to divide it into its floater and inverse IO components as illustrated in Exhibit 35.

The coupon on the inverse IO is the amount generated by the fixed position in excess of that which is required to be paid to the floater. The amortization of the notional principal balance on the Inverse IO depends on the paydown of the underlying CMO class.

Since the inverse IO bond can be thought of as the residual cash flow from the fixed-rate bond and the floater, it is easy to understand its investment characteristics by studying Exhibit 36. As can be seen, all the negative convexity risk (discussed in Chapter 8) of the premium bond is transferred to the inverse IO since the floater is structured as a par bond.

The formula for the inverse IO coupon is determined as follows:

Inverse IO coupon = (Fltr cap − Fltr margin) − LIBOR

Exhibit 37: Allocation of Inverse IO Coupon

LIBOR (%)	Fixed coupon (%)	Floater Coupon (%)	Inverse IO coupon (%)
4	9.5	4.5	5.0
5	9.5	5.5	4.0
6	9.5	6.5	3.0
7	9.5	7.5	2.0
8	9.5	8.5	1.0
9	9.5	9.5	0.0

Exhibit 38: Inverse Floaters versus Inverse IOs

Characteristic	Inverse Floaters	Inverse IOs
Yield	High	Very high
Prepay sensitivity	High	Very high
Convexity profile	Discount bond	Premium bond
Leverage	Low-moderate	High/very high
$ Invested at risk?	No	Yes
Can be hedged?	Yes	No
Bond liquidity	Good	Fair

For the hypothetical inverse floater created in Exhibit 35, the coupon formula is:

$$\text{Inverse IO coupon} = (9.5\% - 0.5\%) - \text{LIBOR}$$
$$= 9.0\% - \text{LIBOR}$$

Using this formula, the coupon allocation between the inverse IO and the floater is shown in Exhibit 37.

The primary difference between an inverse IO and an inverse floater is the degree of leverage. That is, most newly constructed inverse floaters have leverage of 2.0 to 4.0, whereas the effective leverage for inverse IOs is much higher (usually 10 times or more). Moreover, an inverse IO is much more sensitive to prepayments than an inverse floater. If the underlying premium fixed-rate bond were to pay down completely, the inverse IO's value would decline to zero since there is no receipt of any principal.

Exhibit 38 summarizes some of the differences in investment characteristics of inverse floaters and inverse IOs.

Chapter 5

Nonagency Residential MBS

In the previous chapter, our focus was solely on carving up the cash flows of a pool of mortgage loans to redistribute prepayment risk. Credit risk was not a consideration because the CMOs discussed in the previous chapter were those guaranteed by a federally related institution (Ginnie Mae) or issued by a government sponsored enterprise (Fannie Mae and Freddie Mac). In this chapter and the two that follow, we turn our focus to mortgage-related products where an investor is concerned with both prepayment risk and credit risk. In this chapter, we cover nonagency mortgage-backed securities — products that the market participants view as part of the MBS market. In Chapter 6 we cover products backed by a pool of residential loans classified as part of the ABS market. Securities backed by commercial mortgages are covered in Chapter 7.

COLLATERAL FOR NONAGENCY MBS

Mortgage loans used as collateral for an agency security are conforming loans. That is, they must meet the underwriting standards of the agency. The collateral for a nonagency MBS consists of nonconforming loans. A loan may be nonconforming for one or more of the following reasons (see Exhibit 1 also):

1. The mortgage balance exceeds the amount permitted by the agency.
2. The borrower characteristics fail to meet the underwriting standards established by the agency.
3. The loan characteristics fail to meet the underwriting standards established by the agency.
4. The applicant fails to provide full documentation as required by the agency.

There are alternative lending programs for borrowers seeking nonconforming loans for any of the above reasons.

A mortgage loan that is nonconforming merely because the mortgage balance exceeds the maximum permitted by the agency guideline is called a *jumbo loan*. With respect to the characteristics of the borrower, a loan may fail to qualify because the borrower's credit history does not meet the underwriting standards or the *payment-to-income* (PTI) *ratio* exceeds the maximum permitted. Borrowers who do satisfy the underwriting standards with respect to borrower characteristics are referred to as A credit borrowers or prime borrowers. An *Alter-*

native A loan is a loan of an A credit borrower that has a mortgage balance that is below or above the amount necessary to be conforming, but for various reasons fails to qualify to meet the underwriting standards of either the agencies or originators of jumbo loans. For example, the loan could fail to qualify for inclusion in an agency pool because the property is non-owner occupied, the property could be a second home, or the documentation is not complete. We will discuss Alternative A loans and nonagency CMO deals backed by such loans in more detail at the end of this chapter.

B and C borrowers or sub-prime borrowers are borrowers who fail to satisfy the underwriting standards of the agencies because of borrower characteristics. These characteristics include credit history and maximum PTI. The loans are actually scaled by originators from B to D. Every originator establishes its own profiles for classifying a loan into a rating category.

A characteristic that may result in a loan failing to meet the underwriting standards is that the *loan-to-value* (LTV) *ratio* exceeds the maximum established by the agency or the loan is not a first-mortgage lien. There are lenders who specialize in loans that exceed the maximum LTV. These lending programs are sometimes referred to as *125 LTV programs* because the lender may be willing to lend up to 125% of the appraised or market value of the property. Basically, the lender is making a consumer loan based on the credit of the borrower to the extent that the loan amount exceeds the appraised or market value. For this reason, lenders with 125 programs have limited these loans to A credit borrowers. Mortgage-related products in which the underlying loans are 125 LTV loans are considered part of the ABS market and are discussed in the next chapter.

Exhibit 1: Agency/Non-Agency Pools

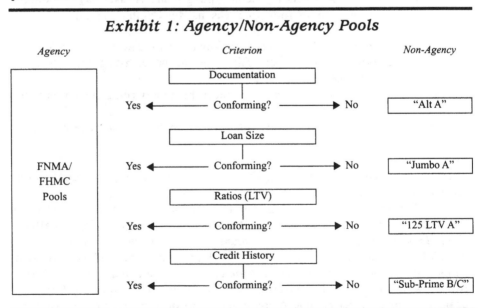

For borrowers seeking a loan that is not a first lien on the property, a consumer loan in the form of a home equity loan can be obtained. A growing number of home equity loans are now first liens. There are two types of home equity loans, closed-end and open-end loans. With closed-end home equity loans the lender provides the proceeds at the closing and the borrower must make scheduled monthly payments to amortize the loan as with a standard mortgage loan. In an open-end home equity loan, the lender provides a line of credit and the borrower takes down the line as needed. Mortgage-related products backed by home equity loans are considered part of the ABS market and will be covered in the next chapter.

In assessing whether a loan qualifies for conforming classification, the agencies require documentation (verification) of the information provided in the loan application. These include documents to verify the PTI and the LTV. To verify the PTI, documents to verify income (e.g., pay stubs or tax returns) and employment are needed, as well as a credit report. To verify the LTV, a property appraisal report and documentation of the source of the down payment are required. Failure to provide adequate documentation will result in a loan failing to conform. There are originators who will provide a loan based on no documentation ("no-doc loan") or limited documentation ("low-doc loan") with respect to verification of income. The borrowers are not necessarily subprime borrowers. They may be self-employed individuals or owners of a business where the amount reported in tax returns or paid as income would not meet the PTI standard of the agencies. Originators of no doc and low doc loans rely on the collateral (by limiting the LTV to 80% or less) and verification of significant assets that can be used to make the mortgage payments.

DIFFERENCES BETWEEN AGENCY AND NONAGENCY SECURITIES

As with agency MBS, there are nonagency passthrough securities and nonagency CMOs. Agency CMOs are created from pools of passthrough securities. In the nonagency market, a CMO can be created from either a pool of passthroughs or unsecuritized mortgage loans. It is uncommon for nonconforming mortgage loans to be securitized as passthroughs and then the passthroughs carved up to create a CMO. Instead, in the nonagency market a CMO is carved out of mortgage loans that have not been securitized as passthroughs. Since a mortgage loan is commonly referred to as a whole loan, nonagency CMOs are commonly referred to as *whole-loan CMOs*.

Differences between agency and nonagency MBS are discussed below.

Guarantees

With a nonagency MBS there is no explicit or implicit government guarantee of payment of interest and principal as there is with an agency security. Thus, there is credit risk. The nationally recognized statistical rating organizations rate nonagency securities.

Dispersion of Characteristics of Underlying Collateral

While both agency and nonagency MBS are backed by 1- to 4-single family residential mortgages, the underlying loans for nonagency securities will typically be more heterogeneous with respect to coupon rate and maturity of the individual loans. For example, a nonagency MBS might include both 15-year and 30-year mortgages in the same mortgage pool. The greater dispersion of the coupon rate means that it is more difficult to predict prepayments due to refinancing based on the pool's weighted average coupon.

Moreover, there are issues in which the underlying collateral is mixed with various types of mortgage-related loans. That is, the collateral backing a deal may include collateral that is a combination of first-lien mortgages, home equity loans, manufactured housing loans, and home improvement loans. The Securities Data Corporation (SDC) has established criteria for classifying a mortgage product with mixed collateral as either a nonagency MBS or an ABS. The purpose of the classification is not to aid in the analysis of these securities, but rather to construct the so-called "league tables" for ranking investment banking firms by deal type. SDC's rules for classifying a deal as either a nonagency MBS or an ABS are as follows. If at the cut-off date more than 50% of a deal consists of either manufactured housing loans, home equity loans, second mortgage loans, or home improvement loans, then the deal is classified as an ABS. For deals in which more than 50% of the loans are first liens, SDC uses a size test to classify the deal. If more than 50% of the aggregate principal balance of the loans have a loan balance of more than $200,000, the deal is classified as a nonagency MBS. A deal in which 50% of the loans are first liens, but more than 50% of the aggregate principal balance of the loans is less than $200,000 is classified as an ABS.

Servicer Advances

The servicer is responsible for the collection of interest and principal, which is passed along to the trustee. The servicer also handles delinquencies and foreclosures. Typically, there will be a master servicer and subservicers. These entities play a critical role and in assessing the credit risk of a nonagency MBS, the rating agencies look carefully at the quality of the servicers.

When there is a delinquency by the homeowner, the investor in a nonagency MBS may or may not be affected. This depends on whether a servicer is required to make advances. Thus, the financial capacity of the servicer to make advances is critical. Typically, a back-up servicer is used just in case the master servicer cannot meet its obligation with respect to advances. The servicer recovers advances when delinquent payments are made or the property is foreclosed and proceeds received.

There are different forms of advancing: (1) mandatory advancing, (2) optional advancing, and (3) limited advancing. The strongest form from the investor's perspective is mandatory advancing wherein failure to advance by a servicer is an event of default. However, a servicer need not advance if it can show that there is not a strong likelihood of recovery of the amount advanced when the property is ultimately disposed of. In an optional or a voluntary advancing, the servicer is not legally obligated to advance so that failure to do so is not an event of default. In a limited advancing the issuer is obligated to advance, but the amount it must advance is limited.

Compensating Interest

A feature unique to nonagency MBS is compensating interest. MBS pay principal and interest on a monthly basis. While homeowners may prepay their mortgage on any day throughout the month, the agencies guarantee and pay investors a full month of interest as if all the prepayments occur on the last day of the month. This guarantee does not apply to nonagency MBS. If a homeowner pays off a mortgage on the tenth day of the month, he will not have to pay interest for the rest of the month. Because of the payment delay (for example, 25 days), the investor will receive full principal but only 10 days of interest on the 25th of the following month.

This phenomenon is known as *payment interest shortfall* or *compensating interest* and is handled differently by different issuers. Some issuers will only pay up to a specified amount and some will not pay at all. Actually, it is the servicers who will pay any compensating interest. The servicer obtains the shortfall in interest from the servicing spread. The shortfall that will be made up to the investor may be limited to the entire servicing spread or part of the servicing spread. Thus, while an investor has protection against the loss of a full month's interest, the protection may be limited.

We look further at compensating interest later in this chapter.

Clean-Up Call Provisions

All nonagency CMOs are issued with "clean-up" call provisions. The clean-up call provides the servicers or the residual holders (typically the issuer) the right, but not the obligation, to call all the outstanding tranches of the CMO structure when the CMO balance is paid down to a certain percentage of the original principal balance. The servicer typically finds it costs more than the servicing fee received to service the CMO when the balance is paid down to a small amount. For example, suppose a $100 million CMO was originally issued with a 10% clean-up call. When the entire CMO balance is paid down to $10 million or less, the servicer can exercise the clean-up call to pay off all outstanding tranches regardless of the percentage balance of the individual tranches.

The call provision, when exercised, shortens the principal paydown window and the average life of the back-end tranches of a CMO. This provision is not unique to nonagency CMO structures. It is mandatory, however, for all nonagency CMO structures while agency CMOs may or may not have clean-up calls. Typically, Freddie Mac CMOs have 1% clean-up calls and Fannie Mae CMOs do not have clean-up calls.

Credit Enhancements

To obtain a specific credit rating for a tranche in a deal, it is necessary for the pool of mortgage loans to be credit enhanced. Credit enhancement levels are determined by the rating agencies from which the issuer seeks a rating for the tranches. This is also the case for real estate backed asset-backed securities described in the next chapter.

Credit enhancement mechanisms can take various forms. As explained later in this chapter, credit enhancement can be classified as either internal or external. External credit enhancement mechanisms are third-party guarantees, such as corporate guarantees, letters of credit, pool insurance policies, and bond insurance policies. External credit enhancements do not materially alter the cash flow characteristics of a CMO structure except in the form of prepayment. In case of a default resulting in net losses within the guarantee level, investors will receive the principal amount as if a prepayment has occurred. If the net losses exceed the guarantee level, investors will realize a shortfall in the cash flows.

Internal credit enhancement mechanisms involve reserves, overcollateralization, and senior/subordinated structures. Each of these will be discussed later in this chapter. The combination of credit enhancement mechanisms selected by the issuer will be those that provide the issuer with the best execution. That is, it will maximize proceeds from the pool of mortgage loans sold as collateral after credit enhancement expenses (implicit and explicit) are taken into account.

WAC Interest-Only and Principal-Only Securities

In the previous chapter, we explained how a notional interest-only tranche can be created. This is done by stripping the excess interest between the coupon rate of the underlying pool of passthroughs for the CMO and the coupon rate for a particular tranche.

Because of the wide dispersion of the coupon rates on the underlying mortgages for a nonagency security, a different type of IO and PO security can be created. This is done by the issuer first establishing the rate that it wants to pay on the issue. This is called the *remittance rate*. Then from all underlying mortgages with a coupon rate that is in excess of the remittance rate, the excess interest is stripped off to create an IO security. This IO security is called a *WAC IO*. A principal-only security is created from the underlying mortgages for which the coupon rate is less than the remittance rate. The resulting PO security is called a *WAC PO*.

To illustrate this, consider the $200 million 30-year pool described in Exhibit 2 that is going to be used as collateral for a nonagency security. Suppose that the issuer determines that to sell the security a remittance rate of 9% will be required. Of the $200 million in collateral, there is $110 million whose coupon rate is different from the remittance rate. There is $70 million whose coupon rate is above the remittance rate. Since the coupon rate is 10% and the remittance rate is 9%, a WAC IO can be created from the 100 basis points excess interest of the $70 million of mortgages with a 10% coupon rate.

There is $40 million with a coupon rate of 8% which is less than the remittance rate. The issuer can calculate the amount of par value of the $40 million that is needed to generate a 9% coupon. The interest generated from the $40 million of the 8% coupon portion of the collateral is $3.2 million ($40 million times 8%). The amount of par value from the $40 million of the 8% coupon needed to create a 9% coupon is $35.6 million ($3.2 million divided by 9%). The difference of $4.4 million between the $40 million par value of 8% coupon collateral and $35.6 million of par value needed to create a 9% remittance rate is the par amount for a WAC PO.

Other Risks

Losses can also result through (1) borrower bankruptcy, (2) borrower fraud, and (3) special hazard risk.

Borrower Bankruptcy

When a borrower files for personal bankruptcy, there is a risk that a bankruptcy judge could reduce the borrower's mortgage debt. This debt reduction, called a *cramdown*, usually occurs only when the value of the borrower's home has fallen so that the mortgage loan balance exceeds the home's market value. If a cramdown is ordered, the loan's terms can be altered by reducing the unpaid principal balance or the loan's interest rate.

A mortgage borrower can file for personal bankruptcy under Chapter 7, Chapter 11, or Chapter 13. A few cramdowns have occurred in recent years in settling Chapter 13 bankruptcy cases. Chapter 13 allows for restructuring or forgiving debts while letting borrowers retain their assets. However, the 1993 Supreme Court case of Nobelman versus American Savings ruled that a borrower filing under Chapter 13 cannot effectively reduce his or her mortgage debt. In a Chapter 7 bankruptcy filing, a type of bankruptcy that generally involves liquidation of assets to make payments to creditors, cramdowns have also been disallowed under a Supreme Court ruling.

Exhibit 2: Description of Collateral Used to Create a WAC IO and WAC PO

Remittance rate: 9%
Collateral description: $200 million, 30-year nonconforming mortgages

Dispersion of collateral:

Coupon rate (%)	Par amount
8	$40,000,000
9	90,000,000
10	70,000,000

Finally, cramdown filings under Chapter 11 are more rare than those under Chapter 7 or Chapter 13 because of their cost and complexity. Jumbo loan borrowers are more likely to file under Chapter 11 because this section can be used only when the debtor's secured debt exceeds $350,000.

The rating agencies determine the size of the bankruptcy carve-out based on the collateral. For example, Standard & Poor's states that for securities backed by mortgages that exceed 75% LTV, issuers must have a bankruptcy reserve of $100,000 or have cramdown coverage equal to 121 basis points.

Borrower Fraud

Another potential risk to the nonagency investor arises from borrower fraud or misrepresentation during the application process. This type of risk is often not covered by the originator/conduit/sellers' representations and warranties.

Senior/subordinated structures provide a carve-out as protection against the risk of fraud. The risk of losses due to fraud are front-loaded. That is, borrowers who misrepresent their income, employment, or net worth will generally run into payment problems early in the loan's life. Therefore, fraud coverage is largest at issuance — around 2%, declining to 0% by the sixth year.

Special Hazard Risk

Special hazard losses result from properties damaged by earthquakes, mud-slides, tidal waves, volcanoes, or floods. Such losses are excluded from coverage under homeowners' and private mortgage insurance policies.

Subordinated tranches absorb special hazard losses up to a predetermined capped amount that declines as the mortgage pool amortizes. This "capped" amount is determined by the rating agencies. Standard & Poor's requires a triple-A level of special hazard risk equal to the highest of:

- 1% of current mortgage pool balance.
- Twice the principal balance of the pool's largest loan.
- The principal balance of the highest zip code concentration within California.

Special hazard losses in excess of this capped amount are distributed among the senior and subordinated classes pro-rata.

Historically, losses from special hazards are quite rare because:

- Special casualty insurance is often required on homes in high risk areas (i.e., flood insurance in flood zones, and earthquake insurance along known fault lines).
- Damage caused indirectly by an act of God, such as water damage or fire caused by an earthquake, can be covered under standard homeowners' policies.

Another important factor is land value. In costly areas such as Southern California, the value of land can represent over 50% of the value of a single-family home. Thus, if a home is totally destroyed, the land value acts as a floor in terms of the loan's loss severity.

Finally, where damage to property caused by special hazards is uninsured, the homeowner can often get access to low-cost government funds to help rebuild. Therefore, special hazards have not historically resulted in significant losses. In addition, geographic diversification can help to limit a pool's exposure to special hazard risk.

CREDIT ENHANCEMENTS

All nonagency securities are credit enhanced. Typically a double A or triple A rating is sought for the most senior tranche in a deal. The amount of credit enhancement necessary depends on rating agency requirements and is referred to as "sizing" the transaction. As explained earlier, there are two general types of credit enhancement structures: external and internal. We describe each type below.

External Credit Enhancements

External credit enhancements come in the form of third-party guarantees that provide for first loss protection against losses up to a specified level, for example, 10%. The most common forms of external credit enhancement are (1) a corporate guarantee, (2) a letter of credit, (3) pool insurance, and (4) bond insurance.

Pool insurance policies cover losses resulting from defaults and foreclosures. Policies are typically written for a dollar amount of coverage that continues in force throughout the life of the pool. However, some policies are written so that the dollar amount of coverage declines as the pool seasons as long as two conditions are met: (1) the credit performance is better than expected and (2) the rating agencies that rated the issue approve. Since only defaults and foreclosures are covered, additional insurance must be obtained to cover losses resulting from bankruptcy (i.e., court mandated modification of mortgage debt — "cramdown"), fraud arising in the origination process, and special hazards (i.e., losses resulting from events not covered by a standard homeowner's insurance policy).

Bond insurance provides the same function as in municipal bond structures. Typically, bond insurance is not used as the primary protection but to supplement other forms of credit enhancement.

A nonagency security with external credit support is subject to the credit risk of the third-party guarantor (called *event risk*). Should the third-party guarantor be downgraded, the issue itself could be subject to downgrade even if the structure is performing as expected. This is based on the "weak link" test followed by rating agencies. According to this test, when evaluating a proposed structure, credit quality of the issue is only as good as the weakest link in credit enhancement regardless of the quality of the underlying loans.

External credit enhancements do not materially alter the cash flow characteristics of a CMO structure except in the form of prepayment. In case of a default resulting in net losses within the guarantee level, investors will receive the principal amount as if a prepayment has occurred. If the net losses exceed the guarantee level, investors will realize a shortfall in the cash flows.

Internal Credit Enhancements

Internal credit enhancements come in more complicated forms than external credit enhancements and may alter the cash flow characteristics of the loans even in the absence of default. The most common forms of internal credit enhancements are reserve funds, overcollateralization, and senior/subordinated structures.

Reserve Funds

Reserve funds come in two forms, cash reserve funds and excess servicing spread. *Cash reserve funds* are straight deposits of cash generated from issuance proceeds. In this case, part of the underwriting profits from the deal are deposited into a fund which typically invests in money market instruments. Cash reserve funds are typically used in conjunction with some form of external credit enhancement.

Excess servicing spread accounts involve the allocation of excess spread or cash into a separate reserve account after paying out the net coupon, servicing fee, and all other expenses on a monthly basis. For example, suppose that the gross weighted average coupon (gross WAC) is 7.75%, the servicing and other fees are 0.25%, and the net weighted average coupon (net WAC) is 7.25%. This means that there is excess spread of 0.25%. The amount in the reserve account will gradually increase and can be used to pay for possible future losses.

The excess servicing spread is analogous to the guarantee fee paid to the issuer of an agency mortgage-backed security except that this is a form of self-insurance. This form of credit enhancement relies on the assumption that defaults occur infrequently in the very early life of the loans, but gradually increase in the following two to five years.

Overcollateralization

The total par value of the tranches is the liability of the structure. So, if a structure has two tranches with a par value of $300 million, then that is the amount of the liability. The amount of the collateral backing the structure must be at least equal to the amount of the liability. If the amount of the collateral exceeds the amount of the liability of the structure, the deal is said to be *overcollateralized*. The amount of overcollateralization represents a form of internal credit enhancement because it can be used to absorb losses. For example, if the liability of the structure is $300 million and the collateral's value is $320 million, then the structure is overcollateralized by $20 million. Thus, the first $20 million of losses will not result in a loss to any of the tranches.

Senior/Subordinated Structure

In a senior-subordinated structure there is a *senior tranche* and at least one *junior* or *subordinated tranche*. For example, suppose a deal has $300 million as collateral (i.e., a pool of loans or receivables). The structure may look as follows:

> senior tranche $270 million
> subordinated tranche $ 30 million

This means that the first $30 million of losses are absorbed by the subordinated tranche.

There is no reason why there must be only one subordinated tranche. The structure can have more than one subordinated tranche. For example, the structure could be as follows:

> senior tranche $270 million
>
> subordinated tranche 1 $22 million
> subordinated tranche 2 $8 million

In this structure, the subordinated tranches 1 and 2 are called the *non-senior tranches*. The senior tranche still has protection up to $30 million as in the previous structure with only one subordinated tranche. In the second structure, the first $8 million of losses is absorbed by the subordinated tranche 2. Hence, this tranche is referred to as the *first loss tranche*. Subordinated tranche 1 has protection of up to $8 million in losses, the protection provided by the first loss tranche.

The basic concern in the senior-subordinated structure is that while the subordinated tranches provide a certain level of credit protection for the senior tranche at the closing of the deal, the level of protection changes over time due to prepayments. The objective after the deal closes is to distribute any prepayments such that the credit protection for the senior tranche does not deteriorate over time. There is a well developed mechanism used to address this concern called the *shifting interest mechanism*. We will discuss the shifting interest mechanism when we discuss structural analysis in the next section.

EVALUATING SUBORDINATED TRANCHES

Investors have been increasingly drawn to residential subordinated structures for several reasons:

- Yield advantages versus comparably rated corporates
- Excellent mortgage credit history
- Improving structural protection
- Excellent call protection with limited extension risk

Below we discuss four important factors to consider when evaluating a structure. Next, we show some common methods of stress testing. Finally, other factors such as special hazard, bankruptcy, and fraud risk are analyzed.

Collateral Analysis

The first step in determining the relative value of investing in subordinated tranches is a detailed analysis of the deal's collateral. The collateral represents the raw material from which the deal's final structure is produced. In a typical deal, the collateral might consist of 100 to 400 loans, while for a Re-REMIC structure (a structure created by using tranches from previous deals as collateral) the number of loans constituting the collateral pool could be 1,000 to 5,000. Regardless of the complexity of the structure or the number of loans involved, the steps involved in a collateral analysis are similar.

The factors to examine during a review of a deal's collateral include:

- Loan type (fixed/adjustable)
- Loan-to-value (LTV) ratio
- Property type (single-family, condominium)
- Loan purpose (purchase, refinancing, equity-take out)
- Loan term (30-year, 15-year)
- Geographic diversification
- Seasoning of loans
- Occupancy status

Many of these factors are well known to investors in MBS. We highlight only some important features for analyzing subordinated tranches.

Historical analysis of static-pool data has shown that fixed-rate collateral is considerably safer than adjustable-rate mortgage (ARM) collateral. Hence, the subordinated market for deals backed by ARMs is still largely undeveloped. Therefore, this chapter's discussion focuses on fixed-rate mortgages.

A key variable in any analysis of mortgage loans is the *loan-to-value* (LTV) *ratio*. This ratio provides important information about a borrower's credit quality and net equity in a property. When analyzing a diskette or tape of loan pool information, what is particularly important is the pool's dispersion of LTV, not its weighted average LTV. Further, it is important to know the issuer's policy with regard to requiring private insurance coverage for loans in excess of 80% LTV.

Another variable to examine is the percent of a pool that does not represent single-family detached homes. Single-family homes are the largest and most desirable segment of the housing market and have historically shown the best resale performance. Condominiums, townhouses, and planned unit developments do not enjoy the same record of relative price stability.

Exhibit 3: Loan Balance, Market Value, and LTV Ratio for 30-Year and 15-Year Mortgages for Selected Years*

	30-Year			15-Year		
	Year 0	Year 3	Year 7	Year 0	Year 3	Year 7
Loan Balance ($)	240,000	237,003	231,677	240,000	215,080	170,786
Market Value ($)	300,000	300,000	300,000	300,000	300,000	300,000
LTV Ratio	80.0%	79.0%	77.2%	80.0%	71.7%	56.9%

* Assumes an 8% mortgage rate, full amortization, and 0% housing inflation.

Loan purpose is another category that should be carefully examined. A potential investor should closely examine the exposure, number of loans, and individual LTVs associated with equity-take out loans (also called *cash-out refinancings*). The main risk associated with these loans is that the loan may be initiated to increase a borrower's leverage. This can be problematic particularly since no market transaction is evident to confirm market value; that is, these loans are made solely on the basis of an appraisal.

Loan term is another important factor in collateral analysis. Currently, however, most pools backed by 15-year mortgages are separated from those backed by 30-year mortgages. This is the case because 15-year mortgages amortize much faster than 30-year loans, and therefore present less risk due to rapidly declining LTVs. As shown in Exhibit 3, the LTV ratio is considerably different over time for these two mortgage terms.

A final important consideration is geographic diversification. Pools with the lowest level of default risk have consisted of mortgages distributed over a wide geographic area. Many investors have become particularly concerned about their levels of California exposure. This actual level of exposure should be further divided into a pool's exposure to northern and southern California. Many investors analyze a pool's exposure by zip code and overlay these zip codes by California region or county. Within California, as in the rest of the country, geographic diversification limits risk. Recent estimates show that between 50% and 60% of all nonagency borrowers are in California.

Issuer Analysis

Another important consideration in analyzing collateral risk is the credit risk originating with the issuer and servicer. In this analysis we focus on the following factors:

- Issuer
- Servicer
- Underwriting guidelines
- Written policies
- Credit approval
- Cash management/systems
- Quality control

- Collection procedures
- PMI Policies
- Property management record
- Delinquency/loss history
- Historical track record
- Financial strength

In our discussion, we focus only on the factors that are particularly important in the analysis of subordinated tranches.

Of particular importance are the issuer's underwriting guidelines and delinquency/loss history and the servicer's ROE and collection record. In terms of underwriting guidelines, we think that full documentation or alternative documentation (when underwritten by a reputable originator/issuer) should be emphasized. Limited and no documentation loans have consistently shown a record of higher delinquencies and realized losses. Full documentation originations should fulfill the following criteria:

- Independent property appraisal
- Credit check
- Verification of income (VOI)
- Verification of deposit (VOD)
- Verification of employment (VOE)

Another factor to consider is the issuer's policy on compensating interest. Mortgage borrowers are required to make mortgage interest payments in arrears for the number of days that the mortgage is outstanding in the previous accrual period (one month). Scheduled mortgage payments thus include 30 days interest on the previous month's balance. However, when mortgagors fully prepay a mortgage, they are required only to pay interest on the number of days the loan was outstanding, not for the entire accrual period. The lender/servicer therefore receives less interest than was scheduled, creating an interest shortfall. In a CMO structure, interest shortfalls are allocated pro-rata among the different classes. Some issuers do, however, reimburse investors for this shortfall, by paying compensating interest. Compensating interest is discussed more fully in the structural analysis section of this chapter.

Rating Agency Analysis

The rating agencies determine the appropriate amount of credit enhancement for a given pool of collateral. For example, Standard & Poor's (S&P) developed its rating standards through analysis of the Great Depression of the 1930s and the regional recessions of the 1980s (such as in Houston, Texas). S&P's analysis begins with a "prime pool" of mortgage loans. The criteria for a prime pool are as follows:

- 300 or more loans
- geographically diverse
- first lien
- single-family detached
- purchase mortgage
- 30-year term
- fully amortizing
- fixed-rate
- full documentation
- owner occupied
- 80% LTV
- balances less than $300,000

For a prime pool, S&P has statistics by rating and loan-to-value ratio for (1) foreclosure frequency and (2) loss severity. The product of the foreclosure frequency and loss severity gives the base case loss coverage required for a prime pool. So, for example, if a AA rating is sought for a prime pool and the corresponding foreclosure and loss severity is 10% and 40%, respectively, then:[1]

base case loss coverage required for a AA prime pool = 10% × 40% = 4%

Adjustments are made to the prime pool loss coverage for each deviation from the prime loan criteria. For example, there will be an adjustment based on the loan-to-value ratio. For a prime pool, the LTV criterion is 80%. Suppose that a target rating of AA is sought but that the loans have an LTV of 90% and the loans have private mortgage insurance. Assuming that the frequency foreclosure and severity loss for a AA rating for a pool which is prime except that the LTV is 90% instead of 80% is 15% and 29%, respectively, then the loss coverage required would be 4.4% (= 15% × 29%). That is, base case loss coverage increases from 4% to 4.4%.

After the adjustments for deviations from the prime loss criteria, S&P then scales the base case coverage required for a AA prime loan for any other rating that might be desired. In general, the adjustment is as follows:

base case loss coverage required for a AA prime pool after adjusting for deviations from prime pool × factor based on rating sought

The "factor based on rating sought" will be greater than 1 if a rating higher than AA is sought and less than 1 if a rating lower than AA is sought.

Rating approaches vary by agency. Moody's philosophy is that ratings on mortgage securities are comparable to other types of securities (i.e., corporate and

---

[1] The statistics used in the example are for illustration purposes only. However, they are believed to be close to statistics used by S&P at one time. S&P updates its statistics periodically.

municipal bonds). Therefore, from the analysis of bonds that it has rated, Moody's determines expected credit losses in terms of yield impairment within each rating level. Fitch's approach is similar to S&P's, except Fitch places more emphasis on regional economics.

Structural Analysis

Structural analysis involves an assessment of the type of senior/subordinated structure, class tranching, methods of allocating losses, deal triggers, clean-up calls, and compensating interest.

Shifting Interest Structure

A number of variations of the senior/subordinated structure have been employed since the late 1980s in the nonagency MBS market, but the most popular structure is the shifting interest mechanism discussed earlier in this chapter. The subordinated classes are designed to increase as a percentage of the total outstanding principal (during the early years of the transaction) and to lend additional credit support for the senior tranches.

In shifting interest structures, amortization and interest are allocated pro-rata among all the deal's classes. Prepayments that would normally be allocated to the subordinated tranches are shifted to the senior tranches for a period of time. This is illustrated in Exhibit 4. For example, for an initial period of five years, 100% of all prepayments on the mortgage pool are allocated to the senior tranches. After the initial prepayment lockout period, a smaller percentage of the pro-rata share of the subordinated tranche's prepayment is paid to the senior classes. A typical shifting interest structure is given in Exhibit 5.

Exhibit 4: Shifting Interest Structure

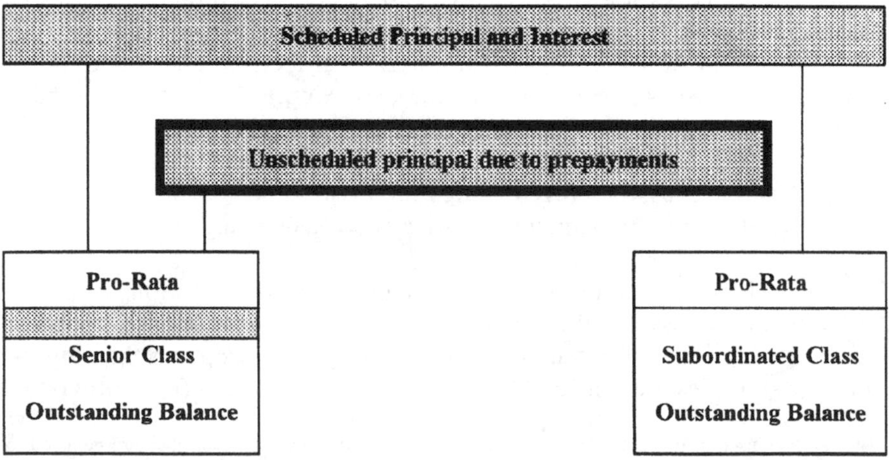

Exhibit 5: Typical Shifting Interest Mechanism Allocation of Cash Flows

	To Subordinated Tranches			To Senior Tranches			
Year	Pro-rata Interest (%)	Pro-rata Scheduled Principal (%)	Pro-rata Prepayment (%)	Pro-rata Interest (%)	Pro-rata Scheduled Principal (%)	Pro-rata Prepayment (%)	Additional Prepayment
1 through 5	100	100	0	100	100	100 +	100% of Sub.'s Share
6	100	100	30	100	100	100 +	70% of Sub.'s Share
7	100	100	40	100	100	100 +	60% of Sub.'s Share
8	100	100	60	100	100	100 +	40% of Sub's Share
9	100	100	80	100	100	100 +	20% of Sub's Share
10 and up	100	100	100	100	100	100 +	0% of Sub's Share

Exhibit 6: A Typical Senior/Subordinated Structure

	Securities/Rating		Class size (%)	Cushion provided by classes below (%)
	Senior class (AAA/AA rated)		94.0	6.0
	B	AA	1.0	4.0
	C	A	1.0	3.0
	D	BBB	1.0	2.0
	E	BB	1.0	1.0
	F	B	0.5	0.5
	G	NR	0.5	0.0

Pool of mortgage loans → Junior classes

In a shifting interest structure, the junior class has a claim not on a particular amount of cash flow, but on a portion of the underlying assets. Realized losses act to reduce the lowest subordinated tranche outstanding on a dollar for dollar basis. Hence, the *first-loss tranche* (also called the *unrated tranche*) will be reduced by losses until its principal balance is exhausted, then the next highest rated tranche will absorb losses, and so on.

Class Tranching

Originators/issuers often sell their subordinated cash flows to Wall Street dealers on a competitive basis. Therefore, the issuer is not always sure how a dealer will end up structuring a pool's cash flows. Further, the subordinated cash flows are often sold separately from a pool's senior (AAA-rated) cash flows. A typical senior/subordinated structure will look like that shown in Exhibit 6.

The dealer may consider whether to create a multi-tranche structure or a single-tranche. The broker/dealer most often chooses the structure which will provide the best all-in execution. Dealers will sometimes go with the higher cost execution when there is a higher probability of successfully selling the B-piece tranches.

Methods of Allocating Losses

Losses within a senior/subordinated structure are absorbed by the most junior tranche, although the timing and allocation of cash flow can vary within a deal structure. There are two traditional methods of allocating losses within a senior/subordinated structure: (1) the waterfall method and (2) the direct write-off method. Exhibit 7 highlights the differences between these two methods.

Several distinctions should be made between the two methods. First, under the waterfall method, multi-tranche subordinated structures can be adversely affected with the accrual of interest payments. For example, in the illustration given in Exhibit 7, the mezzanine tranche receives only $28,333 of its scheduled $67,667 interest payment. Therefore, a shortfall is created that must be repaid in later periods. If credit problems persist, the unpaid interest can amount to several months without any cash flow. This problem, which arises due to the payment of the senior's share of the loss in cash, can severely impact the liquidity of the tranche in accrual status.

These bonds have additional problems: (1) extension of average life and duration; (2) roll-up the yield curve; and, (3) no interest-on-interest potential.

Under the direct write-off method, the senior bond is entitled to the proceeds of the liquidated property, and any loss is written off against the most junior tranche. In addition, all interest and scheduled principal are allocated on a pro-rata basis.

Of the major nonagency issuers, Prudential Home and Residential Funding Corporation (pre-August 1993) use the waterfall loss allocation method. The other major issuers, including Residential Funding Corporation (since August 1993), generally use the direct write-off method.

Deal Triggers

An important component to be considered when analyzing senior/subordinated tranches is the deal's "triggers." Triggers are step-down tests that allow the subordinated tranches to be reduced as a percentage of the overall deal. For example, as illustrated in Exhibit 8, the subordinated bonds in the standard senior/subordinated structure are locked out from unscheduled payments (prepayments) for five years. Following this lockout period, the prepayment protection gradually "steps down" until the subordinated tranches receive their full pro-rata share of prepayments in year 10.

During the initial 5-year lockout period, the subordinated bonds delever, that is, they grow as a percentage of the overall deal. This delevering can occur only if a series of tests (or covenants) are met. These tests address (1) total losses and (2) total delinquencies (60+ days).

These tests are levels of credit performance required before the credit support can be reduced. The tests are applied annually after year 5, and monthly if a test is failed. Of the two tests, the loss test prevents a step-down from occurring if cumulative losses exceed a certain limit (which changes over time). The delinquency test, in its most common form, prevents any step-down from taking place as long as the current over 60-day delinquency rate exceeds 2% of the then-current pool balance.

Exhibit 7: Comparison of Waterfall and Direct Write-Off Methods

Example		Month 1	
Collateral:	$200,000,000	Interest:	$1,333,333
90% Senior:	180,000,000	Scheduled principal:	200,000
5% Mezzanine:	10,000,000	Prepayments:	800,000
5% Subordinated:	10,000,000	Recovery:	100,000
8% Coupon		Total:	2,433,333
		Realized Losses:	150,000
		Reduction Mortgage Balance:	1,250,000

Senior Bonds

	Waterfall Method	Direct Write-Off Method
Interest	$1,200,000	$1,200,000
Scheduled Principal	180,000	180,000
Prepayments	800,000	800,000
Recovery	90,000	100,000
Unrecovered Senior	135,000	0
Total	2,405,000	2,280,000
Beginning Balance	180,000,000	180,000,000
Ending Balance	178,795,000	178,920,000
Change in Balance	−1,205,000	−1,080,000

Mezzanine Bonds

	Waterfall Method	Direct Write-Off Method
Interest	$28,333	$66,667
Scheduled Principal	0	100,000
Prepayments	0	0
Recovery	0	0
Unrecovered Mezzanine	0	0
Payment Unpaid Balance	0	0
Total	28,333	76,667
Write-down Principal	0	0
Ending Unpaid Account Balance	38,334	0
Beginning Balance	10,000,000	10,000,000
Ending Balance	10,000,000	9,990,000
Change in Balance	0	−10,000

Junior Class

	Waterfall Method	Direct Write-Off Method
Interest	$0	$66,667
Scheduled Principal	0	10,000
Prepayments	0	0
Recovery	0	0
Total	0	76,667
Write-down Principal	45,000	150,000
Unpaid Interest	66,667	0
Write-Beginning Balance	10,000,000	10,000,000
Ending Balance	9,995,000	9,840,000
Change in Balance	−45,000	−160,000

Exhibit 8: Average Life at Different Speeds and Step-Down Allowances*

	Prepayment Speed (PSA)		
	250	400	600
All Step-Downs Taken	10.9	9.4	8.2
No Step-Downs Taken	16.0	15.0	13.1

* Assumes 30-year fixed-rate loans, 8.5% gross WAC, 320 WAM, and 4.50% subordinated tranche

The above step-down criteria remain in effect on older deals. However, most deals issued after October 1995 are subject to new step-down tests. Following that date new requirements were adopted by the rating agencies, particularly in the area of delinquencies. This was done largely as a result of the fact that many strong deals have performed well and have, in fact, been upgraded by the agencies, despite running delinquencies above 2% of the current pool balance. Under these new tests, the delinquency measures are less stringent and, as a result, present less extension risk for subordinated CMO tranche holders.

The following are the most recent step-down tests employed by Fitch and Standard & Poor's:

Fitch: Step-down allowed if projected losses, assuming 100% default of all current 60+ day delinquencies and a 45% loss severity, do not exceed 25% of original credit enhancement.

S&P: Step-down allowed if 60+ day delinquencies are less than 50% of current credit support and original loss trigger tests remain unchanged.

As a result, it is important to determine which step-down test applies to a specific issue.

Although most nonagency deals in the market will currently pass the loss test, the delinquency test could be a potential problem for many deals. As the loans season and enter their peak loss years, higher delinquencies can cause a deal trigger to disallow a step-down. This occurrence can lead to a significant extension in average life and a roll-up of the yield curve, as illustrated in Exhibit 8. This potential risk should be carefully considered when evaluating securities.

Clean-Up Calls

Nonagency deals are usually subject to a 5% to 10% clean-up call; that is, the issuer has the right to collapse a deal if the deal factor is down to 0.05 to 0.10. As shown in Exhibit 9, the average life can vary significantly if run to the call date. This option has two major effects on subordinated tranche holders. First, since most subordinated tranches trade at discounts to par, it has a positive impact since par is received. Second, since these calls come into play before maturity, the duration and average life will shorten.

Exhibit 9: Typical Profile of a Subordinated Bond

	225 PSA +100		300 PSA Base		600 PSA − 100	
	Maturity	Call	Maturity	Call	Maturity	Call
Average Life	11.63	9.56	10.54	8.06	8.06	4.31
Modified Duration	6.86	6.33	6.53	5.62	5.62	3.53
Last Pay	6/23	11/05	6/23	4/03	4/23	9/98

Exhibit 10: Likelihood of a Newly Issued Deal Being Eligible for Call During the Initial 5-Year Lockout Period

	25% CPR		35% CPR		45% CPR		55% CPR		65% CPR	
	5%	10%	5%	10%	5%	10%	5%	10%	5%	10%
Year	Call	Call	Call	Call	Call	Call	Call	Call	Call	Call
1	No	No	No	No	No	No	No	No	No	No
2	No	No	No	No	No	No	No	No	No	No
3	No	No	No	No	No	No	No	Yes	Yes	Yes
4	No	No	No	No	No	Yes	Yes	Yes	Yes	Yes
5	No	No	No	No	No	Yes	Yes	Yes	Yes	Yes

Although most deals use a 10% clean-up call, that does not necessarily mean that these deals will be called. Reasons why many deals may not be called include:

1. Advances in computer technology allow servicers to continue to maintain pool servicing functions economically.
2. Adverse selection (last loans in a pool can be the least creditworthy) may prevent the repurchase of these loans.
3. Issuer of pool often retains economic interest in pool by controlling servicing function and/or by owning the IO-tranche.

During the prepayment spike of 1993, investors were shown how negatively convex these securities can be. That is, tranches which were trading above par were being bid by dealers to their calls, despite the 5-year prepay lockouts and the lack of first-hand experience as to the likelihood of the call option actually being exercised.

Exhibit 10 shows the likelihood of a newly issued deal being eligible for calls during the subordinated tranche's initial 5-year lockout period. For both 5% and 10% clean-up calls, if prepayment speeds are 35% CPR or below there is no interruption of the scheduled 5-year subordinated tranche lockout. If the deal prepays at 45% CPR for five years, the structure with the 5% clean-up call is unaffected, but the 10% call could be exercised in year 4. At very fast prepayment speeds (i.e., 55% to 65% CPR or faster), the calls could come into play as early as the third year after issuance.

Although most deals are structured with the 10% call option, the 5% structure can have substantially lower option costs, while trading at the same yield spreads versus the Treasury curve.

Exhibit 11: Compensating Interest Polices for Major Nonagency Issuers

	Max Compensating Interest Paid Annually (bps)	Type of Prepayments Covered:		Prepayment Remittance Cycle
		Prepayments in Full	Curtailments	
Chase	12.5	Yes	Yes	Previous month
CMSI	12.5	Yes	Yes	Previous month
Countrywide	12.5	Yes	Yes	Mid-month to Mid-month
GE	12.5	Yes	Yes	Mid-month to Mid-month
NASCOR	12.5	Yes	No	Mid-month to Mid-month
RFC	12.5	Yes	No	Previous month

Source: Table 1 in "Compensating Interest: Rarely an Issue," *PaineWebber Mortgage Strategist* (September 8, 1998), p. 20.

Compensating Interest

The compensating interest policies of issuers have changed dramatically over the past few years. Whereas at one time some issuers offered no compensating interest, today the compensating interest policies of the major issuers of nonagency CMOs provide at least 12.5 basis points of compensating interest. Exhibit 11 shows the compensating interest policies. There are three aspects of the compensating interest policy that are shown in the exhibit: (1) the maximum compensating interest, (2) the types of prepayments covered — prepayment in full and curtailments, and (3) the prepayment remittance cycle.

Exhibit 12 provides an illustration of the computation of how the maximum compensating interest is computed and how the compensation is determined. The illustration assumes that the issuer will pay compensating interest up to an amount equal to 12.5 basis points per year. Based on the assumptions in the exhibit the maximum compensating interest is $30,880.19. The interest shortfall based on the assumptions is $19,969.68. Since the maximum compensating interest available is greater than the interest shortfall, the interest shortfall will be covered.

The assumption made in Exhibit 12 is that the prepayment rate is 25% CPR for the month. The faster the CPR, the greater the interest shortfall and therefore the greater the possibility that the maximum compensating interest available will not be adequate. What happens for our hypothetical CMO if the CPR is 50% rather than 25%? It can be shown that the interest shortfall before compensating interest is $47,315.47. Under a 50% CPR scenario, the maximum compensating interest available would be $30,373.79 and therefore there would be an uncompensated interest shortfall of $16,941.69.

The illustration demonstrates that in a severe prepayment scenario of 50% CPR, investors in the hypothetical CMO will lose $16,941.69. The question is, how significant is this loss? The PaineWebber Mortgage Strategy Group examined this question by determining how high the prepayment speeds must rise before there will be foregone interest to bondholders resulting from interest shortfall. The prepayment CPR at which there will be foregone interest is referred to as the "breakeven CPR." For prepayment speeds below the breakeven CPR, the bondholder does not realize a loss. Exhibit 13 shows this analysis for different compensating arrangements and bonds with different coupon rates and WAMs. The analysis in Exhibit 13 indicates that it takes a minimum of prepayment speeds of 30% CPR (and for most issuers 50%) even under the most unfavorable compensating interest arrangements before the bondholder will not recover interest.

Exhibit 12: Illustration of the Calculation of Compensating Interest

Assumptions:
   Coupon rate = 6.75%
   WAM = 357
   Servicing = 0.125%

Beginning principal balance:	$300,000,000.00
Accrued bondholder interest:	1,687,500.00
Scheduled amortization:	257,044.75
Prepayments at 25% CPR, 2.3688% SMM:	7,100,438.28

Interest shortfall to bondholder before compensating interest:

$$= \frac{15}{30} \times \frac{1}{12} \times \frac{6.75}{100} \times 7,100,438.28 = 19,969.98$$

Maximum compensating interest available:

$$= \frac{0.125}{100} \times \frac{1}{12} \times (300,000,000 - 7,100,438.28) + \frac{0.125}{100} \times \frac{15}{30} \times \frac{1}{12} \times 7,100,438.28 = 30,880.19$$

Difference: 30,880.19 − 19,969.98 = 10,910.20
   Source: Figure 1 in "Compensating Interest: Rarely an Issue," *PaineWebber Mortgage Strategist* (September 8, 1998), p. 19.

Exhibit 13: Breakeven CPRs for Various Compensating Interest Arrangements

		Breakeven CPR			
		15 days foregone		7.5 days foregone	
Coupon	WAM	12.5*	20*	12.5*	20*
6.75	357	35.91	50.93	58.27	74.94
6.75	300	35.92	50.95	58.28	74.96
7.00	357	34.88	49.66	56.97	73.71
7.00	300	34.89	49.68	56.98	73.72
7.50	330	32.99	47.31	54.52	71.32
7.50	270	33.01	47.33	54.54	71.34
8.00	330	31.29	45.15	52.26	69.05
8.00	270	31.31	45.17	52.27	69.06

* bps servicing that can be used to pay compensating interest.
   Source: Table 2 in "Compensating Interest: Rarely an Issue," *PaineWebber Mortgage Strategist* (September 8, 1998), p. 21.

Exhibit 14: Effect of Different Levels of Compensating Interest at Different PSA Speeds

Assumptions:

Coupon 6.75%   WAM 357 months

	Yield at PSA Level (If full accrued interest is paid)			
	100	275	500	1000
3-yr	6.66	6.50	6.35	6.10
10-yr	6.89	6.91	6.96	7.03
Long	6.96	6.99	7.12	7.34
NAS	6.72	6.69	6.67	6.51

	Foregone Yield at PSA Level											
	100% PSA			275% PSA			500% PSA			1000% PSA		
Comp. Int.	0	12.5	20	0	12.5	20	0	12.5	20	0	12.5	20
3-yr	1.5	0.0	0.0	3.5	0.0	0.0	5.5	0.0	0.0	8.8	1.2	0.2
10-yr	1.6	0.0	0.0	4.4	0.0	0.0	7.6	0.0	0.0	13.9	4.3	1.3
Long	1.7	0.0	0.0	4.7	0.0	0.0	8.2	0.0	0.0	15.5	5.4	1.9
NAS	1.6	0.0	0.0	4.4	0.0	0.0	8.5	0.0	0.0	16.9	6.6	2.5

Source: Table 4 in "Compensating Interest: Rarely an Issue," *PaineWebber Mortgage Strategist* (September 8, 1998), p. 22.

The analysis in Exhibit 13 simply indicates at what prepayment speeds the bondholder is not compensated for interest shortfall. A further analysis is required to show the extent to which prepayment speeds greater than the breakeven CPR impact the bond's yield. The PaineWebber study investigated this question by structuring a typical deal with 6.75% coupon collateral and a pricing speed of 275% PSA. The tranches in this hypothetical deal included a 3-year sequential, a 10-year sequential, a long securities, and an non-accelerating senior (NAS) bond. The NAS bond is discussed later in this chapter. The difference between the yield assuming full accrued interest is paid and the yield based on different prepayment speeds and compensating interest levels was analyzed. These results are reported in Exhibit 14 based on different PSA speeds and compensating interest (0, 12.5, and 20 basis points). As can be seen, even at prepayment speeds as high as 500% PSA, there is no impact on yield for any of the tranches if the compensating interest arrangement is for 12.5 or 20 basis points. At extreme levels of 1,000% PSA there is an impact.

From their analysis, the authors of the PaineWebber study on compensating interest conclude that: "in most new structures, there's little impact from standard compensating interest features... It will rarely impact a decision to buy or not to buy a bond." However, as can be seen in Exhibit 14, for structures with no compensating interest, the impact on yield can be significant. Such arrangements exist in older deals and therefore the investor must recognize the potential adverse impact.

Exhibit 15: Flowchart of the Way Losses Occur

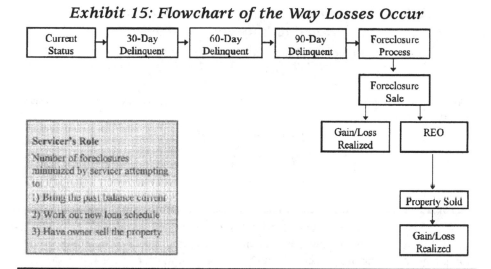

SUBORDINATED TRANCHE STRESS TESTING

After getting comfortable with a deal's collateral and structure, the next step is to perform stress testing to evaluate the adequacy of a tranche's credit protection.

How Do Losses Occur?

Before we can perform a meaningful stress test for subordinated tranches, we must understand how losses occur. As shown in the flowchart in Exhibit 15, before a pool loss can occur a loan must pass from current status into 30-, 60-, and 90-day delinquency status before finally entering the foreclosure process. During this process, the servicer plays a very important function.

It should be pointed out that the servicer will commonly advance (principal and interest) to bondholders all the way through foreclosure. These advances, which will be reimbursed once the property is liquidated, will be paid before any pool losses are calculated.

The servicer also will work to prevent any losses from occurring to bondholders. The servicer will attempt to minimize losses, once a loan becomes delinquent, by:

1. Contacting the borrower and seeking to bring the balance current.
2. Providing the borrower with a new loan schedule (to bring the balance current).
3. Encouraging owners with equity to sell the property.

If any of these strategies are successful, the servicer has prevented a delinquent loan from resulting in a pool loss.

Exhibit 16: Impact of Principal Amortization and Housing Inflation on LTV

Principal Amortization: Impact on LTV

	Year 0	Year 5	Year 10
LTV	75.0%*	71.4%	66.1%

* Assumes gross weighted average coupon (GWAC) of 8.24% and 30-year weighted average maturity (WAM).

Housing Inflation: Impact on LTV

	Year 0	Year 5	Year 10
LTV	75.0%*	64.8	54.2

* Assumes gross weighted average coupon (GWAC) of 8.24% and 30-year weighted average maturity (WAM) and 2% housing inflation.

The best defense against pool losses adversely impacting the subordinated tranches is homeowner's equity in the property. That is, the homeowner's down payment or actual perceived equity in a particular property is the first line of defense against default. Defaults rationally occur only when a negative equity condition exists. Otherwise the homeowner would sell the property to prevent default.

Empirical studies of homeowners in negative equity situations show that only a small portion of this universe will default. Statistics show that it requires a period of severe borrower stress (i.e., divorce or unemployment) coupled with a negative equity condition to result in significant levels of default. Mortgage borrowers have resisted default in most negative equity situations due to: (1) the social stigma of losing one's home, (2) fear of tarnishing one's credit rating, and (3) the ongoing need for housing. Furthermore, negative equity/default conditions are not that common to begin with because of annual versus fixed-debt burden.

As shown in Exhibit 16, for a typical loan with a 75% LTV ratio, the LTV ratio will decline to 71.4% after five years and 66.1% after ten years, assuming no housing inflation. This occurs due to normal amortization of principal over the loan's 30-year life. If any improvement in housing values is assumed (i.e., 2% housing inflation) the LTV ratio will decline to 64.7% after five years and 54.2% after ten years. Thus credit mortgage pools have a normal tendency to improve with time.

Timing and Extent of Losses

The most widely accepted loss curve is the Moody's curve. This loss curve, which is shown in Exhibit 17, highlights the expected timing of losses for 30-year collateral fixed-rate single-family pools. The shape of the curve highlights the fact that losses do not typically occur during the first year (since the foreclosure process can often last more than one year), but are typically concentrated in years 3 through 7. During these years the homeowner has not had substantial time to amortize principal or enjoy the benefit of housing inflation. This is in direct conflict with the longer part of the loss curve, where losses become quite rare due to seasoning and the build-up of the homeowner's equity.

Exhibit 17: Moody's Loss Curve

Age	Losses	Cumulative
1	0.5%	0.5%
2	3.5%	4.0%
3	11.0%	15.0%
4	21.5%	36.5%
5	13.5%	57.5%
6	13.5%	71.0%
7	11.5%	82.5%
8	7.5%	90.0%
9	7.0%	97.0%
10+	3.0%	100.0%

Most conservative investors will perform their stress testing assuming that the allocation of a pool's total losses will be front-loaded. That is, 100% of total losses will occur between years 2 through 4 or 2 through 6.

An important factor in making new subordinated investors comfortable has always been historical pool losses. Historical pool numbers reported in a deal prospectus can be misleading, however, and we do not advocate using these statistics. An important and unbiased measure of historical pool performance is static-pool statistics. These statistics represent all losses that have occurred during the particular year of origination. Investors can use static pool data as a way of extrapolating the extent of total pool losses.

More recently, Standard & Poor's produced a study which contained historical loss data. S&P's numbers, however, track losses by year of origination and by product type: 30- and 15-year fixed-rate loans and adjustable-rate mortgages.

The study found an average loss on transactions backed by 30-year fixed-rate pools, originated between 1986 to 1990, of 0.71%. Meanwhile, the loss experience of 15-year fixed-rate mortgages was 0.20%, or less than one-third of 30-year product. Finally, average losses from adjustable-rate mortgages over the same 5-year period were 1.69%, or more than twice the loss experience of 30-year fixed-rate mortgages.

The S&P study by rating category found that the rate of default by credit rating compared favorably with corporate defaults (as also reported by a 1970 to 1994 study by Moody's). According to the S&P study, no tranche originally rated A or higher backed by 30-year collateral has ever defaulted. Similarly, no BB or higher-rated tranche backed by 15-year collateral has defaulted.

Estimating Potential Pool Losses

In order to assess the potential risk of a non-agency pool, an investor has to address three key issues:

1. Amount of loans that will default (foreclosure frequency).

2. The amount of the loss on default (loss severity).
3. The timing of the loss.

There are two quick and simple methods to estimate what total losses will be on a pool. The first estimates expected losses using the Moody's loss curve. Assume a 1991 originated Pru-Home pool has had the following loss record:

1996 losses	Cumulative losses	Number of years seasoned
0.25%	0.15%	5

According to the Moody's loss curve, pools that are five years seasoned should have experienced 57.5% of the lifetime losses, and losses occurring during the fifth year should represent 21% of total lifetime losses. Therefore, the investor can get a range of losses based on this seasoned pool's actual performance:

Projected losses (cumulative) = 0.25/0.575 = 0.43%

Projected losses (5th year) = 0.15/0.21 = 0.71%

Under this method, estimated lifetime losses would range between 43 and 71 basis points.

Another popular method, illustrated in Exhibit 18, takes recent pool performance and estimates cumulative losses by assigning a probability factor to each category. In the exhibit, we are using Citicorp's estimated cure rates to calculate estimated pool losses. This example shows that loans in the 30-day delinquent category default approximately at a rate of 5%, while loans in foreclosure default 50% of the time. After coming up with a foreclosure frequency, we would apply a loss severity rate of 30%. The result is an estimated lifetime cumulative loss of 17 basis points.

This method, if used, should be updated often to reflect changes in loan categorization. That is, as a loan moves from 30 days to 60 days delinquent, the estimated losses will increase due to the lower assumed cure rate.

Exhibit 18: Estimating Pool Losses by Assigning Cure Rates by Delinquency Category

	Delinquencies (%)					
	30-Day	60-Day	90-Day	Foreclosures	REO	Total
Status (1)	2.05	0.77	0.53	0.14	0.10	3.59
Est. Non-cured Default % (2)	5.00	15.00	30.00	50.00	100.00	
Foreclosure Frequency						
(1) × (2) = (3)	0.10	0.12	0.16	0.07	0.10	
Loss Severity (4)	30.00	30.00	30.00	30.00	30.00	
Estimated Loss						
(3) × (4) = (5)	0.03	0.04	0.05	0.02	0.03	0.17

Exhibit 19: Annual Default Rate, 100% SDA

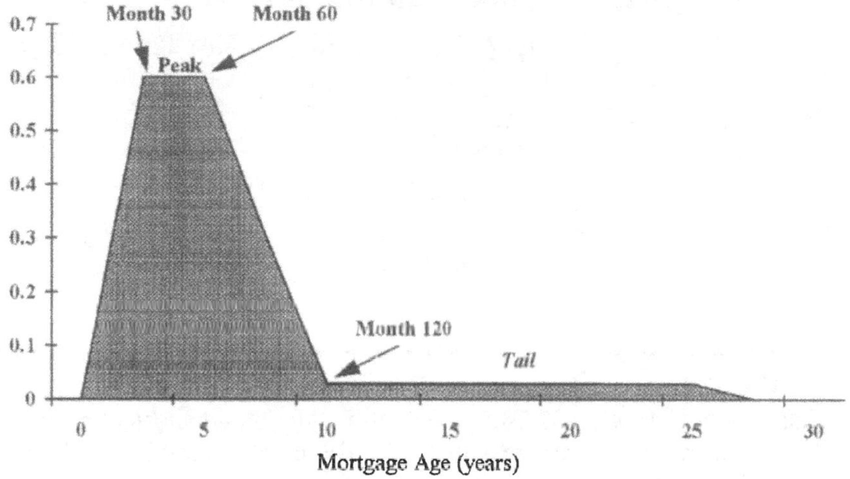

Exhibit 20: Cumulative Default Rates (%)*

	50 SDA	100 SDA	200 SDA
100 PSA	1.56	3.09	6.08
150 PSA	1.40	2.78	5.47
400 PSA	0.88	1.74	3.45

*Assume 30-year fixed loans with 360 WAM and 8% coupon.

SDA Model

In May 1993, the Public Securities Association (PSA) came up with a benchmark default standard for evaluating the credit risk of nonagency MBS (see Exhibit 19). The model is designed along the same lines as the PSA's prepayment curve, which is used by investors to analyze prepayment risk in mortgage securities. Investors can use multiples of the Standard Default Assumption (SDA) curve to stress test mortgage securities.

As shown in Exhibit 19, the SDA curve begins with an assumed default rate of 0.02% in month 1 and increases by 0.02% per month until it reaches a peak of 0.60% in month 30. This peak level default is maintained through the 60th month and then subsides monthly until reaching its constant level of 0.03% for the pool's remaining life.

An important point to remember is that the SDA default curve in any month is applied to the remaining balance of the performing loans at the end of the month. Therefore, the cumulative default rate over the life of the pool depends not only on the assumed monthly default rate, but also on the prepayment assumption. This is illustrated in Exhibit 20. Note that the larger the assumed prepayment speed, the lower the cumulative default level for a given percentage of the SDA model.

Exhibit 21: Loss Adjusted Yield Matrix for
Typical "B" Rated Subordinate Tranche

Scenario	SDA (%)	Loss Severity	100 PSA			250 PSA			400 PSA		
			Yield (%)	A/L	Cum Loss	Yield (%)	A/L	Cum Loss	Yield (%)	A/L	Cum Loss
1	0	20	14.2	15.2	0.00	15.0	11.4	0.00	15.6	9.6	0.00
2	40	20	14.1	15.4	0.37	15.0	11.4	0.24	15.6	9.6	0.16
3	50	20	13.6	16.2	0.47	14.8	11.6	0.29	15.5	9.6	0.20
4	75	20	12.0	17.8	0.69	13.8	12.4	0.43	14.8	10.0	0.30
5	100	20	10.8	19.7	0.92	12.8	13.2	0.58	14.1	10.4	0.40
6	150	20	6.7	25.8	1.36	10.9	16.0	0.87	12.9	11.3	0.60

The SDA curve's basic assumption of 100 SDA and 150 PSA produces cumulative default levels of 2.78% — which is high on a historical basis. Only high LTV loans have generally experienced this type of default levels. Most historical studies show that for loans with LTV ratio ranging between 70 and 80, defaults have ranged between 0.5% and 1.5%, which would equate to less than 50% SDA.

To use the SDA model properly, the investor must provide input assumptions for:

• Loss severity level
• Servicer advancing
• Time to liquidation on defaults

The final step in our analysis of a subordinated tranche is stress testing to determine the impact on credit-adjusted yield. The idea is to break the collateral into different groupings that can then be stressed in different ways. The most common grouping is by LTV ratio. That is, the loans are broken into LTV clusters and stressed at different foreclosure frequencies and loss severities. One method is to apply the Texas scenario to these LTV clusters. The idea, of course, is to ensure that the security in question can survive these stress testings.

Stress testing also involves the testing of housing values. The idea is to calculate a credit-adjusted yield on the individual tranche. Therefore, the investor will need a model that can calculate the yield impact of losses, payment delays, and "trigger" events. Most investors, when calculating credit-adjusted yields, will assume a front loading of defaults and cumulative losses.

The final step is the production of a loss matrix, which will show the credit-adjusted yield under a variety of scenarios. Exhibit 21 is a loss-adjusted yield matrix for a typical "B" rated subordinated tranche.

Exhibit 22: Development of NAS Market

Phase				
Super Senior		Mezzanine AAA		
1 —————————		————————————————		
2			NAS	
3				Super-NAS
1990	1992	1994	1996	1998

Exhibit 23: Creating Super-Senior Bonds

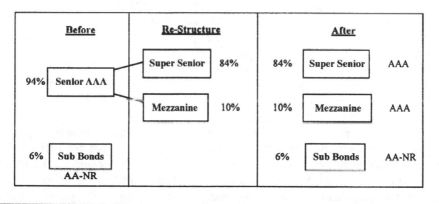

NAS AND SUPER-NAS BONDS

There have been three generations of structural development with regard to the NAS market. These phases of development are shown in Exhibit 22. The first generation of NAS development was the *super-senior bond*, which was common in nonagency CMO deals during the early 1990s. The super-senior bond was created in order to ease senior investor fears about the credit risk inherent in nonagency pools which had relatively high California loan concentrations. The thought process was that if the rating agency required 6% subordination on a deal with a high California concentration, then any potential investor credit concerns should be eased if the subordination level were raised to 16%. (See Exhibit 23.)

Exhibit 24: Mezzanine Bond Schedule for Prepayment Allocation

Year	Months	Mezzanine Bond % of Pro Rata Share
1-5	1-60	0
6	61-72	30
7	73-84	40
8	85-96	60
9	97-108	80
10+	+109	100

Super-senior bonds are created by splitting the senior bonds into two parts: the *super-senior* and the *mezzanine bonds*. The mezzanine bonds, despite the fact that they enjoy AAA ratings, were subordinated to the other AAA bonds in terms of loss priority.

The AAA mezzanine bonds do, however, enjoy the same hard lockout features as the subordinated bonds in the structure. That is, during the first five years, 100% of unscheduled principal payments (i.e., the prepayments) from the collateral pool go to paydown the senior bonds. (See Exhibit 24.) However, unlike traditional subordinated bonds, not all mezzanine bonds are required to pass the loss and delinquency trigger tests in order to begin to receive their pro rata share of unscheduled principal payments.

The super-senior structure was phased out around 1992-1993 as the California housing market improved, but the AAA mezzanine concept reappeared in 1994 as a method to structure AAA rated bonds with call protection superior to those available in the planned amortization class (PAC) market.

Despite the popularity of the AAA mezzanine structure, the second phase of development occurred because AAA mezzanine bonds were not ERISA eligible. ERISA eligibility was an important factor in bringing pension fund investors into this market. ERISA guidelines state that the subordinated status of AAA mezzanine bonds would make them ineligible investments for pension funds. Therefore, Wall Street came up with the *non-accelerated senior* (NAS) *bond*.

The NAS bond had all the benefits of the AAA mezzanine plus ERISA eligibility. This was the case since the NAS bond shared losses *pari-pasu* with all other senior bonds in the structure (i.e., it was not subordinated).

The NAS bond is created in a similar way to the PAC bond in that the bond has a schedule which leads to more average life volatility in the other senior bonds. Because of this schedule (i.e., complete 5-year prepay lockout followed by subordinated-like step down schedule), the NAS bond can only receive principal ahead of schedule if all other senior bonds are completely retired. Thus, all senior bonds act to buffer the NAS bond.

The latest or third state of NAS development is the *super-NAS*. The super-NAS was created in order to further stabilize the average life profile of the NAS bond. Structurally the super-NAS was created as shown in Exhibit 25.

Exhibit 25: Creating Super-NAS Bonds

Before		Re-Structure		After	
80%	Senior			Senior	84%
		Super NAS	10%		
14%	NAS			Super NAS	10%
		Senior	4%		
6%	Sub Bonds			Sub Bonds	6%

Source: "Super-NAS Bonds: Required Summer Reading," *PaineWebber Mortgage Strategist* (June 9, 1998), p. 16.

The super-NAS is a bond with less average life variability than an ordinary NAS. The super-NAS bond is created by time tranching the NAS cash flows such that the shorter bond becomes the "super-NAS" and the longer bond cash flows are returned to the senior bonds. The result is a shorter and less volatile super-senior with a tighter principal payment window.

NAS Valuation Basics

In determining the relative value of any NAS bond, the investor should consider the following factors: (1) collateral characteristics, (2) tranche coupon, and (3) percentage of NAS size.

In general, collateral which is more predictable with regard to its prepayment profile, such as 15-year collateral, Alternative-A programs, and/or collateral with low dispersion, should trade better than 30-year, Jumbo-A, and collateral with a high degree of dispersion. A predictable pattern of mortgage prepayments is important to achieving the lowest option costs or highest OAS (option-adjusted spread) on a NAS investment.

Another important factor for NAS valuation is the tranche's coupon. All things being equal, most traditional investors prefer to own discount or par mortgage bonds. Premium bonds, particularly NAS tranche coupons which would equate to dollar prices above $104, will trade at significant yield concessions to lower dollar price bonds.

Another important NAS valuation factor is the size of the NAS relative to the overall deal size. That is, NAS bonds are referred to as 10% NAS bonds, 20% NAS bonds, and so forth. This percentage represents the NAS tranche size as a percentage of the overall deal. For example, assume two NAS bonds are created, one a 10% NAS and the other a 20% NAS. (See Exhibit 26.) Additionally, assume both structures have 6% subordination below the NAS bonds.

Exhibit 26: NAS Bond Comparison

	10% NAS	20% NAS
NAS Bonds	10%	20%
Sr Bonds	84%	74%
Sub Bonds	6%	6%
	100%	100%
Senior/NAS Ratio	8:4:1	3:7:1

Exhibit 27: NAS Average Life Comparison

Description	75 PPC*	100 PPC	150 PPC	Avg Life Range
Deal with 10% NAS				
10-year sequential	13.7	9.4	5.0	8.7
NAS Bond	12.2	11.0	9.4	2.8
Deal with 20% NAS				
10-year sequential	17.5	9.4	4.2	13.3
NAS Bond	12.2	11.0	7.6	4.6

* PPC refers to the prospectus prepayment speed assumption. For example, 100 PPC is the assumed pre-payment vector.

Comparing the structure of the two deals, the larger NAS bonds (i.e., 20% NAS) has a lower senior bonds/NAS bond ratio which results in fewer bonds to support or buffer the cash flow variability of the NAS. This means that a smaller NAS, with its lower average life variability, is a better NAS bonds.

NAS Bond Profile

Because of its schedule, the NAS bond will have a more stable average life profile than a comparable duration sequential-pay bond from the same deal. Exhibit 27 shows the average life profile for two recent Alternative A deals, one with 10% NAS and one with 20% NAS.

As shown above, the lower the percentage NAS within the deal the more stable the average life profile of all bonds within the deal. Additionally, NAS bonds have significantly lower cash flow variability than comparable duration sequential-pay bonds. This lower variation in cash flow average lives results in lower option costs on the NAS bonds

Comparing Super-NAS Bonds with NAS Bonds

As mentioned earlier, super-NAS bonds are a shorter, more stable version of the standard NAS bond. Super NAS bonds also have a tighter principal payment window, since the tail NAS cash flows are placed into the senior bonds.

Exhibit 28 compares the average life variability and principal windows of a 20% NAS bond with a similar sized Super-NAS Alternative A collateralized bond.

Exhibit 28: Super NAS versus NAS

Description	75 PPC	100 PPC	150 PPC	Avg Life Range
Deal with 20% NAS				
NAS – Avg Life	12.2	11.0	7.6	4.6
Window	8/03-6/28	8/03-6/28	8/03-6/28	
Super-NAS – Avg Life	9.4	8.7	7.7	1.8
Window	8/03-6/13	8/03-9/12	8/03-6/28	

Exhibit 29: Super NAS at Faster Prepay Speeds

Description	100 PPC	125 PPC	150 PPC	250 PPC
Deal with 20% NAS				
NAS – Avg Life	11.0	9.4	7.6	4.1
Window	8/03-6/28	8/03-6/28	8/03-6/28	7/01-11/04
Super-NAS – Avg Life	8.7	9.1	7.6	4.1
Window	8/03-9/12	8/03-1/20	8/03-6/28	7/01-11/04

The first factor to notice is that the super-NAS has much lower average life dispersion (or range), between 75 PPC and 150 PPC, than does the NAS bond. (PPC is the prospectus prepayment curve and is discussed in the next chapter.) Additionally, the base case principal window is much narrower (August 2003-September 2012) than the traditional NAS bond (August 2003-June 2028).

At slower prepayment speeds (i.e., 75 PPC), the super-NAS bond extends less than the traditional NAS bond. This is due to the fact that the bond maintains its schedule while the tail cash flow was structured into other senior bonds. This is apparent in the principal window as the final payment date extends only from September 2012 to June 2013 when prepayments slow from 100 PPC to 75 PPC.

Similarly, the super-NAS bond is subject to less contraction risk since it is a shorter average life bond in the base case. It is also apparent from Exhibit 28 that the average lives of both bonds at 150 PPC is 7.6 years. Additionally, note that the principal payment window under both bond structures is identical (August 2003-June 2028). The payment window on the super-NAS bond shifts out due to the fact that at these fast prepayment speeds, all of the senior bonds will be paid down prior to the end of the 10-year NAS bond shifting interest schedule. In this scenario, the super-NAS bond becomes the only AAA or senior bonds remaining in the deal and must therefore assume the principal window of the underlying collateral.

As shown in Exhibit 29, at fast prepayment speeds, the average lives and principal windows of both the NAS and super-NAS are the same. However, at moderately faster speeds, such as at 125 PPC, the super-NAS actually extends due to the NAS tail (which was combined with the other senior bonds) providing added call protection to the super-NAS. At faster speeds, this tail is paid down and the super-NAS and NAS bonds assume the same profile.

ALTERNATIVE A DEALS

"Alternative-A" or "Alt-A" loans are mortgage loans made to borrowers who have excellent credit histories, but do not meet the Freddie Mac or Fannie Mae conforming agency loan guidelines. These guidelines are shown in Exhibit 30. "Alternative A" borrowers are deemed to be non-conforming under the agency guidelines for one or more of the following reasons:

- Limited/low documentation loans
- Non-conforming ratio loans
- Investor property loans
- Second home/vacation property loans
- Self employed/foreign national loans
- Cash-out refinancing

How are "Alt-A" Deals Created?

As mentioned above, "Alt-A" borrowers are usually deemed non-conforming from agency guidelines for reasons other than for size and/or credit quality. (See Exhibit 31.)

Exhibit 30: Traditional Agency Loan Guidelines

Conforming Factor	Conforming Guideline
Loan Size	< $227,500
Documentation	Full Documentation
	• Verify Income (VOI)
	• Verify Employment (VOE)
	• Verify Deposit (VOA)
	• Appraisal
Ratios	28% Mortgage Payment/Monthly Inc.
	36% Total Debt /Monthly Inc.
Loan-To-Value (LTV	Maximum 80% w/o PMI
	(Private Mortgage Insurance)
Property Type	Single-Family
Credit Score	FICO score > 660

Exhibit 31: Reasons Other Than for Size and/or Credit Quality Loans are Alternative A

Non-Conforming Reason	Mortgage Program	Typical Lenders
Size	Jumbo-A	GE, Nascor, RFC, Countrywide
Credit	Home Equity	Aames, Conti, Moneystore
Property-Type	Alt-A	RASTA, RALI, Headlands
Documentation	Alt-A	RASTA, RALI, Headlands
Ratios	Alt-A	RASTA, RALI, Headlands
LTV	Alt-A	RASTA, RALI, Headlands

The "Alternative A" loan market began following the fast prepayment period of 1992-1993. Due to the high volume of refinancings, overcapacity became a problem in 1994. Certain traditional lenders, such as INMC and RFC, recognized that increased specialization and standardization of mortgage underwriting had created a significant void in the market for underserved and unserved borrowers. These borrowers are those with conforming credit histories, but required special or non-standard credit underwriting.

Because "Alt-A" loans fall into special "buckets," the lenders serving this market segment can charge higher mortgage rates. For example, the largest "Alt-A" lender — RASTA — charges rate adjustments which average 60-80 basis points above jumbo mortgage rates or 80-105 basis points more than prevailing agency mortgage rates. Similarly, RFC's RALI program charges 45-55 basis points more than prevailing jumbo mortgage rates.

The "Alt-A" market continues to grow rapidly.

Attractiveness of "Alt-A" Subordinated Bonds

Alt A subordinated bonds have attractive investment characteristics relative to other subordinated CMOs (such as "Jumbo A" subordinated tranches) for the following reasons. First, Alt-A collateral offers better convexity than other types of mortgage loans. This attribute leads to a more stable and predictable cash flow, which in turn leads to tranches with less average life volatility. Second, Alt-A collateral enjoys a higher base case prepayment speed, which leads to a more rapid de-leveraging of the subordinated tranches. Finally, historically Alt-A subordinated tranches have offered a most attractive combination of more spread and more credit enhancement than jumbo-A subordinated bonds.

Alt-A Collateral Deals have Greater Convexity

Alt-A deals are more convex than those comprised of jumbo A collateral. This convexity reflects a more controlled prepayment profile when rates decline and a faster prepayment speed when rates are flat or rise. First, Alt-A faster base case speeds reflect a faster seasoning ramp than for other types of mortgage collateral.

This faster seasoning ramp is due to the "curing effect" associated with these loans. That is, once an Alt-A loan develops a positive track record, it becomes a candidate for a lower rate loan from a more traditional lender. This faster seasoning also takes place in a rising rate environment. Conversely, when rates decline Alt-A loans tend to prepay at a slower rate of speed. This is the case due to two factors. First, these loans are generally smaller balance loans which means the dollars saved are lower than with a jumbo loan. Second, during periods of heavy refinancings, the channels of loan origination clog with easily underwritten standard refinancings (thus Alt-A loans are bypassed).

The fact that the prepayment risk is more understandable and predictable creates a mortgage deal structure which is more cash flow certain. This certainty increases the desirability of the tranches created from the collateral pool.

Faster Base Case Speeds Result in De-Leveraging of Deals

As mentioned above, "Alt-A" deals prepay faster in the base case than traditional mortgage deals. According to Morgan Stanley data, new issue CPR speeds approach 10%-16%. We attribute these faster speeds to the curing effect mentioned above.

Additionally, the faster speeds can result in a more rapid de-leveraging of the deal structure. This de-leveraging results in increased upgrade opportunities for the Alt-A subordinated bonds. We believe that this opportunity is greater than it is in the jumbo-A market since prepayment speeds tend to be faster in an unchanged or rising rate environment. Additionally, as previously mentioned, Alt-A subordinated tranches are larger than jumbo-A subordinated bonds. We believe that the amount of subordination required for Alt-A deals will decrease with time, as the rating agencies become more familiar with the credit histories of the major issuers. This "learning curve" factor will further increase the upgrade potential of "Alt-A" subordinated bonds.

Higher Spread and Credit Enhancement

Alt-A subordinated tranches tend to enjoy both the benefit of higher spreads and higher subordination levels than jumbo-A subordinated tranches. This spread advantage, although historically very modest, has ranged between 0 basis points for the most highly rated bonds to 100 basis points for bonds at the single-B level.

In addition to the aforementioned spread advantage, the subordination levels on Alt-A deals tend to be 25%-33% greater than on more traditional deals. The rating agencies state that this increased subordination is due to non-conforming factors. For example, although Alt-A borrowers have similar credit scores as jumbo-A borrowers, there are distinctly different attributes to the "Alt-A" pools as shown in Exhibit 32.

Among the non-conforming factors mentioned above, the rating agencies require the highest additional credit enhancement for investor properties. In contrast to the rating agency view, DLJ recently released some historical "Alt A"-like credit statistics using Prudential Home collateral. The study concludes that either no additional credit enhancement or minimal additional enhancement should be given to "Alt-A" pools. This further supports our belief that the "Alt-A" sector is both misunderstood and potentially undervalued.

Exhibit 32: Typical "Alt-A" Loan Pools

Loan Type	Avg. Loan Balance	% Deal < 227,150	% Limit Doc Loan	% Invest Property	% Single Family	% Cash Out-Refi
Jumbo-A	$281,902	25.2	20.7	0.1	95.4	8.9
Alt-A	133,574	85.0	56.1	22.1	81.3	25.2

Source: "Alt-A Prepayment Speeds: What's the Buzz?" *PaineWebber Mortgage Strategist* (June 2, 1998), p. 12.

Chapter 6

Real Estate Backed
Asset-Backed Securities

In this chapter we discuss mortgage-related products that are classified in the marketplace as asset-backed securities. The products include bonds backed by home equity loans, 125 loans, and manufactured housing loans. In practice, the classification of a mortgage-related product is not always simple. There are issues in which the underlying collateral is mixed with various types of mortgage-related loans. That is, the collateral backing a deal may have a combination of non-conforming first-lien mortgages, home equity loans, and manufactured housing loans. As explained in the previous chapter, the Securities Data Corporation has established criteria for classifying a mortgage-related product with mixed collateral as either a nonagency MBS or an ABS.

HOME EQUITY LOAN-BACKED SECURITIES

A *home equity loan* (HEL) is a loan backed by residential property. At one time, the loan was typically a second lien on property that was already pledged to secure a first lien. In some cases, the lien was a third lien. In recent years, the character of a home equity loan has changed. Today, a home equity loan is often a first lien on property where the borrower has either an impaired credit history and/or the payment-to-income ratio is too high for the loan to qualify as a conforming loan for securitization by Ginnie Mae, Fannie Mae, or Freddie Mac. Typically, the borrower used a home equity loan to consolidate consumer debt using the current home as collateral rather than to obtain funds to purchase a new home.

Home equity loans can be either *closed end* or *open end*. Our focus in this chapter is on securities backed by closed-end HELs. A closed-end HEL is structured the same way as a fully amortizing residential mortgage loan. That is, it has a fixed maturity and the payments are structured to fully amortize the loan by the maturity date. There are both fixed-rate and variable-rate closed-end HELs. Typically, variable-rate loans have a reference rate of 6-month LIBOR and have periodic caps and lifetime caps. The cash flow of a pool of closed-end HELs is comprised of interest, regularly schedule principal repayments, and prepayments, just as with mortgage-backed securities. Thus, it is necessary to have a prepayment model and a default model to forecast cash flows. The prepayment speed is measured in terms of a conditional prepayment rate (CPR).

With an open-end HEL the homeowner is given a credit line and can write checks or use a credit card for up to the amount of the credit line. The amount of the credit line depends on the amount of equity the borrower has in the property. There is a revolving period over which the homeowner can borrow funds against the line of credit. At the end of the term of the loan, the homeowner either pays off the amount borrowed in one payment or the outstanding balance is amortized.

Originators of HELs look at three key ratios when deciding to underwrite a loan — *combined loan-to-value ratio* (CLTV), *second-lien ratio*, and *payment-to-income ratio*. The CLTV looks at the ratio of all mortgage liens relative to the appraised value of the property. For example, suppose that an applicant seeking a $10,000 second mortgage lien via a HEL on property with an appraised value of $100,000 has a first mortgage-lien on that property of $80,000. Then the CLTV is 90% [($80,000 + $10,000)/$100,000]. The second lien ratio is found by dividing the amount of the second lien sought by the applicant by the combined mortgage liens. In our example, the second lien ratio is 11.11% [$10,000/($80,000 + $10,000)]. In calculating the payment-to-income ratio, the monthly mortgage payment includes all mortgage payments.

Prepayments

There are differences in the prepayment behaviors for home equity loans and traditional residential mortgage loans. In general it is expected that prepayments due to refinancings would be less important for HELs than for traditional residential mortgage loans because typically the average loan size is less for HELs. In general it is also thought that interest rates must fall considerably more for HELs than for traditional residential mortgage loans in order for a borrower to benefit from refinancing.

Wall Street firms involved in the underwriting and market making of home equity loan-backed securities have developed prepayment models for these loans. Several firms have found that the key difference between the prepayment behavior of HELs and traditional residential mortgages is the important role played by the credit characteristics of the borrower.[1]

A study by Bear Stearns strongly suggests that borrower credit quality is the most important determinant of prepayments. The study looked at prepayments for four separate deals. The underlying HELs for each deal had a different level of borrower credit quality (with the credit quality of the loans being classified by the issuer). The four deals whose prepayments were analyzed were FICAL 90-1 (dominated by the highest credit quality borrowers, A++), GE Capital 91-1 (A- borrowers), Fleet Finance 90-1 (B/C borrowers), and Goldome Credit 90-1 (D borrowers). Prepayments were analyzed from the third quarter of 1991 to the third quarter of 1995, a period which encompassed the refinancing wave of 1992 and 1993. The main focus was on how borrower credit quality affected prepayments. The study

---

[1] Dale Westhoff and Mark Feldman, "Prepayment Modeling and Valuation of Home Equity Loan Securities," Chapter 16 in Frank J. Fabozzi, Chuck Ramsey, Frank Ramirez, and Michael Marz (eds.), *The Handbook of Nonagency Mortgage-Backed Securities* (New Hope, PA: Frank J. Fabozzi Associates, 1997).

found that prepayments for the Goldome Credit 90-1 deal (which was comprised of D borrowers) were completely uncorrelated to changes in interest rates. The deal with the highest credit quality borrowers, FICAL 90-1, exhibited prepayments similar to those of agency mortgage-backed securities in terms of their sensitivity to interest rates. The correlation between prepayments and interest rates for the deal with A– borrowers (Capital 91-1) was less than for FICAL 90-1, but greater than for the deal with B/C borrowers (Fleet Finance 90-1). Consequently, the sensitivity of refinancing to interest rates is reduced the lower the credit quality of the borrower.

Prudential Securities has developed a prepayment benchmark for closed-end, fixed-rate HELs. The benchmark reflects Prudential Securities findings that such loans season much faster than traditional single-family mortgage loans. The benchmark, referred to by Prudential Securities as the *home equity prepayment curve* (or *HEP curve*), assumes that the loans become seasoned after 10 months (as opposed to residential mortgage loans which are assumed by the PSA prepayment benchmark to season after 30 months). The HEP curve is expressed in terms of the terminal CPR and assumes a linear increase in the CPR each month up to month 10. For example, 10% HEP means a CPR of 1% in month 1 with the CPR for each subsequent month increasing by 1% until month 10 when the CPR is 10%. An 18% HEP means a CPR of 1.8% in month 1 with the CPR for each subsequent month increasing by 1.8% until month 10 when the CPR is 18%.

Bear Stearns found that seasoning depends on the credit quality of the borrowers and the attributes of the loans. Some loans season in 10 months and some take as long as 30 months. The study by Bear Stearns found that the seasoning process consists of two phases. The first phase exhibits rapid seasoning and an eventual plateau in prepayments. In this phase, all other factors equal, lower credit quality loans tend to season faster and plateau at a higher level than loans of higher credit quality. Bear Stearns found the following pattern in a no-change interest rate scenario:

Borrower credit quality	Seasoning	CPR at Plateau
A	30 months	18% to 20% CPR
B	15 to 18 months	24% CPR
C	12 to 15 months	30% CPR

The reason for the more rapid seasoning and higher plateau for pools of lower credit quality borrowers is because of the curing effect — those borrowers that make timely payments become eligible to move up in credit quality rating and can thereby take advantage of lower loan rates that may be available. Loan originators monitor such loans and solicit loan applications from these potential borrowers.

In the second phase there is a longer period of steadily declining prepayments. For lower credit quality loans, there is a significant slowdown in prepayments that lasts three to four years. Bear Stearns believes that this is due to the fact that borrowers who have improved their credit quality refinance in the first phase, which leaves in the remaining pool borrowers who are less able to refinance, as well as those who may exhibit a greater tendency to be delinquent. This phase is referred to as the "credit inertia" effect.

Prospectus Prepayment Curve

Borrower characteristics and the seasoning process must be kept in mind when trying to assess prepayments for a particular deal. In the prospectus of an offering a base case prepayment assumption is made — the initial speed and the amount of time until the collateral is expected to be seasoned. Thus, the prepayment benchmark is issue specific. The benchmark speed in the prospectus is called the *prospectus prepayment curve* or *PPC*. As with the PSA benchmark, slower or faster prepayments speeds are a multiple of the PPC.

Since HEL deals are backed by both fixed-rate and variable-rate loans, a separate PPC is provided for each type of loan. For example, in the prospectus for the Contimortgage Home Equity Loan Trust 1998-2, the base case prepayment assumption for the fixed-rate collateral begins at 4% CPR in month 1 and increases 1.45455% CPR per month until month 12, at which time it is 20% CPR. Therefore, if an investor analyzed the deal based on 200% PPC, this means doubling the CPRs cited and using 12 months for seasoning. For the variable-rate collateral, 100% PPC assumes seasoning after 18 months with the CPR in month 1 being 4% and increasing 1.82353% CPR each month. From month 18, the CPR is 35%. Thus, the variable-rate collateral is assumed to season slower but has a faster CPR when the pool is seasoned.[2]

Payment Structure

As with nonagency mortgage-backed securities discussed in the previous chapter, there are passthrough and paythrough home equity loan-backed structures.

Typically, home equity loan-backed securities are securitized by both closed-end fixed-rate and adjustable-rate (or variable-rate) HELs. The securities backed by the latter are called HEL floaters and most are backed by non-prime HELs. The reference rate of the underlying loans typically is 6-month LIBOR. The cash flow of these loans is affected by periodic and lifetime caps on the loan rate. To increase the attractiveness of home equity loan-backed securities to investors, the securities typically have been created in which the reference rate is 1-month LIBOR. Because of (1) the mismatch between the reference rate on the underlying loans and that of the HEL floater and (2) the periodic and life caps of the underlying loans, there is a cap on the coupon rate for the HEL floater. Unlike a typical floater, which has a cap that is fixed throughout the security's life, the effective periodic and lifetime cap of a HEL floater is variable. The effective cap, referred to as the *available funds cap* or *net funds cap*, will depend on the amount of funds generated by the net coupon on the principal, less any fees.

Let's look at one issue, Advanta Mortgage Loan Trust 1995-2 issued in June 1995. At the offering, this issue had approximately $122 million closed-end

---

[2] For an explanation as to how issuers develop a prospectus prepayment curve, see Bradley Adams and Glenn Schultz, "Developing The Prospectus Prepayment Curve for Real Estate Backed Structured Products," in Frank J. Fabozzi (ed.), *Selected Topics in Securitization for Issuers* (New Hope, PA: Frank J. Fabozzi Associates, 2001).

HELs. There were 1,192 HELs — 727 fixed-rate loans and 465 variable-rate loans. There were five classes (A-1, A-2, A-3, A-4, and A-5) and a residual. The five classes are summarized below:

Class	Par amount ($)	Passthrough coupon rate (%)
A-1	9,229,000	7.30
A-2	30,330,000	6.60
A-3	16,455,000	6.85
A-4	9,081,000	floating rate
A-5	56,917,000	floating rate

As explained below, class A-5 had two sub-classes, A-5-I and A-5-II.

The collateral is divided into group I and group II. The 727 fixed-rate loans are included in group I and support Classes A-1, A-2, A-3, and A-4. The 465 variable-rate loans are in group II and support Classes A-5-I and A-5-II certificates. All classes receive monthly principal and interest (based on the passthrough coupon rate).

The initial investors in the A-5 floating-rate certificates were given a choice between two sub-classes that offered different floating rates. Sub-class A-5-I has a passthrough coupon rate equal to the lesser of (1) 12% or (2) 1-month LIBOR plus 32 basis points with a cap of 12%. Sub-class A-5-II has a passthrough coupon rate equal to the lesser of (1) the interest rate for sub-class A-5-I or (2) the group II available funds cap. The available funds cap is the maximum rate payable on the outstanding Class A-5 certificates principal balance based on the interest due on the variable-rate loans net of fees and minus 50 basis points.

The Class A-4 certificate also has a floating rate. The rate is 7.4% subject to the net funds cap for group I. This is the rate that is paid until the outstanding aggregate loan balances in the trust have declined to 10% or less. At that time, Class A-4 will accrue interest on a payment date that depends on the average net loan rate minus 50 basis points and the net funds cap rate for group I.

PAC/NAS Structures

As explained in the previous chapter, tranches with greater prepayment protection have been created for the senior tranches in a paythrough structure. These tranches are referred to as non-accelerating senior (NAS) structures in the nonagency MBS market. In the agency market they are called planned amortization class (PAC) tranches. In the HEL structures, they are referred to as both PAC and NAS tranches. Unlike agency CMO PAC tranches that are backed by fixed-rate loans, for HEL deals the collateral is both fixed-rate and adjustable-rate.

An example of a HEL PAC tranche in a HEL-backed deal is tranche A6 in ContiMortgage 1998-2. We described the PPC for this deal above. There is a separate PAC collar for both the fixed-rate and adjustable-rate collateral. For the fixed-rate collateral the PAC collar is 125%-175% PPC; for the adjustable-rate collateral the PAC collar is 95%-130% PPC. The average life for tranche A6 (a tranche backed by the fixed-rate collateral) is 5.1 years. As explained in Chapter 4, the effective collar for shorter tranches can be greater than the upper collar specified in the prospectus. The effective upper collar for tranche A6 is actually 180 PPC (assuming that the adjustable-rate collateral pays at 100 PPC).[3]

For shorter PACs, the effective upper collar is greater. For example, for tranche A3 in the same deal, the initial PAC collar is 125 PPC to 175 PPC with an average life is 2.02 years. However, the effective upper collar is 190 PPC (assuming the adjustable-rate collateral pays at 100 PPC).

The effective collar for PAC tranches changes over time based on actual prepayments and therefore as the amount of the support tranches change. For example, if for the next 36 months after the issuance of the ContiMortgage 1998-2 actual prepayments are a constant 150 PPC, then the effective collar would be 135 PPC to 210 PPC.[4] That is, the lower and upper collar will increase. If the actual PPC is 200 PPC for the 10 months after issuance, the support bonds will be fully paid off and there will be no PAC collateral. In such situations the PAC is said to be a broken PAC.

Credit Enhancement

All forms of credit enhancement described in Chapter 5 have been used for home equity loan-backed securities. HEL issuers typically have two alternatives when it comes to structuring an ABS transaction. The issuer can pay a premium to an insurer and have the bonds "wrapped" with a AAA guarantee, or try to sell a senior/subordinated deal where the major form of credit protection is internal credit enhancement. Exhibit 1 shows a diagram of these alternatives.

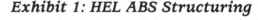

Exhibit 1: HEL ABS Structuring

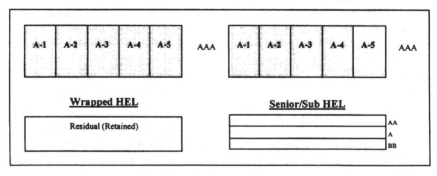

---

[3] For a more detailed analysis of this tranche, see Charles Schorin, Steven Weinreich, and Oliver Hsiang, "Home Equity Loan PAC and TAC Bonds," Chapter 20 in Frank J. Fabozzi, Chuck Ramsey, and Michael Marz (eds.), *Handbook of Nonagency Mortgage-Backed Securities* (New Hope, PA: Frank J. Fabozzi Associates, 1999).

[4] Schorin, Weinreich, and Hsiang, "Home Equity Loan PAC and TAC Bonds."

If the issuer tries to have his deal wrapped, the insurer will charge the issuer a premium (which is based on the credit quality of the underlying collateral) in order to obtain the insurer's guarantee of the timely payment of interest and the ultimate payment of principal on all wrapped bonds.[5]

Wrap insurers look at their business like catastrophe insurance; that is, they only expect a minute probability of having to pay a claim. This is the expectation for three reasons. First, HEL ABS transactions are structured so that the internal credit enhancement (i.e., the residual B-pieces, over-collateralization, and reserve accounts) would achieve an investment grade rating on a stand-alone basis. This is called a "shadow rating."

Second, the deal's servicer will perform the insurer's role of advancing interest and principal due but not collected. Additionally, the servicer will pay compensating interest on prepayment interest rate shortfalls. Finally, if the deal does start to underperform, "triggers" will protect the insurer by allowing excess spread to be diverted back into the deal.

The other form of HEL ABS, the senior/subordinated structure, does not have any external form of credit protection. That is, the collateral pool itself will determine whether a deal can maintain its existing ratings. It is therefore logical that if "headline risk" were to impact the market view of an issuer, the underlying bonds — both the senior bonds and the B-pieces (AA, A, and BBB) — would be expected to experience spread widening.

Structural Trends

Wrapped HEL deals comprised virtually all HEL ABS issuance during the 1994-1996 period. According to Prudential Securities, wrapped deals comprised 94.6% of all HEL issuance during 1996. However, beginning in 1997 the trend began to shift toward senior/subordinated structures. Two factors explain this trend. First, major institutional investors began to reach their credit exposure limits with respect to the insurers. Second, faced with a rapidly growing pipeline of deals, insurers began to raise their premiums. At the same time, credit spreads were tight which allowed subordinated investors to find the B-pieces attractive on a relative value basis.

The popularity of the senior/subordinated structure varies with the credit environment. For example, during the second quarter of 1997, 63.7% of new HEL deals were senior/subordinated structures. This trend began to reverse itself by the fourth quarter of 1997, when the Asian crisis led to the widening of credit spreads. During periods of tighter credit spreads (i.e., lower credit risk), senior/subordinated structures become more popular since they offer investors a spread advantage. However, when perceived credit risk increases, as it did during the 1998 Russian debt crisis, investors prefer the safety of insurance wraps.

---

[5] For most insurers, the ABS market is part of a diversification strategy from their traditional business of wrapping municipal bond obligations. The municipal business, although now a mature business, does provide the insurer a solid and recession-proof business and lessens the downgrade exposure from the ABS sector.

Other Advantages of "Wraps"

There are three additional advantages of investing in wrap deals versus senior/subordinated structures — liquidity, credit protection, and expertise. Wrap deals have the benefit of added liquidity since investors look first to the credit of the insurer rather than to the characteristics of the pool. This factor leads to much more liquidity and ability to trade in the underlying bonds.

As mentioned previously, the insurer will guarantee the timely payment of interest and the ultimate full payment of principal. Additionally, the obligation is unconditional and irrevocable. This guaranty also covers instances of fraud on the part of the issuer, originator, and/or servicer. These added protections should be of great comfort to the investor and mitigate headline or pool risk. Additionally, since the pool has an investment grade shadow rating, if the AAA insurer is ever downgraded, internal credit enhancement should be adequate to maintain an investment grade rating. Wrap deals can be thought of as "belt and suspenders" protection.

Finally, wrap providers bring an added layer of expertise to a transaction. That is, they perform pre-closing due diligence and review individual loan files. Additionally, the insurer monitors collateral performance and oversees the activities of the servicer. This added protection should give the investor comfort in wrapped HEL transactions.

Open-End Home Equity Loan-Backed Securities

Our discussion thus far has focused on ABS backed by a pool of closed-end home equity loans. The other type of home equity loan is an open-end home equity loan which is a line of credit — popularly referred to as a *home equity line of credit* or HELOC. It has been estimated that in the 1990s, HELOCs have been 20% to 25% of all home equity originations.[6] However, only 7% of HELOCs have been securitized.

The revolving period for a HELOC is the period where the borrower can take down all or part of the line of credit. The revolving period can run from 10 to 15 years. At the end of the revolving period, the HELOC can specify either a balloon payment or an amortization schedule (of up to 10 years). Almost all HELOCs are floating-rate loans. The interest rate paid by about 75% of HELOC borrowers is reset monthly to the prime rate (as reported in *The Wall Street Journal*) plus a spread.[7]

The bonds created in HELOC deals are floating-rate tranches. While the underlying loans are priced based on a spread over the prime rate as reported in *The Wall Street Journal*, the securities created are based on a spread over 1-month LIBOR.

---

[6] David Olson Research. As reported in W. Alexander Roever, John N. McElravey, and Glenn M. Schultz, "Home Equity Line of Credit (HELOC) Securitizations," Chapter 7 in Frank J. Fabozzi (ed.), *The Handbook of Nonagency Mortgage-Backed Securities* (New Hope, PA: Frank J. Fabozzi Associates, 1999).

[7] Richard F. DeMong and John H. Lindgren, *1998 Home Equity Loan Study*, Consumer Bankers Association, 1998.

Because HELOCs are for revolving lines, the deal structures are quite different for HELOCs and closed-end HELs. As with other ABS involving revolving credit lines such as credit card deals, there is a revolving period, an amortization period, and a rapid amortization period.

SECURITIZATION OF LOANS BACKED BY "125 LOANS"

One of the newer segments of the mortgage market is low/no equity second mortgages. These loans have high loan-to-value (LTV) ratios which generally range between 95% to 125% (hence the name "125 LTV loans"). The origination process involved in these loans focuses on credit rather than property value. That is, 125 LTV loans target prime borrowers or borrowers who have strong credit histories (i.e., "A" or "A-borrowers").

125 LTV loans are an outgrowth of home improvement lending programs. Home improvement loans are either made under FHA Title 1 or conventional programs to finance property improvements. Generally, loans made under the FHA Title 1 program can be made without regard for the market value of the property. One home improvement lender, FirstPlus, decided to tighten the credit restrictions on this program and began making home improvement and debt consolidation loans to creditworthy borrowers. Since that time several other issuers have entered into the market with similar 125 LTV programs.[8]

The well-publicized increase in consumer debt, as well as the attractive economics of the debt consolidation loan, are the basis of the rapid growth of the 125 LTV market. Exhibit 2 illustrates the attractiveness of the debt consolidation loan structured as a second mortgage. The economics of the debt consolidation loan are very attractive to the high quality borrower. In the example in Exhibit 2, the borrower not only eliminates his or her high cost debt, but also reduces monthly payments by 62% and frees up credit lines to use in the event of an emergency.

Exhibit 2: An Example of the Economics of Debt Consolidation

	Before 125 Loan			After 125 LTV Loan			
	Total Debt	Terms	Monthly Payment	Total Debt	Terms	Monthly Payment	Pre-Tax Savings
Credit card debt	$20,000	20%/3 Yr.	$743.31	0	—	0	—
Used car loan	$5,000	15%/4 Yr	$139.15	0	—	0	—
125 LTV 2nd mtg.	$0	—	—	$26,750*	13%/15 Yr	$338.48	—
Total	$25,000	—	$882.46	—	—	$338.48	$544.01

* Includes 7 point origination fee

---

[8] They include Empire Funding, MEGO, Residential Funding, DiTech, Preferred Mortgage, and Master Financial.

Exhibit 3: Comparison of Underwriting for 125 LTVs Pools versus Jumbo Nonagency and FHLMC Pools

Characteristic	125 LTV Pool	Jumbo Nonagency Pool	FHLMC Pool
Gross WAC	Jumbo Rate +5%	FHLMC Rate + 1/8%	Current Coupon (10 Yr + 135)
WAM	235	360	360
% Loan w/Prepay Penalty	60%	0%	0%
Avg. Loan Size	$30,000	$260,000	$150,000
Origination Fee	7.0 Pts	1.5 Pts	1.5 Pts
First Lien %	0%	100%	100%
Electronic Funds Trans.?	Yes-60%	No	No
Typical LTV	112%	78%	80%
FICO Scores			
Avg	685	720	680
% Below 620	0%	10%	5% to 15%
AAA Credit Support	24% to 30%	4% to 6%	N/A

Exhibit 4: "Three Cs" of Mortgage Lending

	Measures	Typical Guideline
C-credit reputation	Willingness to pay (based on credit history)	FICO score > 620
C-capacity	Ability to pay (based on debt/inc ratios)	Front ratio <28% Back ratio < 36%
C-collateral	Security in loan (based on appraisal)	LTV < 80%

Typical 125 LTV Guidelines and Loan Philosophy

FirstPlus, considered the 125 LTV industry leader, has been making loans to consumers with average FICO scores (a credit scoring model discussed in the next section) of 680. Exhibit 3 compares a typical FirstPlus pool with a typical jumbo nonagency and a FHLMC (Freddie Mac) agency mortgage pool.

The "three Cs" of traditional underwriting — *credit reputation, capacity,* and *collateral* — are modified in formulating 125 LTV loan guidelines (see Exhibit 4). The primary difference in focus on 125 LTV loans is that the third "C" (collateral) is often missing in the underwriting process. Despite this fact, 125 LTV lenders do file a lien against the borrower's home. The process of securing the loan with a lien creates for most borrowers a sense of obligation. Thus, in the underwriting process, borrower credit is of utmost importance and rates are assigned assuming little or no value can be obtained by foreclosing on the property.

FICO Scoring System

Developed by Fair Isaacs & Company, FICO is a credit scoring system that is used by lenders in the credit card, auto, home equity, and home mortgage markets. The system was developed to use past credit data in order to determine the likelihood of an individual borrower default over the next two years. FICO scores are based on the following variables:

- previous credit history
- current level of indebtedness
- length of credit history
- number of new credit inquiries
- type of credit available

The range of FICO scores is from a low of 365 (highest risk) to a high of 840 (lowest risk). Freddie Mac uses FICO scores as an important component in its underwriting process. For example, Freddie Mac breaks all mortgage loans into the following three buckets:

Bucket	FICO Range	Underwriting Method
1	less than 620	Cautious review
2	620 to 660	Comprehensive review
3	greater than 660	Basic review

The review that is necessary to approve a mortgage application generally increases as FICO scores decline (that is, credit risk increases). This is the case since historically default experience increases as FICO scores decline. As shown below, according to Fair Issacs & Company, historical default experience increases as FICO scores decline:

	FICO Score				
	<579	580 – 619	620 – 659	660 – 730	740+
% Defaults	9.5%	5.9%	2.7%	1.0%	0.1%

Further, according to Standard & Poor's, 75% of the U.S. population has FICO scores above 660, while only 25% of the population has FICO scores below 660. 125 LTV loans seek to attract a borrower with a good credit history with FICO scores in the high 680s. It is for this reason that one might expect defaults within the sector to be consistent with other high quality mortgage products (i.e., agencies and jumbo loans). See Exhibit 5.

Exhibit 5: MBS/ABS Product Grid — Typical FICO Scores

	FICO Scores					
	Credit Cards	Home Equity	Agencies	125 LTV	Jumbo Mortgage	
Lower			Product			Higher
FICOs			Type			FICOs

Exhibit 6: Typical 125 LTV Transaction

Rating	Tranching				% Deal
AAA	A1	A2	A3	A4	77.5
AA	M-1				10.0
A	M-2				5.25
BBB	B-1				4.75
BB	B-2				2.5

125 LTV Loan Structure

The most common structure for 125 LTV loan transactions is the senior-subordinated structure. This structure is diagrammed in Exhibit 6. The basic structure of the deal includes a series of AAA-rated sequential-pay bonds. These bonds achieve their AAA rating by virtue of the subordinated tranches M-1 through B-2 (rated AA to BB).

In a typical 125 LTV transaction, credit support comes from the following three sources: (1) excess spread, (2) overcollateralization, and (3) subordination. We discuss each below.

Excess Spread

Excess spread represents the difference between the collateral's gross weighted average coupon (gross WAC) and the servicing and coupon expenses associated with the transaction. Below is an example of the typical excess spread calculation on a 125 LTV transaction.

Gross WAC	13.75%
Less deal expenses	
Servicing	(0.75%)
Wgt avg deal coupon	(6.88%)
Excess spread	6.12%

Excess spread acts as the first line of defense against any cash flow shortfalls (i.e., delinquencies and/or losses). Excess spread, for 125 LTV products, is very powerful due to its magnitude (i.e., over 600 basis points annually) combined with the good credit quality of the receivables (i.e., high FICO scores).

Overcollateralization

The second line of credit protection available to investors is *overcollateralization* (called *O/C*). Overcollateralization is a reserve account funded by excess spread (not needed to cover losses). The O/C target for a transaction (usually 3.0% to 4.5% of the deal size) will be determined by the rating agencies. The amount of time necessary to fund this reserve account becomes a function of the size of the excess spread cash flow and the actual O/C target. Exhibit 7 shows the time needed to fund a typical reserve account at various levels of excess spread. From Exhibit 7 it can be seen that in the previous example a deal with excess spread of approximately 600 basis points and an O/C target of 3.0%, the O/C target should be fully funded within 6 months.

Exhibit 7: Number Months Needed to Fund Reserve

O/C Target	Excess Spread (b.p.)						
	350	400	450	500	550	600	650
3.0%	10.3	9.0	8.0	7.2	6.5	6.0	5.5
3.5%	12.0	10.5	9.3	8.4	7.6	7.0	6.5
4.0%	13.7	12.0	10.7	9.6	8.7	8.0	7.4

Exhibit 8: Typical 125 LTV Subordination Levels

Rating	% Deal	Subordination %
AAA	77.58	22.50
AA	10.00	12.50
A	5.25	7.25
BBB	4.75	2.50
BB	2.50	0.00

Exhibit 9: Total Required Credit Enhancement for a Typical 125 LTV Transaction

Rating	Sub %	O/C %	Total %
AAA	22.5	3.0	22.5
AA	12.5	3.0	15.5
A	7.25	3.0	9.25
BBB	2.50	3.0	5.50
BB	0.00	3.0	3.0

Subordination

The third line of defense for the 125 LTV investor is subordination. Losses can be charged against the principal balance of the lowest rated outstanding subordinated tranche. It is important to note, however, that losses will not be charged against the subordination tranches unless they exceed both the monthly excess spread as well as the outstanding balance of the reserve account. In addition, charge-offs can be reversed in subsequent periods after restoring the reserve account. This rejuvenation can occur due to a decline in default losses and/or the improvement in excess spread. Exhibit 8 shows typical levels of subordination on 1997 First-Plus transactions.

Total Required Credit Enhancement

The total required credit enhancement is the sum of the subordination plus the required reserve (or O/C target). These numbers are shown in Exhibit 9.

Prepayment Assumptions

Most recent 125 LTV deals are priced on a prepayment ramp beginning in month 1 at 2% CPR and increase linearly to a level of 12% or 15% by the 12th month (referred to as 100% PPC). These prepayment assumptions are considerably slower than other types of mortgage structures, such as home equity loans, nonagency jumbo loans, and agency MBS.

The reasons for these slow prepayment assumptions are threefold. First, the typical 125 LTV borrower has a negative equity situation in his or her primary asset (the house). Therefore, the borrower would be ineligible to refinance for most home loan programs. Second, the 125 LTV borrower has recently paid substantial upfront costs (i.e., 5 to 8 points) in order to get into the loan. Therefore, the economics of a rate refinancing would have to be significant given the average balance of the loan (average loan size of $30,000) to justify the refinancing. Third, most new 125 LTV loans contain prepayment penalties which make rate refinancing most uneconomical.

Additionally, prepayments on 125 LTV deals impact the structure differently than on nonagency mortgage deals. That is, like on nonagency deals, subordinated tranches are locked out from prepayments. However unlike nonagency deals, fast prepayments — particularly when they occur early in the deal's life (i.e., while the reserve fund is being built) — can weaken the overall credit structure of the deal. That is, excess spread (which is the primary credit protection on 125 LTV deals) is really like a WAC-IO. Therefore, prepayments lessen the scope of the excess spread protection by shrinking the amount of cash available to protect against losses.

On the other hand, deleveraging occurs at the subordinated tranche level when prepayments occur. This is the case since the senior bonds must absorb all prepayments for a minimum of 36 months, which causes the subordinated bonds to grow as a percentage of the overall deal. The impact of prepayments on the deal's subordinated bonds is illustrated more fully below.

Call Provisions

125 LTV deals often have two call provisions which can result in an early termination of the transaction. The first call provision is the *10% clean up call*. This provision allows the issuer to call out all the tranches at par when the deal factor drops to 0.10. Some deals also allow for a 50 basis point coupon step-up on remaining tranches if the deal is not cleaned up when the deal factor drops to 0.10 or lower.

The second call provision allows the deal to be called at par when the deal factor drops to 0.15. However, this provision can only be applied if the collateral is put out for auction (called an *auction call*). That is, the issuer must sell the underlying collateral to a third party. Most analysts do not expect the auction call to be exercised since it takes the process out of the issuer's hands.

Subordinated Tranche Provisions

The subordinated tranches of 125 LTV deals have some of the same important structural provisions as contained in nonagency subordinated tranches. These structural provisions include *lockout protection* and *step-down mechanisms*.

Exhibit 10: Sample Delinquency Test

	(A)	(B)	(C)	(D)	(E)	(F)	(G)	(H)
Scenario	Multiplier	Current 60+ Day %	(A) × (B)	Qtrly Excess Spread	(C) − (D)	O/C	Pass/Fail	New O/C Level
1	1.5	1%	1.5	1.5	0.0	3.0	Pass	3.0
2	1.5	2%	3.0	1.5	1.5	3.0	Pass	3.0
3	1.5	3%	4.5	1.0	3.5	3.0	Fail	3.5
4	1.5	4%	6.0	1.0	5.0	3.0	Fail	5.0

Lockouts

125 LTV deals contain a hard lockout provision for 36 months. However, given the slow pay nature of the collateral, investors can normally expect the actual lockout to be much longer (i.e., usually 58 to 63 months at 100% PPC). During the hard lockout period, the first payment date can only be breached by the exercise of the clean-up call provision. This would imply a 650% PPC speed or more than 6.5 times the expected prepayment speed.

In addition, the payment window in 125 LTV subordinated bonds is tighter (i.e., 5 to 7 years) than with a comparable nonagency subordinated bond. This is due to two factors. First, the weighted average maturity (WAM) on the loans is shorter on 125 LTV loans (i.e., 235 months) than with traditional 30-year mortgage products. This shorter WAM reduces the tail associated with the subordinated bond's cash flow. Second, 125 LTV deals do not pay scheduled principal payments on a pro-rata basis to the subordinated bonds. This factor has the effect of shortening the payment window by 3 to 5 years.

Step-Down Mechanisms

The step-down mechanism allows for the paydown of principal for the subordinated bonds. The step-down mechanism is comprised of two tests. The first test allows for the pro-rata return of principal for the subordinated bonds if the credit enhancement available to the AAA bondholders has doubled. For example, return of principal to the subordinated bonds will occur when the credit support available to the AA tranches has increased from 22.5% (as in our example) to 45%. This first test is known as the *doubling test*.

The second step-down test is a form of *delinquency test*. This test which must be met in conjunction with the doubling test measures the 60+ day delinquency levels relative to the deal's current reserves. An example of this test is shown in Exhibit 10. The step-down is allowed in the example if the product of columns A and B minus the quarterly excess spread (column E) is less than the overcollateralization (column F). Note that the multiplier is determined by the rating agencies. As shown above in scenario 3, when the product of columns A and B minus the quarterly excess spread is more than the quarterly excess spread, the test is failed and a new higher overcollateralization target is set (i.e., see column H in Exhibit 10).

Stress Testing 125 LTV Subordinated Bonds

Before performing extensive stress testing it is important to explain some critical assumptions used in the 125 LTV loan section.

Assumptions

First, *loss severity* is most often assumed to be 100%. This is the case since most loans within the sector are made with the knowledge that there is little or no equity available in the home. However, FirstPlus data have shown recent recovery rates within the sector to be between 0% and 15%. Positive recovery rates recently observed within the sector are a function of three factors. First, most loans have relatively short amortization periods (i.e., 15 years) which can lead to a more rapid amortization of loan balance than with traditional 30-year mortgages. Second, housing inflation continues to help resale values which have improved default recovery rates. Finally, a new market called the "re-performing" loan market has created a floor for non-performing unsecured loans at 5% to 10% of their loan balance.

Another critical assumption deals with the issue of advancing. Servicers within the 125 LTV market routinely do not advance delinquent payments to investors. The reason for this policy is twofold. First, the amount of excess spread in these transactions is usually adequate to cover reasonable levels of delinquencies. Second, advancing of payments is the one policy which could result in a loss severity in excess of the loan amount (i.e., loss severity greater than 100%).

Default Stress Testing

For each of the stress tests performed below we used the two most junior tranches off a 1997 FirstPlus transaction (1997-3). These two tranches, the B1 and B2 bonds, are rated BBB and BB, respectively.

Exhibit 11 shows these two bonds run at 100% PPC at various levels of CDR (conditional default rates). The CDR model assumes defaults occur monthly at an annual rate assuming these monthly defaults are applied to the then outstanding loan balance. For example, 2% CDR implies 2% of the pool will default over the next 12 months. That is, 0.167% (2%/12) defaults will apply in a particular month against the outstanding principal balance. This outstanding principal balance is regularly reduced by prepayments, principal payments, and defaults.

Based on the results of the stress tests reported in Exhibit 11, three trends are observable. First, the stability of the BBB yields given a changing average life profile is a function of the fact that the investment grade subordinated bonds are typically priced as par bonds at issue. In contrast, the BB bond's yield volatility is a function of the fact that it is structured to be a bond priced in the low 90s at issue.

A second observable trend between the two bonds is the fact that the BB bond has a shorter average life and a tighter principal payment window. This is a function of the fact that after the step-down dates, the overcollateralization is gradually allowed to be reduced. Any reduction of the O/C reserve is first used to retire the lowest rated debt (i.e., the BB rated bond). Consequently, the BB bond is a consistently shorter bond than the BBB bond. Likewise, the BBB bond will have a shorter average life and a tighter window than the A rated bond, etc.

The third observable trend is that both BBB and BB bonds are unaffected by credit losses at all stress levels (up to 5% CDR or 26% cumulative lifetime defaults) assuming no advancing, 100% PPC, and 100% loss severity. In fact, the subordinated tranche does not begin to suffer credit losses until between 5.5% CDR and 6% CDR for the BB bond (cumulative defaults between 27% and 29%) and between 6% and 6.5% CDR on the BBB rated bond (29% and 31% cumulative lifetime defaults).

The key factor when analyzing the results of these stress tests is the magnitude of the default protection mentioned above. One method of analysis is to look at FirstPlus historical data to gauge how this type of collateral has performed in the past. Exhibit 12 shows historical defaults for high LTV products broken out by FICO score.

Exhibit 11: Stress Tests

BBB – B1 Tranche

	CDR %					
	0	1	2	3	4	5
Yield	7.89%	7.89%	7.89%	7.89%	7.89%	7.89%
Avg Life	10.80	10.30	9.80	9.4	9.00	8.60
Window-Yrs	5.25-19.80	4.90-19.40	4.70-18.90	4.40-18.40	4.30-17.90	4.10-17.40
Window Months	176	175	172	169	165	161
Cum Losses	0.00%	6.40%	12.10%	17.20%	21.90%	26.10%

BB – B2 Tranche

	CDR %					
	0	1	2	3	4	5
Yield	9.79%	9.83	9.87%	9.91%	9.95%	9.99%
Avg Life	10.70	10.10	9.60	9.20	8.80	8.40
Window-Yrs	5.25-19.80	4.90-17.80	4.70-17.30	4.40-16.70	4.30-16.10	4.10-15.60
Window Months	159	156	152	148	143	139
Cum Losses	0.00%	6.40%	12.10%	17.20%	21.90%	26.10%

Exhibit 12: Analysis of Projected Defaults

	(A)	(B)			(A) × (B)
FICO Range	% Pool	Historical Defaults	Bank Card	First Mortgage	Expected Defaults
620-639	5.5%	5.3%	9.4%	5.0%	0.3%
640-659	17.7%	3.4%	6.6%	2.9%	0.6%
660-679	23.7%	2.9%	5.4%	2.6%	0.7%
680-699	22.9%	2.0%	3.7%	1.8%	0.5%
700-719	16.3%	1.5%	2.5%	0.8%	0.2%
720+	13.9%	1.3%	1.5%	0.4%	0.2%
	100.0%				2.5%

Source: FirstPlus, Lehman Brothers, and Fair Issacs & Company

Exhibit 13: Prepayment Stress Testing

BBB – B1 Tranche

	PPC %				
	0	50	100	150	200
Yield	7.79%	7.79%	7.79%	7.79%	7.79%
Avg Life	17.30	12.40	9.00	6.70	5.40
Window-Yrs	11.90-22.10	6.40-20.70	4.70-17.90	3.10-14.40	3.20-11.50
Window Months	123	172	165	137	101
Cum Losses	45.90%	30.60%	21.90%	16.60%	13.20%

BBB – B2 Tranche

	PPC %				
	0	50	100	150	200
Yield	9.51%	9.69%	9.95%	10.24%	10.54%
Avg Life	17.30	12.30	8.80	6.50	5.20
Window-Yrs	11.90-22.10	6.40-19.70	4.30-16.10	3.10-12.50	3.20-9.90
Window Months	123	160	143	137	83
Cum Losses	45.90%	30.60%	21.90%	16.60%	13.20%

It should be noted that the FirstPlus default statistics shown in Exhibit 12 represent defaults over a 2-year period. Therefore, to equate this with a CDR level the number would have to be annualized. The result of this exercise would put historical FirstPlus defaults between 1.0% and 1.3% CDR, or 76% below the *maximum CDR* level which can be absorbed at the BB tranche level without taking credit losses.

Another important observation from Exhibit 12 is that the FirstPlus 125 LTV product consistently has had fewer defaults than unsecured credit cards. Additionally, FirstPlus defaults at the lower FICO score ranges are close to the historical performance of first mortgage loans (i.e., A quality mortgage loans).

Prepayment Stress Testing

Exhibit 13 shows the impact of varying prepayment speeds given a constant default assumption (i.e., 4% CDR). The major observation from the data shown in Exhibit 13 is that prepayments have not impacted the two bonds' abilities to buffer against losses. It is interesting to note that at 0% PPC, despite a significant extension of average life for both bonds, the tranches (due to the improved "IO-like" cash flows) are absorbing losses of nearly 46% without credit losses.

As previously mentioned, many analysts believe that after reviewing all previous 125 LTV transactions and studying the underlying collateral characteristics, that 100% PPC (based on a 2% to 12% CDR ramp over 12 months) is a reasonable prepayment speed forecast. We therefore gain comfort from the above stress tests, particularly given the fact that they were all run assuming a relatively fast CDR assumption (defaults are also a form of collateral prepayment).

Exhibit 14: Manufactured Housing Loan Characteristics

	Single-Wide	Multi/Double-Wide	U.S. Average Site-Built
Average Home Size	1,065 Sq. Ft.	1,525 Sq. Ft.	1,945 Sq. Ft.
Average Sales Price	$26,000	$50,000	$143,000
Loan Rate vs. Conventional	+338 bps	+288 bps	—
Average Loan Term	200 mo.	240 mo.	360 mo.
Average Monthly Payment	$260	$406	$831

Source: Green Tree Financial

MANUFACTURED HOUSING-BACKED SECURITIES

Manufactured housing are single-family detached homes constructed off-site and transported to a plot of land or to a manufactured housing community (park). There are two types of manufactured housing (MH) units: (1) single-section (also known as "single-wides") and (2) multi-sections. Single-wide units, which are transported to their site in one piece, average 1,065 square feet. Multi-section units are assembled at the site after being transported in pieces, and average 1,525 square feet. Exhibit 14 summarizes the manufactured housing loan characteristics. The senior bonds of manufactured housing ABS are both SMMEA and ERISA eligible.

The typical manufactured housing loan is a 15- to 20-year fully amortizing retail installment loan. Therefore, as with residential mortgage loans and HELs, the cash flow of a pool of MH loans consists of net interest, regularly scheduled principal, and prepayments. Single-section units are usually financed over 15-year terms at rates between 300 to 350 basis points above conventional 30-year rates. Multi-section units are usually financed over 20-year terms at rates between 250 to 300 basis points over conventional 30-year rates. Currently, only 10% of all units financed are written as mortgage loans (i.e., financed with the unit's land).

Prepayments

Manufactured housing has proven to be a market which is largely interest rate insensitive. We believe that this is the case for the following reasons. First, MH loans have small balances resulting in minimal saving from refinancings. (See Exhibit 15.) Even a decline of 200 basis points for a typical $35,000 MH loan would result in only a $44 monthly savings.

Second, manufactured housing units, like cars, are subject to depreciation. In the early years of a loan's life, depreciation exceeds amortization leaving the borrower with little equity which is needed to refinance. Third, few refinancing options are currently available for used manufactured housing units. Finally, MH borrowers may not qualify for alternative financings because of their limited financial resources.

Exhibit 15: Manufactured Housing Refinancing Incentive

	MH	Single-Family
Loan Balance	35,000	150,000
Term	200 mo.	360 mo.
Current Rate	11%	8%
Monthly Payment	$382	$1,100
-100 b.p.		
New Rate	10%	7%
New Payment	$360	$998
Savings	$22	$102
−200 b.p.		
New Rate	9%	6%
New Payment	$338	$899
Savings	$44	$201

Exhibit 16: Prepayment Sensitivity to Rate Movements (CPR)

	+300	+200	+100	0	−100	−200	−300	+300 BP Range (CPR)
Mfd Housing ABS	10.9	11.5	12.3	14.1	15.3	16.2	17.0	6.1
Home Equity ABS	7.2	7.9	9.0	12.9	17.1	21.7	31.2	24.0

Source: *Lehman Brothers ABS Quarterly Outlook* (September 18, 2000), p. 18 and
Lehman Brothers MBS & ABS Strategies (August 21, 2000).

Several Wall Street firms have reported their research findings on the prepayment behavior of MH loans. Exhibit 16 shows the interest rate sensitivity of manufactured housing prepayments to interest rate movements based on the research by Lehman Brothers. Manufactured housing loans have a CPR prepayment range (+300 to −300) of 9.8% CPR which was substantially lower than the 26.0 CPR and 58.1 CPR range for home equity ABS and 30-year FNMAs, 6.5s, respectively.

The results of a Morgan Stanley study analyzing the factors driving refinancings and turnover in MH loans are summarized in Exhibits 17 and 18.[9] The study also finds that monthly defaults in many MH loan securitizations are about 0.1% to 0.2% of the original loan principal.

Lehman Brothers has developed a benchmark curve for describing the prepayment pattern of MH loans. The benchmark curve, called the *Manufactured Housing Prepayment curve* (MHP curve), starts at 3.7% CPR in the first month and increases by 0.1% CPR each month until month 24. Thus, seasoning is complete in 24 months. From month 24 on the CPR is constant at 6%. This benchmark is referred to as the "100% MHP curve." As with the PSA prepayment benchmark curve, multiples of the curve are determined by multiplying the CPR for each

[9] Steven Abrahams, Howard Esaki, and Robert Restrick, "Manufactured Housing: Overview, Securitization, and Prepayments," Chapter 17 in Frank J. Fabozzi, Chuck Ramsey, Frank Ramirez, and Michael Marz (eds.), *The Handbook of Nonagency Mortgage-Backed Securities* (New Hope, PA: Frank J. Fabozzi Associates, 1997), p. 294.

month accordingly. So, a 200% MHP curve means in month 1 the CPR is 7.4% and increases by 0.2% per month until month 24. From month 24 on the CPR is 12%.

Credit Performance

In evaluating the credit performance of manufactured housing-backed ABS it is important to consider delinquencies, loss statistics, and rating agency upgrade/downgrade data.

Exhibit 17: Morgan Stanley Findings on the Factors Driving Refinancings in Manufactured Housing Loans

Factor	Factor Levels	Proportional Prepayment Impact (% CPR)				
		Interest Rates Shift (bp from loan mortgage rate)				
		0	−50	−100	−200	−300
Refinancing Incentive and Loan Size	$18,000 balance (< avg size loan)	6	7	9	12	14
	$24,000 balance (avg size loan)	6	8	10	13	16
	$30,000 balance (> avg size loan)	6	9	12	14	17
Loan Age	< 24 Months	80% of average life speed				
	> 24 Months	105% of average life speed				
Seasonality	January, February	80% of average life speed				
	Other Months	105% of average life speed				
The Economy	0.8 Million New Home Sales	Slower				
	1.0 Million New Home Sales	Average				
	1.2 Million New Home Sales	Faster				
Lender Competition	More	Raises prepayments				
	Less	Lowers prepayment				

Source: Exhibit 10 in Steven Abrahams, Howard Esaki, and Robert Restrick, "Manufactured Housing: Overview, Securitization, and Prepayments," Chapter 17 in Frank J. Fabozzi, Chuck Ramsey, Frank Ramirez, and Michael Marz (eds.), *The Handbook of Nonagency Mortgage-Backed Securities* (New Hope, PA: Frank J. Fabozzi Associates, 1997), p. 294.

Exhibit 18: Morgan Stanley Findings on the Factors Driving Turnovers in Manufactured Housing Loans

Factor	Factor Levels	Prepayment Impact
Loan Age	Month 1	3.7% CPR
	Months 2-23	Increases 0.1% CPR a month
	Months 24 and beyond	6.0% CPR
The Economy	0.8 Million New Home Sales	Slower
	1.0 Million New Home Sales	Average
	1.2 Million New Home Sales	Faster
Seasonality	January Low	80% of average annual speed
	July High	120% of average annual speed
Setting	On Borrower-Owned Land	Seasons over 36 Months
	In an MH Park	Seasons over 24 Months

Source: Exhibit 12 in Steven Abrahams, Howard Esaki, and Robert Restrick, "Manufactured Housing: Overview, Securitization, and Prepayments," Chapter 17 in Frank J. Fabozzi, Chuck Ramsey, Frank Ramirez, and Michael Marz (eds.), *The Handbook of Nonagency Mortgage-Backed Securities* (New Hope, PA: Frank J. Fabozzi Associates, 1997), p. 296.

Exhibit 19: Green Tree MH Static Pool Losses

Year	Orig. Pool Size ($ billion)	Pool Factor	Loss % of Orig. Pool
1991	$0.6	0.47	4.55%
1992	1.4	0.58	2.16
1993	2.1	0.80	0.67
1994	3.2	0.90	0.16
1995	4.0	0.98	0.02

Various sources including Bloomberg

In terms of delinquencies, the American Bankers Association (ABA) statistics show that total delinquencies were running at around 3% during 1995 (slightly higher than single-family mortgages), higher than the 1% to 1.5% delinquency rates for automobiles, recreational vehicles, and boat loans. According to the Manufactured Housing Institute, delinquency levels since 1990 have ranged between 2.25% and 3.50%. Based on Green Tree static pool data, losses by cohort year are reported in Exhibit 19.

The default curve for manufactured housing starts off at a very low rate and peaks by year 3. After year 3 the default rate will decline gradually until leveling off at about 50% of its peak level in year 10. Historical experience shows that loss severity ranges between 30% and 60% (double-wide units have the highest recovery rates).

Finally, the credit record for the manufactured housing sector has been excellent. For example, manufactured housing-backed securities have had more upgrades than any other ABS sector. The rating agency criteria for ABS appears very conservative.

MH Structures

A typical MH structure is shown in Exhibit 20. The deal outlined in the exhibit was priced at a prepayment assumption of 100 MHP. The deal also assumes a 10% cleanup call. This is the same assumption used in non-agency CMOs, as well as many other ABS sectors.

The deal has sequential-pay priorities for classes A1 through A5 until the first crossover date. The crossover date refers to the date when the lockout period ends and the subordinated tranches (M and B1) begin to receive their pro-rata share of principal payments. Exhibit 21 shows the payment priority for Green Tree 1995-10.

As previously noted, the senior bonds pay sequentially until the crossover date, which is the latter month of 49 or when the deal's "step-down" tests (discussed below) are met. Exhibit 22 shows how losses are allocated within the structure. If losses were to exceed the first four loss priorities, then a pro-rata principal write-off would occur among the A1 to A6 tranches.

Mezzanine and Subordinated Bonds

Before analyzing the lower rated tranches on manufactured housing ABS, the investor must be sure to understand the priorities of cash flow which flow to these bonds. For example, the step-down tests used for the Green Tree 1995-10 deal are given in Exhibit 23. Likewise, the B1 and B2 tranches have to pass a similar series of tests in order to begin to receive principal.

The investor should know when the expected crossover date will occur. For example, Green Tree 1995-10 M1, although locked out for 48 months, is not scheduled to receive any principal until month 63. This 100 MHP pricing assumption (138 MHP is needed to accelerate the principal date on M1 to month 49) is too slow to achieve step-down in month 49.

Exhibit 20: Green Tree 1995-10 MH Structure

Class	Size ($MM)	% Deal	Rating	A/L	Window (Months)	Spread
A1	48.0	11.9%	AAA	1.05	1-24	+47
A2	63.0	15.5%	AAA	3.06	24-57	+48
A3	41.0	10.1%	AAA	5.07	41-73	+55
A4	33.0	8.1%	AAA	7.09	73-98	+71
A5	59.0	14.6%	AAA	10.25	98-152	+94
A6	92.0	22.7%	AAA	17.24	152-241	+145
M1	37.0	9.1%	AA–	12.57	63-241	+145
B1	16.0	4.0%	BBB+	8.30	63-143	+145
B2	16.0	4.0%	BBB+	17.20	143-241	+177
Total	405.0			9.25		

Collateral
No. Loans   11,805   New Unit %   83%
Avg. Size $34,134   Non-Park Unit %   72%
WAC   10.05%   WA LTV%   76%
WAM   280 M   Geographics·
                            10% North Carolina,
                            8% Michigan,
                            7% Texas

Various sources including Bloomberg

Exhibit 21: Typical Green Tree MH Payment Priority

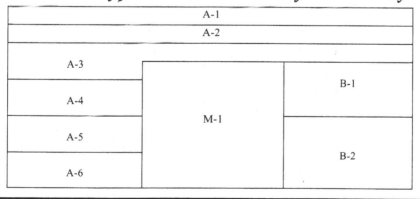

Exhibit 22: Typical Green Tree MH Loss Allocation

Loss Priority	Tranche	Credit Source	Credit
5th	A1-A6	Subordination	16%
4th	M1	Subordination	8%
3rd	B1	Subordination	4%
2nd	B2	Green Tree Guarantee	4%
1st	—	Excess Spread	349 bps

Exhibit 23: Green Tree 1995-10 Step-Down Tests

M-1

Principal lockout until 12/99 (48 months)

Then must pass the following five tests:

1. Average 60-day delinquency ratio <3.5% of orig. pool balance
2. Average 30-day delinquency ratio <5.5% of orig. pool balance
3. Current losses <2.25% of orig pool balance
4. Cumulative losses must be less than:
   48-59 months <5.5% of orig. pool balance
   60-71 months <6.5% of orig. pool balance
   72-83 months <8.5% of orig. pool balance
   84+ months <9.5% of orig. pool balance
5. De-leveraging test
   M1 + B principal >25.5% of orig. pool balance

Chapter 7

Commercial Mortgage-Backed Securities

In previous chapters we covered mortgage-related products backed by a pool of residential mortgage loans. Residential mortgages are for properties with 1- to 4- single family units. In this chapter, we look at commercial mortgage-backed securities (CMBS). These securities are backed by a pool of commercial mortgage loans on income-producing properties — multifamily properties (i.e., apartment buildings), office buildings, industrial properties (including warehouses), shopping centers, hotels, and health care facilities (i.e., senior housing care facilities). Unlike residential mortgage loans where the lender relies on the ability of the borrower to repay and has recourse to the borrower if the payment terms are not satisfied, commercial mortgage loans are non-recourse loans. This means that the lender can only look to the income-producing property backing the loan for interest and principal repayment.

The basic building block of the CMBS transaction is a commercial loan which was originated either to finance a commercial purchase or to refinance a prior mortgage obligation. Many types of commercial loans can be either sold by the originator as a commercial whole loan or structured into a CMBS transaction. The whole loan market, which is largely dominated by insurance companies and banks, is focused on loans between $10 and $50 million issued on traditional property types (multifamily, retail, office, and industrial). CMBS transactions, on the other hand, can involve loans of virtually any size (from conduit loans as small as $1 million to single property transactions as large as $200 million) and/or property type.

As indicated in Chapter 1, the CMBS market is about equal to the size of the nonagency MBS market and roughly a quarter of the size of the ABS market. The growth in the CMBS market has been spurred by the ability of Wall Street to securitize real estate and real estate loans, and transform equity into real estate investment trusts (REITs) and debt into CMBS. This market is expected to grow and liquidity improve with the introduction of CMBS indexes in 1999 by Lehman Brothers and Merrill Lynch. These indexes are discussed at the end of this chapter.

INDICATORS OF POTENTIAL PERFORMANCE

As just noted, commercial mortgages are non-recourse loans and therefore the lender looks only to the property to generate sufficient cash flow to repay principal and to pay interest. If there is a default, the lender looks to the proceeds from the sale of the property for repayment and has no recourse to the borrower for any unpaid balance. Basically, this means that the lender must view each property as a stand-alone business and evaluate each property using measures that have been found useful in assessing credit risk.

While there are fundamental principles of assessing credit risk that apply to all property types, traditional approaches to assessing the credit risk of the collateral differ for CMBS than for nonagency MBS and real estate related ABS. For MBS and ABS backed by residential property, typically the loans are lumped into buckets based on certain loan characteristics and then assumptions regarding default rates are made regarding each bucket. In contrast, for commercial mortgage loans, the unique economic characteristics of each income producing property in a pool backing a CMBS deal require that credit analysis be performed on a loan-by-loan basis not only at the time of issuance, but monitored on an on-going basis.

Regardless of the property type, the two measures that have been found to be key indicators of the potential credit performance are the debt-to-service coverage ratio and the loan-to-value ratio.

The *debt-to-service coverage* (DSC) ratio is the ratio of a property's *net operating income* (NOI) divided by the debt service. The NOI is defined as the rental income reduced by cash operating expenses (adjusted for a replacement reserve). A ratio greater than 1 means that the cash flow from the property is sufficient to cover debt servicing. The higher the ratio, the more likely it is that the borrower will be able to meet debt servicing from the property's cash flow.

For all properties backing a CMBS deal, a weighted average DSC ratio is computed. An analysis of the credit quality of an issue will also look at the dispersion of the DSC ratios for the underlying loans. For example, one might look at the percentage of a deal with a DSC ratio below a certain value. Recognizing that each deal should be analyzed on its own merits, Brian Lancaster of Bear Stearns suggests a guide for quality based on an average DSC ratio and dispersion (as measured by the percentage of the deal with a DSC ratio less than 1.25) as shown in Exhibit 1.[1]

Studies of residential mortgage loans have found that the key determinant of default is the loan-to-value ratio. The figure used for "value" in this ratio is either market value or appraised value. For income producing properties, the value of the property is based on the fundamental principles of valuation. As will be explained in Chapter 8, the value of an asset is the present value of the expected cash flow. This involves projecting an asset's cash flow and discounting at an appropriate interest rate(s). In valuing commercial property, the cash flow is the future NOI. Then a discount rate (a single rate), referred to as the *capitalization rate*, reflecting the risks associated with the cash flow is used to compute the present value of the future NOI. Consequently, there can be considerable variation in the estimates of NOI and the appropriate capitalization rate in estimating a property's market value. Thus, analysts are skeptical about estimates of market value and the resulting LTVs reported for properties.[2]

---

[1] Brian P. Lancaster, "Introduction to Commercial Mortgage-Backed Securities," Chapter 23 in Frank J. Fabozzi, Chuck Ramsey, and Michael Marz (eds.), *The Handbook of Nonagency Mortgage-Backed Securities* (New Hope, PA: Frank J. Fabozzi Associates, 2000).

[2] For a discussion of the pitfalls in calculating NOI, see David P. Jacob, Galia Gichon, Dan Lee, and Lynn Tong, "A Framework for Risk and Relative Value Analysis of CMBS: Theory," Chapter 16 in Frank J. Fabozzi (ed.), *The Handbook of Commercial Mortgage-Backed Securities: Second Edition* (New Hope, PA: Frank J. Fabozzi Associates, 1999).

Exhibit 1: A Quick Guide to CMBS Quality

Average DSCR	Good	Fair	Poor	
	1.45	1.45-1.35	1.35	

% of Deal with DSCRs below 1.25	Good	Fair	Poor	
	Under 5%	10%	>10%	

Average LTV	Very Good	Good	Fair	Poor
	<65%	65%	75%	>75%

% of Deal with LTVs >75%	Excellent	Very Good	Good	Fair
	<5%	6%-10%	11%-15%	>16%-20%

Prepayment Protections	Excellent	Very Good	Good	Fair
	Treasury Defeasance - Lockout	Yield Maintenance	Prepayment Penalty Points	

Geographic Concentration	Acceptable	High
	<40% in one state	40% or greater in one state

Property Type Concentration	Acceptable	High
	<40% in one property type	40% or greater in one property type

This exhibit is designed to serve as a rough guide to quality in the CMBS market. There are of course, exceptions to these basic indicators. As such each deal should be analyzed on its own merits.

Source: Exhibit 3 in Brian P. Lancaster, "Introduction to Commercial Mortgage-Backed Securities," Chapter 23 in Frank J. Fabozzi, Chuck Ramsey, and Michael Marz (eds.), *The Handbook of Nonagency Mortgage-Backed Securities: Second Edition* (New Hope, PA: Frank J. Fabozzi Associates, 2000).

The lower the LTV, the greater the protection afforded the lender. Given the LTV for the properties in the pool, the average LTV can be determined and the dispersion can also be computed. Exhibit 1 shows guides for CMBS quality based on average LTV and the percentage of the deal with LTVs greater than 75%.

Another characteristic of the underlying loans that is used in gauging the quality of a CMBS deal is the prepayment protection provisions. We will discuss these provisions later in this chapter. Finally, there are characteristics of the property that affect quality. Specifically, analysts and rating agencies look at the concentration of loans by property type and by geographical location. Exhibit 1 provides a guide to quality based on these characteristics.

BASIC CMBS STRUCTURE

While there are five basic types of CMBS transactions, we will concentrate on the three types of CMBS deals which are greatly impacted by structure. The CMBS transaction structure takes shape when the owner of the commercial loans has a potential transaction "sized" by the rating agencies. As with any structured finance transaction, sizing will determine the necessary level of credit enhancement to achieve a desired rating level. For example, if certain DSC and LTV ratios are needed, and these ratios cannot be met at the loan level, then subordination is used to achieve these levels. In Exhibit 2, a simple example demonstrates how a CMBS transaction can be structured to meet the rating agencies required DSC and LTV ratios. For example, prior to its acquisition by Fitch IBCA, Duff & Phelps required a 1.51× coverage and a 62.1% LTV to achieve a single-A rating on a regional mall deal. Since that level could not be obtained at the collateral level (coverage of 1.25× and 75% LTV), a CMBS structure with 17.2% subordination could be created.

Paydown Priority

The rating agencies will require that the CMBS transaction be retired sequentially with the highest rated bonds paying off first. Therefore, any return of principal caused by amortization, prepayment, or default will be used to repay the highest rated tranche.

Interest on principal outstanding will be paid to all tranches. In the event of a delinquency resulting in insufficient cash to make all scheduled payments, the transaction's servicer will advance both principal and interest. Advancing will continue from the servicer for as long as these amounts are deemed recoverable.

Losses arising from loan defaults will be charged against the principal balance of the lowest rated CMBS bond tranche outstanding. The total loss charged will include the amount previously advanced as well as the actual loss incurred in the sale of the loan's underlying property.

Finally, the investor must be sure to understand the cash flow priority of any prepayment penalties and/or yield maintenance provisions, as this can impact a particular bond's average life and overall yield.

Exhibit 2: How a CMBS Transaction can be Structured to Satisfy Required DSC and LTV Ratios of Duff & Phelps

Loan Information	
Assume $100 million Regional mall loan	DSC 1.25×
	LTV 75%
Market value	$133.3 million
Debt service	$10.0 million
NOI	$12.5 million

CMBS Structure	Required Subordination (%)*	Tranche Size	Tranche LTV (%)	Tranche DSC
AAA	31.4	68.6	51.5	1.82×
AA	23.3	8.1	57.5	1.63×
A	17.2	6.1	62.1	1.51×
BBB	12.0	5.2	66.0	1.42×
BB	6.6	5.4	70.1	1.34×
B	2.6	4.0	73.1	1.28×
NR	0.0	2.6	75.0	1.25×
		100.0		

This example is based on Duff & Phelps criteria.

Structural Call Protection

The degree of call protection available to a CMBS investor is a function of the following two characteristics:

1. call protection available at loan level
2. call protection afforded from the actual CMBS structure

At the commercial loan level, call protection can take the following forms:

1. prepayment lockout
2. defeasance
3. prepayment penalty points
4. yield maintenance charges

Prepayment Lockout

A *prepayment lockout* is a contractual agreement that prohibits any prepayments during a specified period of time, called the *lockout period*. The lockout period at issuance can be from two to 10 years. After the lockout period, call protection usually comes in the form of either prepayment penalty points or yield maintenance charges. Prepayment lockout and defeasance (discussed next) are the strongest forms of prepayment protection.

Defeasance

With *defeasance* — a method that has long been used by municipal issuers — rather than prepaying a loan, the borrower provides sufficient funds for the servicer to invest in a portfolio of Treasury securities that replicates the cash flows that would exist in the absence of prepayments. Unlike the other call protection provisions discussed next, there is no distribution made to the bondholders when the defeasance takes place. So, since there are no penalties, there is no issue as to how any penalties paid by the borrower are to be distributed amongst the bondholders in a CMBS structure. Nor are there any additional taxes imposed because there is no distribution. Moreover, the substitution of the cash flow of a Treasury portfolio for that of the borrower improves the credit quality of the CMBS deal.

Prepayment Penalty Points

Prepayment penalty points are predetermined penalties which must be paid by the borrower if the borrower wishes to refinance. For example, 5-4-3-2-1 is a common prepayment penalty point structure. That is, if the borrower wishes to prepay during the first year, he must pay a 5% penalty for a total of $105 rather than $100; in the second year, a 4% penalty would apply, and so on.

When there are prepayment penalty points, there are rules for distributing the penalty amongst the CMBS bondholders. Prepayment penalty points are not common in new CMBS structures. Instead, the next form of call protection discussed, yield maintenance charges, is more commonly used.

It has been argued that the prepayment penalty points are not an effective means for discouraging refinancing. However, prepayment penalty points may be superior to yield maintenance charges in a rising rate environment.[3] This is because prepayments do occur when rates rise. With yield maintenance, the penalty will be zero (unless there is a yield maintenance floor that imposes a minimum penalty). In contrast, with prepayment penalty points, there will be a penalty even in a rising rate environment.

Yield Maintenance Charge

Yield maintenance charge, in its simplest terms, is designed to make the lender indifferent as to the timing of prepayments. The yield maintenance charge, also called the *make whole charge,* makes it uneconomical to refinance solely to get a lower mortgage rate. The simplest and most restrictive form of yield maintenance charge ("Treasury flat yield maintenance") penalizes the borrower based on the difference between the mortgage coupon and the prevailing Treasury rate.

There are several methods that have been used in practice to compute the yield maintenance charge. These methods include the simple model, the bullet model, the single discount factor model, the multiple discount factor model, the interest difference model, and the truncated interest difference model.[4] To provide further protection to lenders, there are often *yield maintenance floors* that impose a minimum charge.

The purpose of each of the methods for calculating the yield maintenance charge is to make the lender whole. However, when a commercial loan is included as part of a CMBS deal, there must be an allocation of the yield maintenance charge amongst the bondholders. There are several methods that are used in practice for distributing the yield maintenance charge and, depending on the method specified in a deal, not all bondholders may be made whole. These methods include the principal allocation method, base interest method, bond yield maintenance method, and present value yield loss method.[5]

Structural Protection

The other type of call protection available in CMBS transactions is structural. That is, because the CMBS bond structures are sequential-pay (by rating) the AA rated tranche cannot paydown until the AAA is completely retired, and the AA rated bonds must be paid off before the A rated bonds, etc. (see Exhibit 3). However, as mentioned earlier, principal losses due to defaults are impacted from the bottom of the structure upward.

---

[3] Da Cheng, Adrian R. Cooper, and Jason Huang, "Understanding Prepayments in CMBS Deals," Chapter 24 in *The Handbook of Nonagency Mortgage-Backed Securities: Third Edition.*

[4] These methods for computing the yield maintenance charge are discussed in Cheng, Cooper, and Huang, "Understanding Prepayments in CMBS Deals."

[5] These methods for allocating the yield maintenance charge among bondholders are discussed in Cheng, Cooper, and Huang, "Understanding Prepayments in CMBS Deals."

Exhibit 3: Sequence of Principal Paydowns

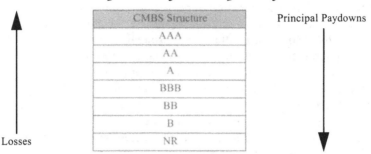

Exhibit 4: Types of CMBS Balloon Provisions

Method	Description	Examples
Time matched	Balloon maturity and bond maturity are the same	CMBS deals pre-RTC
Internal tail	Balloon maturity and bond maturity same but provisions for refinancing begin 1 to 2 years prior to maturity	DLJ 1992 and 1993 "M" series
External tail	Balloon maturity occurs before bond maturity	Most 1995 conduit deals and secured REIT debt transactions

Balloon Maturity Provisions

Many commercial loans backing CMBS transactions are balloon loans which require substantial principal payment at the end of the balloon term. If the borrower fails to make the balloon payment, the borrower is in default. The lender may extend the loan and in so doing will typically modify the original loan terms. During the work-out period for the loan, a higher interest rate will be charged, the *default interest rate*.

The risk that a borrower will not be able to make the balloon payment because either the borrower cannot arrange for refinancing at the balloon payment date or cannot sell the property to generate sufficient funds to pay off the balloon balance is called *balloon risk*. Since the term of the loan will be extended by the lender during the work-out period, balloon risk is also referred to as extension risk.

Although many investors like the "bullet bond-like" paydown of the balloon maturities, it does present difficulties from a structural standpoint. That is, if the deal is structured to completely paydown on a specified date, an event of default will occur if any delays occur. However, how such delays impact CMBS investors is dependent on the bond type (premium, par, or discount) and whether or not the servicer will advance to a particular tranche after the balloon default.

Another concern for CMBS investors in multi-tranche transactions is the fact that all loans must be refinanced to pay off the most senior bondholders. Therefore, the balloon risk of the most senior tranche (i.e., AAA) may be equivalent to that of the most junior bond class (i.e., B).

Currently, there are three types of structural provisions that can be present in CMBS transactions. These provisions are summarized in Exhibit 4.

The first provision — *time matched method* — is no longer used in CMBS transactions because it often results in actual defaults upon balloon maturity. This method was common prior to the real estate recession which began in the late 1980s. Prior to this national real estate downturn, extension risk was not a primary concern for traditional lenders (i.e., insurance companies and banks). However, the real estate recession caused a rapid decline in property values which in turn caused many loans to be non-refinanceable under the original loan terms. Many of these deals did contain default rate provisions. That is, an extension could be granted in exchange for an increase in the interest rate. Further, many deals of this type also had a "cash-trap" mechanism which captured all excess cash flow and used it to paydown debt.

The second type of balloon loan provision is the *internal tail*. The internal tail requires the borrower to provide ongoing evidence of its efforts to refinance the loan. For example, the following procedures would have to be undertaken within one year of the balloon date:

- appraisals on all properties
- Phase I environmental reports
- engineering reports

Finally, within six months prior to balloon maturity, the borrower must obtain a refinancing commitment.

The third type of balloon loan provision is the *external tail*. This provision is preferred by the major rating agencies since it gives the borrower the most time to arrange refinancing while avoiding default on the bond obligations. The external tail method, as shown in Exhibit 5, sets the maturity date of the CMBS issue longer than that of the underlying loans. The difference between these two dates acts as a buffer to arrange loan refinancing. Moreover, the CMBS investor does not suffer an interruption in cash flow during this period since the servicer advances any missing interest and scheduled principal (but not the balloon payment).

Servicer's Role

The servicer on a CMBS deal can play a key role in the overall success of the transaction. The key responsibilities of the servicer are to:

- collect monthly loan payments
- keep records relating to payments

Exhibit 5: External Tail Time Line

	Loan Balloon Date	CMBS Maturity Date
t_0	t_7	t_{10}
	Year	

Exhibit 6: Types of Servicers

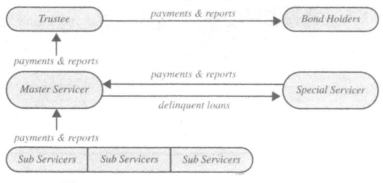

- maintain property escrows (taxes and insurance)
- monitor condition of underlying properties
- prepare reports for trustee
- transfer collected funds to trustee for payment

There are different types of servicers, and their roles can vary from deal to deal. In general, we will discuss three types of servicers: the sub-servicer, the master servicer, and the special servicer. These different servicers are highlighted in Exhibit 6.

The sub-servicer is usually the originator of the loan in a conduit deal who has decided to sell the loan but retain the servicing. All payments and property information will then be sent by the sub-servicer to the master servicer. The master servicer oversees the deal and makes sure the servicing agreements are maintained. In addition, the master servicer must facilitate the timely payment of interest and principal. That is, when a loan goes into default, the master servicer has the responsibility to provide for servicing advances. This role is critical to the success of a deal; therefore, it is important for an investor to be comfortable with both the financial strength and the overall experience of the master servicer.

A special servicer also plays a vital role within a CMBS transaction. The special servicer is usually engaged whenever a loan becomes more than 60 days past due. The special servicer usually has the following powers:

- extend the loan
- make loan modifications
- restructure the loan
- foreclose on the loan and sell the property

The special servicer is important to subordinated buyers because the timing of the loss can significantly impact the loss severity, which in turn can greatly impact subordinated returns. Therefore, first loss investors usually want to either control the appointment of the special servicer or perform the role themselves.

Exhibit 7: CMBS Deal Structures

	Liquidating Trusts (Non-Performing)	Multi-Property Single-Borrower	Multi-Property Conduit	Multi Property Non-Conduit	Single-Property Single-Borrower
Sample deals	-RTC N-Series -Lennar -SKW -Kearny Street	-Belaire -Factory Stores	-Nomura -Megadeal -DLJ Conduit	-RTC C-Series -New England	-Danbury Mall -Freehold Mall
Key risks	Structural	Structural/Credit	Structural/Credit	Credit	Credit
Loan age	Seasoned	New	New	Seasoned	New
Available ratings	AA-B	AAA-NR	AAA-NR	AAA-B	AAA-NR

DIFFERENT TYPES OF CMBS DEALS

Exhibit 7 shows the five types of CMBS deal structures. The first three types — liquidating trusts, multi-property single borrower, and multi-property conduit — will be discussed in detail in this section. These three deal types, which allow investors to focus more attention on structural aspects, have been the focus of most fixed-income money managers' CMBS activity. The latter two deal types — multi-property non-conduit and single-property single borrower — have been the focus of real estate money managers' activity within CMBS.

Liquidating Trusts (Non-Performing CMBS)

A small but interesting segment of the CMBS market is the non-performing or liquidating trusts. This segment, as the name implies, represents CMBS deals backed by non-performing commercial mortgage loans. This market segment contains several structural nuances which must be analyzed when deciding upon the relative attractiveness of a particular tranche. Some of the features are discussed below.

Fast Pay Structure

The so-called *fast-pay structure* requires that all cash flows from both asset sales and ongoing debt service, after bond interest payments, be used to retire the most senior bond class outstanding. The fast-pay structure prevents the equity holder from receiving any cash flow until all bond classes are retired. Since equity holders are highly sensitive to internal rate of return (i.e., they want to retire the bond classes quickly), the bondholders' interests are aligned with those of the equity holder.

Overcollateralization

Liquidating trusts are structured so that the debt obligations (bond classes) are less than the actual receivables outstanding (loan note amount). This creates a level of overcollateralization which can be used to offer discounted payoffs in order to accelerate the retirement of the bond classes. As an example, the first non-performing CMBS transaction — RTC 1992-N1 — had the following attributes:

Exhibit 8: Asset Disposition Strategy by Servicer

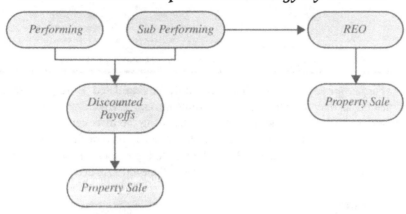

- Estimated market value: $155.3 million (derived investment value)
- Bond classes issued: $110.0 million
- Original loan balances: $345.8 million
- Equity contribution: $61.8 million

These transactions have proven to work well since structurally the acquisition price or derived investment value (DIV) is often 60% or less of the current balance of the mortgage collateral. In this case the DIV was 45% of the original loan balances ($155.3/$345.8), while the bond classes issued were only 71% of the estimated market value or DIV.

Servicer Flexibility

Liquidating trust structures generally allow the servicer maximum flexibility to liquidate the pool's underlying assets. Non-performing loans are generally grouped into three categories: performing, sub-performing, and real estate owned (REO).

As shown in Exhibit 8, the servicer (who is often also the transaction's equity holder) will work to carry out an asset disposition strategy which was designed at the deal's inception. The servicer's ability to dispose of property is paramount to maximizing value for bondholders. To help ensure that bondholder values are maximized, incentives are built in for the servicer.

Generally, the servicer can use one of two disposal strategies: discounted payoffs or take title of a property through foreclosure, then sell the property from REO. The method employed is a function of where the loans are currently situated. That is, if a high percentage of loans are already in REO, the investor will expect a shorter average life and less potential extension risk. Deals with a higher percentage of performing loans are expected to have longer average lives and more extension risk.

Exhibit 9: Types of Reserve Funds

	Liquidity	Asset Expenditure
Purpose	Cash flow used to prevent interest shortfalls to investment-grade bonds	Cash flow used to pay taxes, legal fees, and property maintenance
Used for Acceleration	Yes	No

Furthermore, performing loans can only be liquidated using the discounted payoff method, as they have the right to continue through the maturity of the loan. The sub-performing loans can be liquidated either by using the discounted payoff method or by initiating foreclosure proceedings. Foreclosure can be a difficult and expensive undertaking, but when it is successful and the title to the property is obtained, the trust can then liquidate the underlying property to retire the mortgage debt.

Reserve Funds

Another important structural feature found in liquidating trust transactions are reserve funds. Reserve funds are necessary in these transactions since it is difficult to project the timing of asset dispositions and their resulting cash flows. These reserve funds are established at the time of closing and are used to protect bondholders. The two common types of reserve funds are summarized in Exhibit 9.

Usually the asset expenditure reserve can be used to back up the liquidity reserve and make interest payments in the event of interest shortfalls to the investment-grade bonds. However, the asset expenditure reserve is not used to accelerate bond class paydown after the investment-grade bonds are retired.

Required Principal Payments

Non-performing CMBS are structured with relatively short average lives that receive cash flows from some loans while others are being disposed of. Therefore, the deal will be structured to achieve certain principal pay-down targets. In the event these targets are not achieved, often the fixed-rate coupon is scheduled at a preset date (i.e., increased from 10% to 12%). This motivates the borrower not to allow extension on the lower rated bond classes.

Single-Borrower/Multi-Property Deals

The second type of CMBS deal which contains important structural considerations is the single-borrower/multi-property transaction. The following are important structural features which are often contained in these deals:

- cross-collateralization and cross-default feature
- property release provisions
- lock-box mechanism
- cash-trap features

Each of these features is discussed below.

Exhibit 10: Breakeven DSC Ratio

	DSC Ratio (%)				
Number of Properties	1.15 ×	1.25 ×	1.30 ×	1.35 ×	1.50 ×
1	13	20	23	26	33
3	39	60	69	78	100
5	65	100	115	130	167
10	130	200	230	259	333
15	196	300	345	389	500

Exhibit 11: Breakeven LTV Ratio

	LTV Ratio (%)				
Number of Properties	90%	80%	75%	70%	60%
1	10	20	25	30	40
3	30	60	75	90	120
5	50	100	125	150	200
10	100	200	250	300	400
15	150	300	375	450	600

Cross-Collateralization and Cross-Default

Cross-collateralization is a mechanism whereby the properties that collateralize the individual loans are pledged against each loan. *Cross-default*, on the other hand, allows the lender to call each loan within the pool when any one defaults. Thus, by tying the properties together, the cash flow is available to meet the collective debt on all the loans. Therefore, from a credit standpoint, an individual loan should not become delinquent as long as there is sufficient excess cash flow available from the pool to cover this shortfall.

Exhibits 10 and 11 show a simplified example of the power of the cross-collateralization, cross-default mechanism. In our example, we assume that all properties have the same debt service coverage ratio and loan-to-value ratio, except for one distressed loan. In Exhibit 10, we calculate the breakeven DSC ratio possible before a default would be likely to occur.

For example, if a single loan pool had a DSC ratio of 1.30× (that is, it can cover debt service by 1.30 times), then the coverage ratio could decline by 23% before a breakeven level is reached. A further decline could lead to a loan default. However, if the same loan was within a pool of five cross-collateralized, cross-defaulted loans it could experience a complete loss of cash flow (100%) and a second loan could also experience a 15% decline in the cash flow before a similar breakeven point is reached. As can be seen from Exhibit 10, the stronger the overall DSC of the pool and the larger the overall pool, the greater the cushion against a single distressed loan. Similarly, Exhibit 11 shows the buffer of protection available on cross-collateralized, cross-defaulted pools by LTV.

As shown in Exhibits 10 and 11, a five loan pool with an initial LTV of 75% could have a single distressed loan decline in value to zero and have a second loan decline in value by 25% before a zero equity position in the pool is reached.

Exhibit 12: Lock-Box Structure

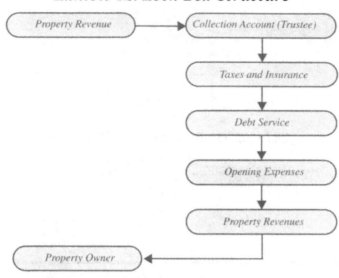

Property Release Provisions

Another structural feature often present in single-borrower/multi-property trans-actions is a *property release mechanism*. The investor should be concerned about the ability of the lender to prepay or otherwise remove the stronger properties from the pool. Various property release provisions will protect the investor against this risk. These provisions usually take the following form:

- If any properties are sold, the borrower must retire 125% of the initial allocatable mortgage amount;
- Resulting DSC ratios cannot be lower than before the sale; and,
- No collateral substitutions are permitted.

These property release provisions are important in order to maintain adequate structural protection in single-borrower transactions. Again, these provisions are to protect the investor from the borrower stripping the pool of its best properties.

Lock-Box Structures

Another structural feature often found in single-borrower transactions is the *lock-box mechanism*. The lock-box mechanism gives the trustee control over the gross revenues of the properties. (See Exhibit 12.)

Just as the cash flow of a CMBS deal flows through a waterfall payment mechanism, the property cash flow in a lock-box structure flows through a waterfall. As shown in Exhibit 12, the owner only has claim to excess cash flow after taxes, insurance, debt service, operating expenses, and property reserves. Likewise, management fees are often subordinate to debt service and operating expenses. The intent of the lock-box structure is not only to insure payment of debt service, but also to provide a strong incentive for owners and property managers to operate the properties efficiently since they have a subordinate claim on cash flow.

Cash-Trap Feature

A *cash trap mechanic* is a structural feature sometimes found in single-borrower/multi-property transactions that is the CMBS equivalent of "early amortization" in the asset-backed securities market. The intent is to penalize the borrower for something he/she has failed to do by amortizing the CMBS debt ahead of schedule. In the process, the cash-trap prevents the borrower from receiving excess cash flow. The most common triggers — which would cause all of the excess cash flow to be trapped for debt reduction — are:

- Failure to maintain pre-determined DSC ratio
- Failure to maintain required minimum debt ratings
- Failure to maintain adequate property reserves

The cash-trap feature works particularly well with a lock-box structure, since the trustee can easily "trap" all of the deal's excess cash. Cash-trap features have not been that common in recent deals (i.e., 1995 vintage) since borrowers have had more funding options (i.e., traditional lenders have returned and REITs which issue this type of debt have recently used unsecured debt issuance).

Multi-Borrower/Conduit Deals

The fastest growing segment of the CMBS is *conduit-originated transactions*.[6] Conduits are commercial-lending entities that are established for the sole purpose of generating collateral to securitize. Most Wall Street houses have established conduits to originate collateral to be used in CMBS transactions. Some important factors when analyzing conduit deals are: origination standards, number of originators, pool diversification, and degree of loan standardization. Each of these considerations will be further discussed below.

Origination Standards

A key consideration in analyzing a conduit CMBS product is understanding how the loans were originated. This analysis must address the following standards:

- Key DSC and LTV ratios
- Cash flow assumptions used in underwriting
- Standards for property reserves
- Method of arriving at appraised values
- Loan terms offered (i.e., amortizing/balloon and call protection terms)

---

[6] Fusion conduit deals are those deals in which there is a large loan (greater than $50 million) included with smaller loans.

• Geographic and property type diversification
• Timing of loan originations (i.e., month and year of origination)

Analyzing the origination standards is important in understanding how the loans were originated. The importance of the origination process in evaluating deals has been emphasized in a study by Fitch.[7] The study found that there is a direct correlation between the performance of a pool and the quality of the origination process. A report on one conduit deal by an analyst of a rating agency stated that while the underlying real estate was average, the overall deal should be viewed positively because the underwriting process was strong.[8]

Number of Originators

Many conduit deals have had more than one originator. This is usually done to speed up the funding period and to accumulate a larger critical mass. Most analysts agree that a minimum issue size of $100 to $125 million is desirable to effectively price a CMBS deal (given the fixed expenses of issuance). However, because multiple lenders may have originated the product, the investor has to get comfortable with the fact that a different lender underwrote the loans in a consistent manner. This can usually only be determined by carefully analyzing the mortgage loan files. It is for this reason that most investors prefer conduit deals originated by a single entity.

Pool Diversification

Another important factor to consider in conduit-originated deals is the diversification of the underlying loans. That is, how geographically and numerically diversified are the loans? Most investors like to see loan originations across several states without any major loan concentrations. One recent conduit deal had a single loan which comprised nearly 15% of the pool. A concentration such as this or a group of similar loans could severely impact the default-adjusted yields of the underlying securities.

Furthermore, the rating agencies have recently given lower overall levels of credit-enhancement to deals which contain diversification across property types. The theory is that because one cannot predict which property type will enjoy the best performance going forward, it is better to be adequately diversified.

Degree of Loan Standardization

It is important to analyze just how "cookie-cutter" a particular mortgage pool is. The higher the homogeneity, the greater the comfort that investors can look to the deal's structural features. For example, if a deal has a large concentration of 10-

---

[7] Jane Klir-Viau and Deborah R. Seife, "Commercial Mortgage Originator Rating Guidelines," Fitch-IBCA (February 24, 1998).
[8] As reported in Galia Gichon, "The CMBS Market: Past, Present, and Future," Chapter 1 in *The Handbook of Mortgage-Backed Securities: Second Edition*, p. 7.

year balloon maturities with seven years of prepayment lockout, then the deal will usually appeal to crossover corporate buyers. Moreover, a highly standardized deal will more easily accept tranches such as bond-IOs (interest only strips). However, a deal which enjoys a high degree of standardization with regard to loan terms may not appeal to below investment-grade buyers. This is because the rating agencies have tended only to upgrade deals due to retirement of debt or de-leveraging. In the example above, the balloon term usually implies interest only (i.e., no debt amortization), while the long lockout period would prevent voluntary prepayments. Thus, the below investment-grade bonds would not be candidates for upgrade.

STRESS TESTING STRUCTURES

As noted earlier in this chapter, an analysis of the credit quality of the CMBS involves looking at the commercial loans on a loan-by-loan basis. Rating agencies and analysts will then stress test the structure with respect to a combination of default and prepayment assumptions.

In stress testing default risk, three key assumptions are made. The first is the annual rate of defaults as measured by the *conditional default rate* (CDR). The benchmark CDRs typically used by rating agencies and analysts are those based on the default experience of commercial loans in the 1970s and 1980s. For example, it is not uncommon for analysts to assume a CDR of 2% to stress test strong deals and 3% for weaker deals.[9] However, Patrick Corcoran and Joshua Phillips have argued that for a variety of reasons the default experience of the 1970s and 1980s is inappropriate for stress testing default risk in today's CMBS market. They believe that "the modern CMBS market has benefited primarily from the tougher oversight and discipline provided by the public markets, and highlighted by rating agency leadership."[10] Specifically, there is much stronger cash coverage in deals today and reduced property cash flows.

A second important assumption is the timing of the defaults. A default can occur sometime early in the term of the loan or at the balloon date (when refinancing is required). The earlier defaults occur, the more adverse the impact will be on the performance of the deal. A third important assumption is the percentage of the loan balance that will be lost when a default occurs. This measure is called the *loss severity*.

To illustrate the importance of the assumptions on stress testing, Corcoran and Phillips used three stress test scenarios for a representative conduit deal to assess the impact on each bond class. Exhibit 13 shows the bond classes in the structure. The loans are 10-year balloon loans with a 30-year amortization. For each scenario, the loss severity assumed was 33% and no voluntary prepayments were assumed (i.e, a CPR of zero is assumed).

---

[9] See Patrick Corcoran and Joshua Phillips, "Stress and Defaults in CMBS Deals: Theory and Evidence," *JP Morgan Credit Research* (June 18, 1999), p. 1.

[10] Corcoran and Phillips, "Stress and Defaults in CMBS Deals: Theory and Evidence," p. 1.

Exhibit 13: Scenario Bond Spreads

Bond Classes	Base Case: 0 CDR 0 CPR	Default Scenarios		
		2 CDR 0 CPR	Model Defaults 0 CPR	Balloon Default Scenario 0 CPR
AAA-5 yr	98	93	97	98
AAA-10 yr	123	123	123	123
AA	137	137	137	137
A	160	160	160	160
BBB	195	195	195	195
BBB–	275	275	275	271
BB	575	575	575	556
B/B–	725	22	443	420
B–	950	−1585	−406	−220
UR	1706	−2921	−16	689
X	450	127	369	475

Source: Table 2 in Patrick Corcoran and Joshua Phillips, "Stress and Defaults in CMBS Deals: Theory and Evidence," *JP Morgan Credit Research* (June 18, 1999), p. 5.

The three stress test scenarios that they analyzed are:

Scenario 1 (2% CDR Scenario): A 2% CDR per year. (For the 10-year loan pool with a 30-year amortization schedule, this means cumulative defaults over the 10-year loan of 16.7%.)

Scenario 2 (Model Default Scenario): Annual default rates over 10 years based on a model developed by Corcoran and Kao.[11] The default model produces a cumulative default rate for 10 years of 14%. However, the pattern of defaults is such that there is a delay or backloading of defaults. This scenario does not allow for the stronger DSC ratios that exist in today's CMBS market compared to those of the 1970s and 1980s.

Scenario 3 (Balloon Default Scenario): Defaults rates from the Corcoran-Kao model are used as in Scenario 1 producing a cumulative default rate for 10 years of 14%. However, the defaults are assumed to occur at the 10-year balloon date. Effectively, this scenario does allow for the stronger DSC ratios in today's CMBS market compared to the 1970s and 1980s.

Exhibit 13 shows the results of the analysis on the spread. The spread reported is a credit-adjusted spread. The second column shows the base case results — a CDR of zero. The next three columns show the results of the 2% CDR Scenario, Model Default Scenario, and Balloon Default Scenario. As can be seen,

---

[11] Patrick Corcoran and Duen-Li Kao, "Assessing Credit Risk of CMBS," Chapter 13 in Frank J. Fabozzi (ed.), *The Handbook of Commercial Mortgage-Backed Securities: Second Edition*.

for the B– rated tranche, the credit-adjusted spread is small in the 2% CDR Scenario but roughly the same in the other two scenarios. However, even though positive in those scenarios, the spread is less than for the BB tranche. For the BBB and higher rated tranches, the credit-adjusted spreads are equal; for the BB tranche the Balloon Default Scenario shows a slightly lower credit-adjusted spread compared to the other two scenarios.

While the scenarios used in the Corcoran-Phillips illustration test solely for defaults, a more complete analysis recognizes that prepayments must be considered and that there is an interaction between default rates and prepayment rates linked by changes in interest rates. In stress testing, it is important to take both defaults and prepayments not due to default into account. For example, Michael Ervolini, Harold Haig, and Michael Megliola of Charter Research Corporation have demonstrated how credit-driven prepayment and default analysis can be used for stress testing.[12]

The model that they present specifies conditions for prepayments and for defaults. Prepayments occur when permitted and when it will result in net proceeds to the borrower (after adjusting for any prepayment penalties). So, assessing prepayments requires modeling how the yield curve will change over the investment horizon. The conditions for default occur when NOI is insufficient to meet debt service. This is modeled to assess the default possibility for each loan rather than an assumed constant CDR. Assumptions regarding when the defaults will occur and the severity loss must be made. In addition, the refinanceability of each property is modeled.

SHORT-TERM CMBS FLOATERS

Recently a new asset class has emerged from within the CMBS market. This asset class, *short CMBS floaters*, offers a combination of two characteristics not previously available to CMBS investors — short average lives and floating-rate cash flows. As shown in Exhibit 14, for the vast majority of the market there are fixed-rate cash flows with long average lives. (This includes conduit-deals and large loan CMBS.)

Exhibit 14: CMBS Product Map

	Avg Life	
	Short	Long
Fixed	RTC "N" Series	Conduit CMBS
	Liquidating Trust	Large Loan CMBS
Floating	New CMBS Short Floaters	Customized CMBS Tranches

[12] Michael A. Ervolini, Harold J. A. Haig, and Michael A. Megliola, "Credit-Driven Prepayment and Default Analysis," Chapter 14 in *The Handbook of Commercial Mortgage-Backed Securities: Second Edition*.

Exhibit 15: Percent Credit Subordination of Short CMBS Floater versus Traditional CMBS Conduit Deal

Rating	DLJ 98-STF1 Short Floater	NASC 98-D6 Conduit	Difference
AAA	43.8%	28.0%	+15.8%
AA	35.5	22.0	13.5
A	26.5	16.5	10.0
BBB	18.5	12.0	6.5
BBB	16.5	10.5	6.0
BB	12.0	4.2	7.8

Floating-rate tranches are rare within the CMBS market. The few that are available were largely created from reverse inquiry by combining fixed cash flows with an interest rate swap. Moreover, short cash flows are quite rare within the CMBS market, usually because of the excellent call protection embedded into the loan agreements. To date the only short cash flows available to CMBS investors have come from sub-performing or non-performing collateral. These deals were structured as liquidating trusts. That is, bond classes were retired in sequential order as the collateral was sold off or liquidated.

Short-CMBS floaters are created as a way to securitize a dealer's CMBS warehouse lines. That is, some CMBS loans are originated as floaters without call protection for the following reasons:

- Borrower's desire to maintain prepayment flexibility as they plan to become a REIT
- Borrower is renovating and/or improving property performance prior to seeking long-term financing

Most of these loans are essentially bridge loans which will ultimately be taken out by permanent CMBS securitizations.

Credit Support for Short CMBS Floaters

Because the rating agencies view floating-rate commercial loans as more transitional in nature and perceive the underlying cash flows as more volatile, they have required larger levels of subordination than on traditional conduit CMBS. Exhibit 15 compares a short CMBS floater deal with a traditional CMBS conduit deal.

Although there is no actual track record for credit performance for this asset class, we believe the extra credit enhancement is quite generous given the dealer's strong incentive to get the loan into a long-term fixed-rate securitization. This incentive is strong since dealers, to date, have retained the lowest rated tranches. This is significantly different from the traditional CMBS transactions where an established market for fixed-rate unrated and single B tranches exist. Because of this, the dealer has a strong incentive to move the loans into permanent CMBS transactions where they do not have this credit risk.

Short CMBS Floater Structure

Short CMBS floater transactions done as of this writing were structured similarly to liquidating trusts. That is, as loans are rolled out of the trust, de-leveraging occurs among the lower rated bonds. This is because the bonds pay down sequentially, which results in the highest rated bonds having the shortest average lives.

CMBS INDEXES

One signal of the maturity of a market sector is the development of a sector index. An index allows managers and their clients to assess performance with respect to that sector. It provides information that is used in asset allocation models. Moreover, an index can be used as the basis of a total return swap. In such a swap, one party pays a fixed or floating rate and receives the return on the index. Effectively, a total return swap allows investors to participate in a market sector without buying or selling individual securities in that sector. Using total return swaps a party can short the market or effectively create a leveraged position. All of this makes a market sector more attractive to a broader range of institutional investors, thereby increasing market liquidity for that sector.

In 1999, two dealers introduced a series of CMBS indexes — Lehman Brothers and Merrill Lynch. The Lehman CMBS Index has four subsectors:

1. *CMBS Investment Grade Index*: Measures return for investment grade classes.
2. *CMBS High Yield Index*: Measures return for non-investment grade and nonrated classes
3. *CMBS Interest Only Index*: Measures return for interest-only classes
4. *Commercial Conduit Whole Loan Index*: Measures return for all bond classes and interest-only classes

Lehman divides the CMBS Investment Grade Index into two components — the ERISA-eligible component and the non-ERISA-eligible component.

The rule for assigning a security that was assigned a split rating is the same rule as used by Lehman for its other indexes. Specifically, the security is categorized according to its Moody's rating. This is consistent with all the other Lehman Brothers indexes. If a security does not have a Moody's rating, then its S&P rating will be used. If the security is not rated by Moody's or S&P, its Fitch rating is used.

A number of specific criteria apply to all the Lehman Brothers CMBS indexes:

"1. All transactions must be private label. No agency transactions will be included.

Exhibit 16: Criteria Specific to Each CMBS Index

Index	Criteria
CMBS Investment Grade Index	All bonds are rated investment grade by Moody's and are offered publicly.
CMBS High Yield Index	All bonds are not rated investment grade by Moody's and can be offered privately and publicly.
CMBS IO Index	Includes all interest only securities.
Commercial Whole Loan Index	Aggregate of all classes that meet the general CMBS Index criteria.

Source: Exhibit 4 in Steven Berkley and Alex Golbin, "Lehman Brothers' CMBS Index," Chapter 5 in Frank J. Fabozzi (ed.), *Investing in Commercial Mortgage-Backed Securities* (New Hope, PA: Frank J. Fabozzi Associates, 2001).

2. The collateral for each transaction must be new origination, that is, originated specifically for securitization.
3. Each original aggregate transaction size must be at least $500 million to be included in the CMBS Index. Aggregate outstanding transaction sizes must be at least $300 million to remain in the CMBS Index.
4. All certificates must be either fixed rate, weighted average coupon (WAC), or capped WAC securities. No floating rate certificates will be included.
5. All certificates must have an expected maturity of at least one year." [13]

The criteria specific to each index are identified in Exhibit 16.

There are five Merrill Lynch CMBS indexes: a 5-year triple A index, a 10-year triple A index, a double A index, a single A index, and a triple B index. In constructing these indexes, Merrill Lynch uses liquid deals brought by high quality issuers that are actively traded.

---

[13] Steven Berkley and Alex Golbin, "Lehman Brothers' CMBS Index," Chapter 5 in Frank J. Fabozzi (ed.), *Investing in Commercial Mortgage-Backed Securities* (New Hope, PA: Frank J. Fabozzi Associates, 2001), p. 86.

Chapter 8

Analysis of
Real Estate-Backed Securities

In this chapter we will look at how to analyze real estate backed structured products. Analysis includes valuing securities, assessing their relative value, and assessing their interest rate risk exposure. We begin with a discussion of the static cash flow yield methodology and its limitations. We then look at a dynamic valuation model for valuing real estate backed structured products (Monte Carlo simulation), a relative value measure that is produced from the valuation model (option-adjusted spread), and measures of interest rate risk (effective duration and effective convexity). At the end of the chapter we present several illustrations of how the dynamic valuation model is applied to several real estate backed structured products.

STATIC CASH FLOW YIELD ANALYSIS

The yield on any financial instrument is the interest rate that makes the present value of the expected cash flow equal to its market price plus accrued interest. For mortgage-backed and asset-backed securities, the yield calculated is called a *cash flow yield*. The problem in calculating the cash flow yield of a mortgage-backed and asset backed security is that because of prepayments (voluntary and involuntary) the cash flow is unknown. Consequently, to determine a cash flow yield some assumption about the prepayment rate must be made.

The cash flow for a mortgage-backed and asset-backed security is typically monthly. The convention is to compare the yield on a mortgage-backed security to that of a Treasury coupon security by calculating the MBS's bond-equivalent yield. The bond-equivalent yield for a Treasury coupon security is found by doubling the semiannual yield. However, it is incorrect to follow that convention for mortgage-backed and asset-backed securities because the investor has the opportunity to generate greater interest by reinvesting the more frequent cash flows. The market practice/convention is to calculate a yield so as to make it comparable to the yield to maturity on a bond-equivalent yield basis. The formula for annualizing the monthly cash flow yield for a mortgage-backed security is as follows:

$$\text{bond-equivalent yield} = 2[(1 + i_M)^6 - 1]$$

where i_M is the monthly interest rate that will equate the present value of the projected monthly cash flow to the market price (plus accrued interest) of the security.

All yield measures suffer from problems that limit their use in assessing a security's potential return. The yield to maturity has two major shortcomings as a measure of a bond's potential return. To realize the stated yield to maturity, the investor must: (1) reinvest the coupon payments at a rate equal to the yield to maturity, and (2) hold the bond to the maturity date. The reinvestment of the coupon payments is critical and for long-term bonds can be as much as 80% of the bond's return. The risk of having to reinvest the interest payments at less than the computed yield is called *reinvestment risk*. The risk associated with having to sell the security prior to the maturity date is called *interest rate risk*.

These shortcomings are equally applicable to the cash flow yield measure: (1) the projected cash flows are assumed to be reinvested at the cash flow yield, and (2) the mortgage-backed or asset-backed security is assumed to be held until the final payout based on some prepayment assumption. The importance of reinvestment risk, the risk that the cash flow will have to be reinvested at a rate lower than the cash flow yield, is particularly important for mortgage-backed and asset-backed securities because payments are monthly and both interest and principal (regularly scheduled repayments and prepayments) must be reinvested. Moreover, an additional assumption is that the projected cash flow is actually realized. If the prepayment experience is different from the prepayment rate assumed, the cash flow yield will not be realized.

Nominal Spread

Given the computed cash flow yield and the average life for a mortgage-backed or asset-backed security based on some prepayment assumption, the next step is to compare the yield to the yield for a comparable Treasury security. "Comparable" is typically defined as a Treasury security with the same maturity as the average life of the security. The difference between the cash flow yield and the yield on a comparable Treasury security is called a *nominal spread*.

Unfortunately, it is the nominal spread that some investors will use as a measure of relative value. However, this spread masks the fact that a portion of the nominal spread is compensation for accepting prepayment risk. For example, CMO support tranches were offered at large nominal spreads. However, the spread embodied the substantial prepayment risk associated with support tranches. An investor who bought solely on the basis of nominal spread — dubbed a "yield hog" — failed to determine whether that nominal spread offered potential compensation given the substantial prepayment risk faced by the holder of a support tranche.

Instead of nominal spread, investors need a measure that indicates the potential compensation after adjusting for prepayment risk. This is the OAS that will be described later. Below we will explain how this measure is computed using the model employed for valuing real estate backed structured products.

Zero-Volatility Spread

The nominal spread is found by spreading the yield to the average life of an interpolated Treasury yield curve or other benchmark. This practice is improper for an amortizing security even in the absence of interest rate volatility because each cash flow should be discounted at its own unique interest rate (i.e., the theoretical spot rate).

What should be done instead is to calculate what is called the *zero-volatility spread, Z spread,* or *static spread.* This is the yield spread in a static scenario (i.e., no volatility of interest rates) of the bond over the entire theoretical Treasury spot rate curve, not a single point on the Treasury yield curve. The magnitude of the difference between the nominal spread and the Z spread depends on the steepness of the yield curve: the steeper the curve, the greater the difference between the two values. In a relatively flat yield curve environment, the difference between the nominal spread and the Z spread will be small.

There are two ways to compute the Z spread. One way is to use today's yield curve to discount future cash flows and keep the mortgage refinancing rate fixed at today's mortgage rate. Since the mortgage refinancing rate is fixed, the investor can usually specify a reasonable prepayment rate for the life of the security. Using this prepayment rate, the bond's future cash flow can be estimated. Use of this approach to calculate the Z spread recognizes different prices today of dollars to be delivered at future dates. This results in the proper discounting of cash flows while keeping the mortgage rate fixed. Effectively, today's prices indicate what the future discount rates will be, but the best estimates of future rates are today's rates.

The second way to calculate the Z spread allows the mortgage rate to go up the curve as implied by the forward interest rates. This procedure is sometimes called the *zero volatility OAS.* In this case a prepayment model is needed to determine the vector of future prepayment rates implied by the vector of future refinancing rates. A money manager using Z spread should determine which approach is used in the calculation.

MONTE CARLO SIMULATION/OAS

In fixed income valuation modeling, there are two methodologies commonly used to value securities with embedded options — the lattice model and the Monte Carlo simulation model. The Monte Carlo simulation model involves simulating a sufficiently large number of potential interest rate paths in order to assess the value of a security along these different paths. This model is the most flexible of the two valuation methodologies for valuing interest rate sensitive instruments where the history of interest rates is important. Mortgage-backed and some asset-backed securities are commonly valued using this model. As explained below, a byproduct of a valuation model is the OAS.

Interest Rate History and Path-Dependent Cash Flows

For some fixed income securities and derivative instruments, the periodic cash flows are *path-dependent.* This means that the cash flow received in one period is determined not only by the current interest rate level, but also by the path that interest rates took to get to the current level.

In the case of mortgage passthrough securities (or simply, passthroughs), prepayments are path-dependent because this month's prepayment rate depends on whether there have been prior opportunities to refinance since the underlying mortgages were originated. Unlike passthroughs, the decision as to whether a corporate issuer will elect to refund an issue when the current rate is below the issue's coupon rate is not dependent on how rates evolved over time to the current level.

Moreover, in the case of securities backed by adjustable-rate mortgages (ARMs), prepayments are not only path-dependent but the periodic coupon rate depends on the history of the reference rate upon which the coupon rate is determined. This is because ARMs have periodic caps and floors as well as a lifetime cap and floor. For example, an ARM whose coupon rate resets annually could have the following restriction on the coupon rate: (1) the rate cannot change by more than 200 basis points each year and (2) the rate cannot be more than 500 basis points from the initial coupon rate.

Pools of passthroughs are used as collateral for the creation of collateralized mortgage obligations (CMOs). Consequently, for CMOs there are typically two sources of path dependency in a tranche's cash flows. First, the collateral prepayments are path-dependent as discussed above. Second, the cash flow to be received in the current month by a tranche depends on the outstanding balances of the other tranches in the deal. Thus, we need the history of prepayments to calculate these balances.

Valuation[1]

Conceptually, the valuation of passthroughs and pools of loans using the Monte Carlo method is simple. In practice, however, it is very complex. The simulation involves generating a set of cash flows based on simulated future mortgage refinancing rates, which in turn imply simulated prepayment rates.

Valuation modeling for CMOs and paythrough structures in home equity loan and manufactured housing ABS is similar to valuation modeling for passthroughs, although the difficulties are amplified because the issuer has sliced and diced both the prepayment and interest rate risk into smaller pieces and distributed these rules among the tranches. The sensitivity of the passthroughs comprising the collateral to these two risks is not transmitted equally to every tranche. Some of the tranches wind up more sensitive to prepayment and interest rate risk than the collateral, while some of them are much less sensitive.

---

[1] Portions of the material in this section and the one to follow are adapted from Frank J. Fabozzi, Scott F. Richard, and David S. Horowitz, "Valuation of CMOs," Chapter 6 in Frank J. Fabozzi (ed.), *Advances in the Valuation and Management of Mortgage-Backed Securities* (New Hope, PA: Frank J. Fabozzi Associates, 1998).

Using Simulation to Generate Interest Rate Paths and Cash Flows

The typical model that Wall Street firms and commercial vendors use to generate random interest rate paths takes as input today's term structure of interest rates and a volatility assumption. The term structure of interest rates is the theoretical spot rate (or zero coupon) curve implied by today's Treasury securities. The volatility assumption determines the dispersion of future interest rates in the simulation. The simulations should be calibrated to the market so that the average simulated price of a zero-coupon Treasury bond equals today's actual price.

Each model has its own model of the evolution of future interest rates and its own volatility assumptions. Typically, there are no significant differences in the interest rate models of dealer firms and vendors, although their volatility assumptions can be significantly different.

The random paths of interest rates should be generated from an arbitrage-free model of the future term structure of interest rates. By arbitrage-free it is meant that the model replicates today's term structure of interest rates, an input of the model, and that for all future dates there is no possible arbitrage within the model.

The simulation works by generating many scenarios of future interest rate paths. In each month of the scenario, a monthly interest rate and a mortgage refinancing rate are generated. The monthly interest rates are used to discount the projected cash flows in the scenario. The mortgage refinancing rate is needed to determine the cash flow because it represents the opportunity cost the mortgagor is facing at that time.

If the refinancing rates are high relative to the mortgagor's original coupon rate (i.e., the rate on the mortgagor's loan), the mortgagor will have less incentive to refinance, or even a positive disincentive (i.e., the homeowner will avoid moving in order to avoid refinancing). If the refinancing rate is low relative to the mortgagor's original coupon rate, the mortgagor has an incentive to refinance.

Prepayments (voluntary and involuntary) are projected by feeding the refinancing rate and loan characteristics, such as age, into a prepayment model. Given the projected prepayments, the cash flow along an interest rate path can be determined.

To make this more concrete, consider a newly issued mortgage passthrough security with a maturity of 360 months. Exhibit 1 shows N simulated interest rate path scenarios. Each scenario consists of a path of 360 simulated 1-month future interest rates. Just how many paths should be generated is explained later. Exhibit 2 shows the paths of simulated mortgage refinancing rates corresponding to the scenarios shown in Exhibit 1. Assuming these mortgage refinancing rates, the cash flow for each scenario path is shown in Exhibit 3.

Calculating the Present Value for a Scenario Interest Rate Path

Given the cash flow on an interest rate path, its present value can be calculated. The discount rate for determining the present value is the simulated spot rate for each month on the interest rate path plus an appropriate spread. The spot rate on a path can be determined from the simulated future monthly rates in Exhibit 1. The relationship that holds between the simulated spot rate for month T on path n and the simulated future 1-month rates is:

$$z_T(n) = \{[1 + f_1(n)][1 + f_2(n)]...[1 + f_T(n)]\}^{1/T} - 1$$

where

$z_T(n)$ = simulated spot rate for month T on path n
$f_j(n)$ = simulated future 1-month rate for month j on path n

Consequently, the interest rate path for the simulated future 1-month rates can be converted to the interest rate path for the simulated monthly spot rates as shown in Exhibit 4.

Exhibit 1: Simulated Paths of 1-Month Future Interest Rates

Month	Interest Rate Path Number						
	1	2	3	...	n	...	N
1	$f_1(1)$	$f_1(2)$	$f_1(3)$	...	$f_1(n)$	...	$f_1(N)$
2	$f_2(1)$	$f_2(2)$	$f_2(3)$	...	$f_2(n)$	...	$f_2(N)$
3	$f_3(1)$	$f_3(2)$	$f_3(3)$	...	$f_3(n)$	...	$f_3(N)$
t	$f_t(1)$	$f_t(2)$	$f_t(3)$	...	$f_t(n)$	...	$f_t(N)$
358	$f_{358}(1)$	$f_{358}(2)$	$f_{358}(3)$	...	$f_{358}(n)$	...	$f_{358}(N)$
359	$f_{359}(1)$	$f_{359}(2)$	$f_{359}(3)$	...	$f_{359}(n)$	...	$f_{359}(N)$
360	$f_{360}(1)$	$f_{360}(2)$	$f_{360}(3)$	...	$f_{360}(n)$	...	$f_{360}(N)$

Notation:
$f_t(n)$ = 1-month future interest rate for month t on path n
N = total number of interest rate paths

Exhibit 2: Simulated Paths of Mortgage Refinancing Rates

Month	Interest Rate Path Number						
	1	2	3	...	n	...	N
1	$r_1(1)$	$r_1(2)$	$r_1(3)$	...	$r_1(n)$	...	$r_1(N)$
2	$r_2(1)$	$r_2(2)$	$r_2(3)$	...	$r_2(n)$	...	$r_2(N)$
3	$r_3(1)$	$r_3(2)$	$r_3(3)$	...	$r_3(n)$	...	$r_3(N)$
t	$r_t(1)$	$r_t(2)$	$r_t(3)$	...	$r_t(n)$	...	$r_t(N)$
358	$r_{358}(1)$	$r_{358}(2)$	$r_{358}(3)$	...	$r_{358}(n)$	...	$r_{358}(N)$
359	$r_{359}(1)$	$r_{359}(2)$	$r_{359}(3)$	...	$r_{359}(n)$	...	$r_{359}(N)$
360	$r_{360}(1)$	$r_{360}(2)$	$r_{360}(3)$	...	$r_{360}(n)$	...	$r_{360}(N)$

Notation:
$r_t(n)$ = mortgage refinancing rate for month t on path n
N = total number of interest rate paths

Exhibit 3: Simulated Cash Flow on Each of the Interest Rate Paths

Month	Interest Rate Path Number						
	1	2	3	...	n	...	N
1	$C_1(1)$	$C_1(2)$	$C_1(3)$	...	$C_1(n)$	...	$C_1(N)$
2	$C_2(1)$	$C_2(2)$	$C_2(3)$	...	$C_2(n)$	...	$C_2(N)$
3	$C_3(1)$	$C_3(2)$	$C_3(3)$	...	$C_3(n)$	...	$C_3(N)$
t	$C_t(1)$	$C_t(2)$	$C_t(3)$	...	$C_t(n)$	...	$C_t(N)$
358	$C_{358}(1)$	$C_{358}(2)$	$C_{358}(3)$	...	$C_{358}(n)$	...	$C_{358}(N)$
359	$C_{359}(1)$	$C_{359}(2)$	$C_{359}(3)$	...	$C_{359}(n)$	...	$C_{359}(N)$
360	$C_{360}(1)$	$C_{360}(2)$	$C_{360}(3)$	...	$C_{360}(n)$	...	$C_{360}(N)$

Notation:

$C_t(n)$ = cash flow for month t on path n

N = total number of interest rate paths

Exhibit 4: Simulated Paths of Monthly Spot Rates

Month	Interest Rate Path Number						
	1	2	3	...	n	...	N
1	$z_1(1)$	$z_1(2)$	$z_1(3)$	...	$z_1(n)$	...	$z_1(N)$
2	$z_2(1)$	$z_2(2)$	$z_2(3)$	...	$z_2(n)$	...	$z_2(N)$
3	$z_3(1)$	$z_3(2)$	$z_3(3)$	...	$z_3(n)$	...	$z_3(N)$
t	$z_t(1)$	$z_t(2)$	$z_t(3)$	...	$z_t(n)$	...	$z_t(N)$
358	$z_{358}(1)$	$z_{358}(2)$	$z_{358}(3)$	...	$z_{358}(n)$	...	$z_{358}(N)$
359	$z_{359}(1)$	$z_{359}(2)$	$z_{359}(3)$	...	$z_{359}(n)$	...	$z_{359}(N)$
360	$z_{360}(1)$	$z_{360}(2)$	$z_{360}(3)$	...	$z_{360}(n)$	...	$z_{360}(N)$

Notation:

$z_t(n)$ = spot rate for month t on path n

N = total number of interest rate paths

Therefore, the present value of the cash flow for month T on interest rate path n discounted at the simulated spot rate for month T plus some spread is:

$$PV[C_T(n)] = \frac{C_T(n)}{[1 + z_T(n) + K]^{1/T}}$$

where

$PV[C_T(n)]$ = present value of cash flow for month T on path n

$C_T(n)$ = cash flow for month T on path n

$z_T(n)$ = spot rate for month T on path n

K = spread

The present value for path n is the sum of the present value of the cash flow for each month on path n. That is,

$$PV[Path(n)] = PV[C_1(n)] + PV[C_2(n)] + ... + PV[C_{360}(n)]$$

where $PV[Path(n)]$ is the present value of interest rate path n.

Determining the Theoretical Value

The present value of a given interest rate path is the theoretical value of a passthrough if that path was actually realized. The theoretical value of the passthrough can be determined by calculating the average of the theoretical values of all the interest rate paths. That is,

$$\text{Theoretical value} = \frac{PV[Path(1)] + PV[Path(2)] + ... + PV[Path(N)]}{N}$$

where N is the number of interest rate paths.

This procedure for valuing a passthrough is also followed for a CMO tranche. The cash flow for each month on each interest rate path is found according to the principal repayment and interest distribution rules of the deal. In order to do this, a model for reverse engineering a CMO deal is needed.

Option-Adjusted Spread

In the Monte Carlo model, the *option-adjusted spread* (OAS) is the spread that when added to all the spot rates on all interest rate paths will make the average present value of the paths equal to the observed market price (plus accrued interest). Mathematically, OAS is the value for K (the spread) that will satisfy the following condition:

$$\frac{PV[Path(1)] + PV[Path(2)] + ... + PV[Path(N)]}{N} = \text{market price}$$

where N is the number of interest rate paths. The left-hand side of the above equation looks identical to that of the equation for the theoretical value. The difference is that the objective is to determine what spread, K, will make the model produce a theoretical value equal to the market price.

The procedure for determining the OAS is straightforward and involves the same search algorithm explained for the zero-volatility spread. The next question, then, is how to interpret the OAS. Basically, the OAS is used to reconcile value with market price. On the right-hand side of the previous equation is the market's statement: the price of a structured product. The average present value over all the paths on the left-hand side of the equation is the model's output, which we refer to as the theoretical value.

Option Cost

The implied cost of the option embedded in any mortgage-backed security can be obtained by calculating the difference between the OAS at the assumed volatility of interest rates and the Z spread. That is,

Option cost = Z spread – OAS

The reason that the option cost is measured in this way is as follows. In an environment of no interest rate changes, the investor would earn the Z spread. When future interest rates are uncertain, the spread is less; however, because of the homeowner's option to prepay, the OAS reflects the spread after adjusting for this option. Therefore, the option cost is the difference between the spread that would be earned in a static interest rate environment (the Z spread) and the spread after adjusting for the homeowner's option.

In general, a tranche's option cost is more stable than its OAS in the face of market movements. This interesting feature is useful in reducing the computationally expensive costs of calculating the OAS as the market moves. For small market moves, the OAS of a tranche may be approximated by recalculating the static spread (which is relatively cheap and easy to calculate) and subtracting its option cost.

Some Technical Issues

In the binomial method for valuing bonds, the interest rate tree is constructed so that it is arbitrage free. That is, if any on-the-run issue is valued, the value produced by the model is equal to the market price. This means that the tree is calibrated to the market. In contrast, in our discussion of the Monte Carlo method, there is no mechanism that will assure that the valuation model will produce a value for an on-the-run Treasury security (the benchmark in the case of agency mortgage-backed securities) equal to the market price. In practice, this is accomplished by adding a *drift term* to the short-term return generating process (Exhibit 1) so that the value produced by the Monte Carlo method for all on-the-run Treasury securities is their market price.[2] A technical explanation of this process is beyond the scope of this chapter.[3]

There is also another adjustment made to the interest rate paths. Restrictions on interest rate movements must be built into the model to prevent interest rates from reaching levels that are believed to be unreasonable (e.g., an interest rate of zero or an interest rate of 30%). This is done by incorporating *mean reversion* into the model. By this it is meant that at some point the interest rate is forced toward some estimated average (mean) value.

The specification of the relationship between short-term rates and refinancing rates is necessary. Empirical evidence on the relationship is also necessary. More specifically, the correlation between the short-term and long-term rates must be estimated.

The number of interest rate paths determines how "good" the estimate is, not relative to the truth, but relative to the valuation model used. The more paths, the

---

[2] This is equivalent to saying that the OAS produced by the model is zero.

[3] For an explanation of how this is done, see Lakhbir S. Hayre and Kenneth Lauterbach, "Stochastic Valuation of Debt Securities," in Frank J. Fabozzi (ed.), *Managing Institutional Assets* (New York: Harper & Row, 1990), pp. 321-364.

more the theoretical value tends to settle down. It is a statistical sampling problem. Most Monte Carlo models employ some form of *variance reduction* to cut down on the number of sample paths necessary to get a good statistical sample. Variance reduction techniques allow us to obtain value estimates within a tick. By this we mean that if the model is used to generate more scenarios, value estimates from the model will not change by more than a tick. So, for example, if 1,024 paths are used to obtain the estimate value for a tranche, there is little more information to be had from the OAS model by generating more than that number of paths. (For some very sensitive CMO tranches, more paths may be needed to estimate value within one tick.)

To reduce computational time, a statistical methodology has been used by vendors that involves the analysis of a small number of interest rate paths. Basically, the methodology is as follows. A large number of paths of interest rates are generated. Using a statistical technique, these paths can be reduced to a small representative number of interest rate paths. These interest rate paths are called *representative paths*. The security is then valued on each representative path. The value of the security is then the weighted average of the representative path values. The weight used for a representative path is determined by the percentage of the interest rate paths it represents. This approach is called the *representative path method*.

For example, suppose that 3,000 interest rate paths are generated and that these paths can be reduced to 10 representative paths. Suppose further that the percentage of the 3,000 interest rate paths for each representative path and the present value for each representative path for some CMO tranche are as follows:

Representative path	Percentage interest rate paths (%)	Present value
1	20	85
2	18	70
3	12	60
4	10	90
5	10	80
6	10	65
7	5	95
8	5	83
9	5	60
10	5	52

The theoretical value of this CMO tranche is 74.8, as shown below:

$$85 (0.20) + 70 (0.18) + 60 (0.12) + 90 (0.10) + 80 (0.10) + 65 (0.10)$$
$$+ 95 (0.05) + 83 (0.05) + 60 (0.05) + 52 (0.05) = 74.8$$

Distribution of Path Present Values

The Monte Carlo method is a commonly used management science tool in business. It is employed when the outcome of a business decision depends on the outcome of several random variables. The product of the simulation is the average value and the probability distribution of the possible outcomes.

Unfortunately, the use of Monte Carlo simulation to value fixed income securities has been limited to just the reporting of the average value, which is referred to as the theoretical value of the security. This means that all of the information about the distribution of the path present values is ignored. Yet, this information is quite valuable.

For example, consider a well protected PAC bond. The distribution of the present value for the paths should be concentrated around the theoretical value. That is, the standard deviation should be small. In contrast, for a support tranche, the distribution of the present value for the paths should be wide, or equivalently, the standard deviation could be large.

Therefore, before using the theoretical value for a mortgage-backed security generated from the Monte Carlo method, a portfolio manager should ask for information about the distribution of the path's present values.

OAS versus the Benchmark

It is important to make sure that OAS is interpreted relative to the benchmark selected. While in our illustrations we have used the on-the-run Treasury rates as the benchmark, many funded investors will use LIBOR as the benchmark. A spot rate curve can be created for LIBOR using bootstrapping.

To see the impact of the benchmark on the computed OAS, the table below shows the OAS computed in November 1999 for a 15-year 6.5% FNMA TBA passthrough (seasoned and unseasoned) and a 30-year 6.5% FNMA TBA using the on-the-run Treasuries and LIBOR:[4]

Issue: 6.5% coupon FNMA TBA	Average life	OAS (bps) benchmark	
		Treasuries	LIBOR
15-year unseasoned	5.9 years	70	−10
15-year seasoned (1994 production)	4.0 years	75	1
30-year	9.5 years	87	−2

As can be seen from the table, the selection of the benchmark has a dramatic impact on the computed OAS. It cannot be overemphasized that the user of an OAS number should make sure that the benchmark is known, as well as the volatility assumption.

Effective Duration

In general, duration measures the price sensitivity of a bond to a small change in interest rates. Duration can be interpreted as the approximate percentage change in price for a 100-basis point parallel shift in the yield curve. For example, if a bond's duration is 4, this means a 100-basis point increase in interest rates will result in a price decrease of approximately 4%. A 50-basis point increase in yields will decrease the price by approximately 2%. The smaller the change in basis points, the better the approximated change in price will be.

---

[4] The table is reported in the November 16, 1999 issue of PaineWebber's *Mortgage Strategist*, p. 10. The values reported were computed on Bloomberg.

The duration for any security can be approximated as follows:

$$\text{Duration} = \frac{P_- - P_+}{2P_0 \Delta y}$$

where

P_- = price if yield is decreased (per \$100 of par value) by Δy
P_+ = price if yield is increased (per \$100 of par value) by Δy
P_0 = initial price (per \$100 of par value)
Δy = number of basis points change used to calculate P_- and P_+

The standard measure of duration is *modified duration*. The limitation of modified duration is that it assumes that if interest rates change, the cash flow does not change. While modified duration is fine for option-free securities such as Treasury bonds, it is inappropriate for mortgage-backed securities because projected cash flows change as interest rates and prepayments change. When prices in the duration formula are calculated assuming that the cash flow changes when interest rates change, the resulting duration is called *effective duration*.

Effective duration can be computed using an OAS model as follows. First the bond's OAS is found using the current term structure of interest rates. Next the bond is repriced holding OAS constant, but shifting the term structure. Two shifts are used; in one yields are increased, and in the second they are decreased. This produces the two prices, P_- and P_+, used in the above formula. Effective duration calculated in this way is often referred to as *option-adjusted duration* or *OAS duration*.

The assumption in using modified or effective duration to project the percentage price change is that all interest rates change by the same number of basis points; that is, there is a parallel shift in the yield curve. If the term structure does not change by a parallel shift, then effective duration will not correctly predict the change in a bond's price.

Effective Convexity

The convexity measure of a security is the approximate change in price that is not explained by duration. *Positive convexity* means that if yields change by a given number of basis points, the percentage increase in price will be greater than the percentage decrease in price. *Negative convexity* means that if yield changes by a given number of basis points, the percentage increase in price will be less than the percentage decrease in price. That is, for a 100-basis point change in yield:

Type of Convexity	Increase in Price	Decrease in Price
Positive convexity	X%	less than X%
Negative convexity	X%	more than X%

Obviously, positive convexity is a desirable property of a bond. A pass-through security can exhibit either positive or negative convexity, depending on the prevailing mortgage rate relative to the rate on the underlying mortgage loans.

When the prevailing mortgage rate is much higher than the mortgage rate on the underlying mortgage loans, the passthrough usually exhibits positive convexity. It usually exhibits negative convexity when the underlying coupon rate is near or above prevailing mortgage refinancing rates.

The convexity of any bond can be approximated using the formula:

$$\frac{P_+ + P_- - 2(P_0)}{2P_0(\Delta y)^2}$$

When the prices used in this formula assume that the cash flows do not change when yields change, the resulting convexity is a good approximation of the standard convexity for an option-free bond. When the prices used in the formula are derived by changing the cash flows (by changing prepayment rates) when yields change, the resulting convexity is called *effective convexity*. Once again, when an OAS model is used to obtain the prices, the resulting value is referred to as the *option-adjusted convexity* or *OAS convexity*.

ILLUSTRATIONS

We will use several deals to show how real estate backed structured products can be analyzed using the Monte Carlo model/OAS procedure discussed above.[5]

Simple CMO Structure

The simple structure analyzed is Freddie Mac (FHLMC) 1915. It is a simple sequential-pay CMO bond structure. The structure includes eight tranches, A, B, C, D, E, F, G, and S. The focus of our analysis is on tranches A, B, and C. All three tranches were priced at a premium.

The top panel of Exhibit 5 shows the OAS, option cost, and effective duration[6] for the collateral and the three tranches in the CMO structure. Tranche A had the smallest effective duration and tranche C had the largest effective duration. The OAS for the collateral is 51 basis points. Since the option cost is 67 basis points, the zero-volatility spread is 118 basis points (51 basis points plus 67 basis points).

At the time this analysis was performed, March 10, 1998, the Treasury yield curve was not steep. When the yield curve is relatively flat the zero-volatility spread will not differ significantly from the nominal spread. Thus, for the three tranches shown in Exhibit 5, the zero-volatility spread is 83 basis points for A, 115 basis points for B, and 116 basis points for C.

---

[5] These illustrations are from Frank J. Fabozzi, Scott F. Richard, and David S. Horowitz, "Valuation of CMOs," Chapter 6 in Frank J. Fabozzi (ed.), *Advances in the Valuation and Management of Mortgage-Backed Securities* (New Hope, PA: Frank J. Fabozzi Associates, 1998).

[6] We will explain how to compute the effective duration using the Monte Carlo model later in this chapter.

Exhibit 5: OAS Analysis of FHLMC 1915 Classes A, B, and C
(As of 3/10/98)

All three tranches were trading at a premium as of the date of the analysis.

Base Case (Assumes 13% Interest Rate Volatility

	OAS (in basis points)	Option Cost (in basis points)	Z-Spread (in basis points)	Effective Duration (in years)
Collateral	51	67	118	1.2
Tranche				
A	32	51	83	0.9
B	33	82	115	2.9
C	46	70	116	6.7

Prepayments at 80% and 120% of Prepayment Model
(Assumes 13% Interest Rate Volatility)

	New OAS (in basis points)		Change in Price per $100 par (holding OAS constant)	
	80%	120%	80%	120%
Collateral	63	40	$0.45	−$0.32
Tranche				
A	40	23	0.17	−0.13
B	43	22	0.54	−0.43
C	58	36	0.97	−0.63

Interest Rate Volatility of 9% and 17%

	New OAS (in basis points)		Change in Price per $100 par (holding OAS constant)	
	9%	17%	9%	17%
Collateral	79	21	$1.03	−$0.94
Tranche				
A	52	10	0.37	−0.37
B	66	−3	1.63	−1.50
C	77	15	2.44	−2.08

Notice that the tranches did not share the OAS equally. The same is true for the option cost. Both the Z-spread and the option cost increase as the effective duration increases. Whether or not any of these tranches were attractive investments requires a comparison to other tranches in the market with the same effective duration. While not presented here, all three tranches offered an OAS similar to other sequential-pay tranches with the same effective duration available in the market. On a relative basis (i.e., relative to the other tranches analyzed in the deal), the only tranche where there appears to be a bit of a bargain is tranche C. A portfolio manager contemplating the purchase of this last cash flow tranche can see that C offers a higher OAS than B and appears to bear less of the risk (i.e., has lower option cost), as measured by the option cost. The problem portfolio managers may face is that they might not be able to go out as long on the yield curve as tranche C because of effective duration, maturity, and average life constraints relative to their liabilities, for example.

Now let's look at modeling risk. Examination of the sensitivity of the tranches to changes in prepayments and interest rate volatility will help us to understand the interaction of the tranches in the structure and who is bearing the risk. How the deal behaves under various scenarios should reinforce and be consistent with the valuation (i.e., a tranche may look "cheap" for a reason).

We begin with prepayments. Specifically, we keep the same interest rate paths as those used to get the OAS in the base case (the top panel of Exhibit 5), but reduce the prepayment rate on each interest rate path to 80% of the projected rate. As can be seen in the second panel of Exhibit 5, slowing down prepayments increases the OAS and price for the collateral. The exhibit reports two results of the sensitivity analysis. First, it indicates the change in the OAS. Second, it indicates the change in the price, holding the OAS constant as in the base case.

To see how a portfolio manager can use the information in the second panel, consider tranche A. At 80% of the prepayment speed, the OAS for this tranche increases from 32 basis points to 40 basis points. If the OAS is held constant, the panel indicates that the buyer of tranche A would gain $0.17 per $100 par value.

Notice that for all of the tranches reported in Exhibit 5 there is a gain from a slowdown in prepayments. This is because all of the sequential tranches in this deal are priced over par. (An investor in a tranche priced at a premium benefits from a slowdown in prepayments because the investor receives the higher coupon for a longer period and postpones the capital loss from a prepayment.) Also notice that while the changes in OAS are about the same for the different tranches, the changes in price are quite different. This arises because the shorter tranches have less duration. Therefore, their prices do not move as much from a change in OAS as a longer average life tranche. A portfolio manager who is willing to go to the long end of the yield curve, such as tranche C, would realize the most benefit from the slowdown in prepayments.

Also shown in the second panel of the exhibit is the second part of our experiment to test the sensitivity of prepayments: the prepayment rate is assumed to be 120% of the base case. The collateral loses money in this scenario because it is trading above par. This is reflected in the OAS of the collateral which declines from 51 basis points to 40 basis points. Now look at the three tranches. They all lost money because the tranches were all at a premium and accelerating prepayments adversely affects the tranche.

Before looking at the last panel, which shows the effect of a change in interest rate volatility on the OAS, let's review the relationship between expected interest rate volatility and the value of a mortgage-backed security. Recall that the investor in a mortgage-backed security has sold an option to homeowners (borrowers). Thus, the investor is short an option. The value of an option depends on expected interest rate volatility. When expected interest rate volatility decreases, the value of the option embedded in a mortgage-backed security decreases and therefore the value of a mortgage-backed security increases. The opposite is true when expected interest rate volatility increases — the value of the embedded option increases and the value of a mortgage-backed security decreases.

Now let's look at the sensitivity to the interest rate volatility assumption, 13% in the base case. Two experiments are performed: reducing the volatility assumption to 9% and increasing it to 17%. These results are reported in the third panel of Exhibit 5.

Reducing the volatility to 9% increases the dollar price of the collateral by $1.03 and increases the OAS from 51 basis points in the base case to 79 basis points. However, this $1.03 increase in the price of the collateral is not equally distributed among the three tranches. Most of the increase in value is realized by the longer tranches. The OAS gain for each of the tranches follows more or less the effective durations of those tranches. This makes sense because the longer the duration, the greater the risk, and when volatility declines, the reward is greater for the accepted risk. At the higher level of assumed interest rate volatility of 17%, the collateral is severely affected. The longer the duration, the greater the loss. These results for a decrease and an increase in interest rate volatility are consistent with what we explained earlier.

Using the Monte Carlo simulation/OAS analysis, a fair conclusion that can be made about this simple structure is: what you see is what you get. The only surprise in this structure is the lower option cost in tranche C. In general, however, a portfolio manager willing to extend duration gets paid for that risk in this structure.

PAC/Support Tranche Structure

Now let's look at how to apply the methodology to a more complicated CMO structure, FHLMC Series 1706. The collateral (i.e., pool of passthroughs) for this structure is Freddie Mac 7s (7% coupon rate). A partial summary of the deal is provided in Exhibit 6. That is, only the tranches we will be discussing in this section are shown in the exhibit.

While this deal looks complicated, it is relatively simple compared to many deals that have been issued. Nonetheless, it brings out all the key points about application of OAS analysis, specifically, the fact that most deals include cheap bonds, expensive bonds, and fairly priced bonds. The OAS analysis helps identify how a tranche should be classified. A more proper analysis would compare the OAS for each tranche to a similar duration tranche available in the market.

At issuance, there were 10 PAC tranches, three scheduled tranches, a floating-rate support tranche, and an inverse floating-rate support tranche. Recall that the "scheduled tranches" are support tranches with a schedule, also referred to in Chapter 4 as "PAC II tranches."

The first two PAC tranches in the deal, tranche A and tranche B, were paid off at the time of the analysis. The other PAC tranches were still available at the time of the analysis. The prepayment protection for the PAC tranches is provided by the support tranches. The support tranches in this deal that are shown in Exhibit 6 are tranches LA, LB, and M. There were other support tranches not shown in Exhibit 6. LA is the shortest average life support tranche (a scheduled (SCH) bond).

Exhibit 6: Summary of Federal Home Loan Mortgage Corporation — Multiclass Mortgage Participation Certificates (Guaranteed), Series 1706

Total Issue: $300,000,000   Issue Date: 2/18/94

Tranche	Original Balance ($)	Coupon (%)	Stated Maturity	Original Issue Pricing (225% PSA Assumed)	
				Average Life (yrs)	Expected Maturity
PAC Tranches					
C (PAC Bond)	25,500,000	5.25	4/15/14	3.5	6/15/98
D (PAC Bond)	9,150,000	5.65	8/15/15	4.5	1/15/99
E (PAC Bond)	31,650,000	6.00	1/15/19	5.8	1/15/01
G (PAC Bond)	30,750,000	6.25	8/15/21	7.9	5/15/03
H (PAC Bond)	27,450,000	6.50	6/15/23	10.9	10/15/07
J (PAC Bond)	5,220,000	6.50	10/15/23	14.4	9/15/09
K (PAC Bond)	7,612,000	7.00	3/15/24	18.8	5/15/19
Support Tranches					
LA (SCH Bond)	26,673,000	7.00	11/15/21	3.5	3/15/02
LB (SCH Bond)	36,087,000	7.00	6/15/23	3.5	9/15/02
M (SCH Bond)	18,738,000	7.00	3/15/24	11.2	10/15/08

The collateral for this deal was trading at a premium. That is, the home-owners (borrowers) were paying a higher mortgage rate than available in the market at the time of the analysis. This meant that the value of the collateral would increase if prepayments slow down, but would decrease if prepayments increase. What is important to note, however, is that a tranche could be trading at a discount, par, or premium even though the collateral is priced at a premium. For example, PAC C had a low coupon rate at the time of the analysis and therefore was trading at a discount. Thus, while the collateral (which was selling at a premium) loses value from an increase in prepayments, a discount tranche such as tranche C would increase in value if prepayments increase. (Recall that in the simple structure analyzed earlier, the collateral and all the tranches were trading at a premium.)

The top panel of Exhibit 7 shows the base case OAS, the option cost, and the effective duration for the collateral and tranches in Exhibit 6. The collateral OAS is 60 basis points, and the option cost is 44 basis points. The Z-spread of the collateral to the Treasury spot curve is 104 basis points.

The 60 basis points of OAS did not get equally distributed among the tranches — as was the case with the simple structure analyzed earlier. Tranche LB, the scheduled support, did not realize a good OAS allocation, only 29 basis points, and had an extremely high option cost. Given the prepayment uncertainty associated with this tranche, its OAS would be expected to be higher. The reason for the low OAS is that this tranche was priced so that its cash flow yield is high. Using the Z-spread as a proxy for the nominal spread (i.e., spread over the Treasury yield curve), the 103 basis point spread for tranche LB is high given that this appears to be a short average life tranche. Consequently, "yield buyers" (i.e., investors with a preference for high nominal yield, who may not be attentive to compensation for prepayment risk) probably bid aggressively for this tranche and thereby drove down its OAS, trading off "yield" for OAS. From a total return perspective, however, tranche LB should be avoided. It is a rich, or expensive, tranche. The other support tranche analyzed, tranche M, had an OAS of 72 basis points and at the time of this analysis was similar to that offered on comparable duration tranches available in the market.

Exhibit 7: OAS Analysis of FHLMC 1706 (As of 3/10/98)
Base Case (Assumes 13% Interest Rate Volatility)

	OAS (in basis points)	Option Cost (in basis points)	Z-Spread (in basis points)	Effective Duration (in years)
Collateral	60	44	104	2.6
PAC Tranches				
C (PAC)	15	0	15	0.2
D (PAC)	16	4	20	0.6
E (PAC)	26	4	30	1.7
G (PAC)	42	8	50	3.3
H (PAC)	50	12	62	4.9
J (PAC)	56	14	70	6.8
K (PAC)	57	11	68	8.6
Support Tranches				
LA (SCH)	39	12	51	1.4
LB (SCH)	29	74	103	1.2
M (SCH)	72	53	125	4.9

Prepayments at 80% and 120% of Prepayment Model
(Assumes 13% Interest Rate Volatility)

	Base Case OAS	New OAS (in basis points)		Change in Price per $100 par (holding OAS constant)	
	OAS	80%	120%	80%	120%
Collateral	60	63	57	$0.17	−$0.11
PAC Tranches					
C (PAC)	15	15	15	0.00	0.00
D (PAC)	16	16	16	0.00	0.00
E (PAC)	26	27	26	0.01	−0.01
G (PAC)	42	44	40	0.08	−0.08
H (PAC)	50	55	44	0.29	−0.27
J (PAC)	56	63	50	0.50	−0.47
K (PAC)	57	65	49	0.77	−0.76
Support Tranches					
LA (SCH)	39	31	39	−0.12	0.00
LB (SCH)	29	39	18	0.38	−0.19
M (SCH)	72	71	76	−0.07	0.18

Exhibit 7 (Continued)
Interest Rate Volatility of 9% and 17%

	Base Case OAS	New OAS (in basis points)		Change in Price per $100 par (holding OAS constant)	
		9%	17%	9%	17%
Collateral	60	81	35	$0.96	−$0.94
PAC Tranches					
C (PAC)	15	15	15	0.00	0.00
D (PAC)	16	16	16	0.00	0.00
E (PAC)	26	27	24	0.02	−0.04
G (PAC)	42	48	34	0.21	−0.27
H (PAC)	50	58	35	0.48	−0.72
J (PAC)	56	66	41	0.70	−1.05
K (PAC)	57	66	44	0.82	−1.19
Support Tranches					
LA (SCH)	39	47	24	0.09	−0.18
LB (SCH)	29	58	−4	0.80	−0.82
M (SCH)	72	100	41	1.80	−1.72

The analysis reported in the top panel of Exhibit 7 helps us identify where the cheap tranches are in the deal. The long average life and effective duration tranches in the deal are the PAC tranches G, H, J, and K. These tranches have high OAS relative to the other tranches and low option cost. They appear to be the cheap tranches in the deal. These PAC tranches had well protected cash flows and exhibited positive convexity (i.e., these tranches lose less in an adverse scenario than they gain in a positive scenario).

The next two panels in Exhibit 7 show the sensitivity of the OAS and the price (holding OAS constant at the base case) to changes in the prepayment speed (80% and 120% of the base case) and in volatility (9% and 17%). This analysis shows that the change in the prepayment speed does not affect the collateral significantly, while the change in the OAS (holding the price constant) and price (holding OAS constant) for each tranche can be significant.

Tranches C and D at the time of the analysis were priced at a discount with short average lives. The OAS and price of these two tranches were not affected by a slowing down or a speeding up of the prepayment model. Tranche H was a premium tranche with a medium-term average life at the time of the analysis. Because tranche H was trading at a premium, it benefits from a slowing in prepayments, as the bondholder will receive the coupon for a longer time. Faster prepayments represent an adverse scenario. The PAC tranches are quite well-protected. The longer average life PACs will actually benefit from a reduced prepayment rate because they will be earning the higher coupon interest longer. So, on an OAS basis, the earlier conclusion that the long PACs were allocated a good part of the deal's value holds up under our first stress test (i.e., changing prepayments).

The sensitivity of the collateral and the tranches to changes in volatility are shown in the third panel of Exhibit 7. A lower volatility increases the value of the collateral, while a higher volatility reduces its value. The long average life PACs continue to be fairly well-protected, whether the volatility is lower or higher. In the two volatility scenarios they continue to get a good OAS on a relative value basis, although not as good as in the base case if volatility is higher (but the OAS still looks like a reasonable value in this scenario). This reinforces the earlier conclusion concerning the investment merit of the long PACs in this deal. Note, however, that PAC tranches H, J, and K are more sensitive to the volatility assumption than tranches C, D, E, and G and therefore the investor is accepting greater volatility risk (i.e., the risk that volatility will change) with tranches H, J, and K relative to tranches C, D, E, and G.

Comparing Products[7]

We will apply the Monte Carlo/OAS analysis to a home equity loan ABS, a manufactured housing ABS, agency passthrough securities, and an agency CMO. Exhibits 8, 9, 10, and 11 provide information about these deals. The analysis was performed on April 14, 2000. Market implied volatility is assumed.

Exhibit 8 shows the information for the home equity loan ABS — the Residential Asset Securities Corp. (RASC) issued in February 2000. The deal has six tranches. The weighted average life of the tranches is 3.2 years and the average option cost is 24 basis points per tranche.

Exhibit 9 shows the information for the Vanderbilt Mortgage and Finance manufactured housing loan deal issued in February 2000. The deal has six tranches with a weighted average life of 6.7 years. The average option cost is 18 basis points per tranche. Notice that the average option cost is lower than in the home equity loan deal. Also note that comparable tranches have lower option costs and a lower standard deviation for the average life in the manufactured housing deal versus the home equity loan deal as shown below:

	Option cost		Average life std. dev.	
Average life	HEL	MH	HEL	MH
3-years	38	27	0.98	0.73
5-years	48	18	2.35	2.18

Information for several agency passthrough securities — Fannie Mae passthroughs with coupon rates from 6% to 8% — is shown in Exhibit 10. Notice from Exhibits 8, 9, and 10 that agency passthrough securities have higher option costs than the weighted average option costs of both the home equity loan deals and manufactured housing deals. Alternatively stated, there is more prepayment volatility in agency passthrough securities. The most relevant passthrough for

---

[7] These illustrations are adapted from Frank J. Fabozzi, Shrikant Ramamurthy, and Laurent Gauthier, "Analysis of ABS," Chapter 28 in Frank J. Fabozzi (ed.), *Investing in Asset-Backed Securities* (New Hope, PA: Frank J. Fabozzi Associates, 2000).

comparison purposes would be the 8% coupon given that the price on this coupon security is comparable to both the home equity loan and manufactured housing loan structures that are presented — they are all slightly above par. The Fannie Mae 8% coupon passthrough has an option cost of 70 basis points versus 24 basis points on the home equity loan deal and 18 basis points on the manufactured housing loan deal.

The CMO deal analyzed is a Fannie Mae deal issued in January 2000 backed by 7% collateral. Information about the deal is presented in Exhibit 11. The weighted average option costs on the collateral as well as option costs on individual tranches are higher in the CMO deal than for the home equity loan deal and the manufactured housing loan deal.

The values of the options embedded in the bonds shown in Exhibits 8, 9, 10, and 11 are mainly driven by two factors: the sensitivity of prepayments to interest rates and the maturity of these options. On one extreme, manufactured housing prepayments are typically insensitive to interest rates, while agency mortgage borrowers are much more able to benefit from refinancing opportunities. Home equity loan borrowers — first-lien mortgages for sub-prime borrowers — are less able to profit from decreasing interest rates to refinance their loans.

The maturity of the loans is important since the longer borrowers possess the option to prepay a loan, the more chances the option has to be exercised. In addition, depending on the seasoning of the underlying loans, prepayments may be more or less interest rate sensitive; after some time, borrowers are more able to refinance. Finally, very seasoned loans exhibit prepayment burnout: the most savvy borrowers have already refinanced if the opportunity presented itself, and the remaining ones are less inclined to do so.

In a structured transaction, depending on the sequencing of cash flows, the value of the option can vary. The very short tranches have low optionality given no seasoning. The highest optionality is on the 3- and 5-year structures where borrowers are at the top of the prepayment ramp and the collateral is slightly seasoned. The longest tranches have low optionality because of prepayment burnout.

Exhibit 8: Analysis of Home-Equity Loan

Issuer	Residential Asset Securities Corp. (RASC)	Prepay. Assumption*	25 HEP
Deal Date	February 2000	Credit Support	Wrapped by AMBAC
Type	HEL REMIC	Volatility Assumption	Market implied

Class	Size ($ mm)	Type	Coupon (%)	Maturity	Avg. Life	Price	Yield (%)	Spread to WAL (bps)	Zero-vol Spd (bps)	OAS** (bps)	Option Cost*** (bps)	Eff. Dur	Eff. Conv	St. Dev. of Avg. Life
A1	220	AAA Seq	7.615	1/15	0.9	100-11	6.585	40****	50	45	5	0.9	-0.3	0.10
A2	100	AAA Seq	7.700	6/21	2.0	100-00	7.525	110	113	93	20	2.1	-0.5	0.45
A3	105	AAA Seq	7.735	11/25	3.1	100-04	7.612	122	130	92	38	3.2	-0.7	0.98
A4	105	AAA Seq	8.040	11/28	5.1	100-16	7.915	163	175	127	48	4.7	-0.6	2.35
A5	55	AAA Seq	8.195	1/31	7.9	100-20	8.126	200	212	176	36	6.3	0.6	2.63
A6	65	AAA NAS	7.905	1/31	6.2	100-24	7.763	155	162	144	18	4.9	0.3	0.74
Weighted avg.			7.794		3.2	100.34	7.358				24	3.0		

Analysis as of 4/4/00

* Yields and spreads are computed relative to a constant prepayment assumption.

** OASs and durations are calculated by a Monte Carlo simulation of rates which utilizes Prudential Securities Inc.'s home equity loan prepayment model.

*** Option cost is defined as the difference between the OAS at market volatility and at zero volatility.

**** The spread to WAL for this class is lower than the OAS because the spread and OAS are computed at different prepayment speeds. The spread is computed at a constant prepayment speed assumption, while the OAS is computed assuming that prepayment speeds vary by time and interest-rate scenario.

Exhibit 9: Analysis of Manufactured Housing

Issuer	Vanderbilt Mortgage and Finance	
Deal Date	February 2000	
Type	MH REMIC	

Prepay. Assumption*	250 MHP	
Credit Support	Senior/sub structure	
Volatility Assumption	Market implied	

Class	Size ($ mm)	Type	Coupon (%)	Maturity	Avg. Life	Price	Yield (%)	Spread to WAL (bps)	Zero-vol Spd. (bps)	OAS** (bps)	Option Cost*** (bps)	Eff. Dur.	Eff. Conv.	St. Dev. of Avg. Life
A2	33.0	AAA Seq	7.580	8/12	3.0	100-16	7.434	103	105	78	27	2.4	-0.3	0.73
A3	32.0	AAA Seq	7.820	11/17	5.1	101-00	7.639	133	145	127	18	3.8	-0.2	2.18
A4	27.2	AAA Seq	7.955	12/24	9.2	101-20	7.877	169	190	175	15	5.8	-0.2	3.76
A5	9.1	AA Seq	8.195	11/32	12.0	102-12	7.989	200	220	212	8	7.9	0.2	3.18
M1	7.3	A Seq	8.635	11/32	8.7	101-16	8.502	240	254	239	15	6.3	0.3	1.53
B1	7.3	BBB Seq	9.250	9/15	6.1	100-09	9.330	310	314	292	22	4.7	0.0	0.54
B2	12.8	BBB Seq	9.250	11/32	10.2	99-02+	9.536	355	363	353	10	6.9	0.4	2.12
Weighted avg.			8.083		6.7	100.90	7.995				18	4.6		

Analysis as of 4/4/00

* Yields and spreads are computed relative to a constant prepayment assumption.

** OASs and durations are calculated by a Monte Carlo simulation of rates which utilizes Prudential Securities Inc.'s manufactured housing prepayment model.

*** Option cost is defined as the difference between the OAS at market volatility and at zero volatility.

Exhibit 10: Analysis of Agency Fixed-Rate MBS

Issuer Fannie Mae Volatility Assumption Market implied

Class	Coupon (%)	Maturity	Avg. Life	Price	Yield (%)	Spread to WAL (bps)	Zero-vol Spd (bps)	OAS* (bps)	Option Cost** (bps)	Eff. Dur.	Eff. Conv.
FNMA	6%	30-year	9.4	91-30	7.40	151	155	125	30	6.0	0.1
FNMA	6.5%	30-year	9.2	94-18	7.46	156	162	122	40	5.6	-0.1
FNMA	7%	30-year	8.7	96-27	7.59	166	174	122	52	5.1	-0.4
FNMA	7.5%	30-year	7.8	98-29	7.74	177	185	122	63	4.6	-0.8
FNMA	8%	30-year	6.7	100-23	7.86	183	194	124	70	3.9	-1.5

Analysis as of 4/4/00

* OASs and durations are calculated by a Monte Carlo simulation of rates which utilizes Prudential Securities Inc.'s Agency prepayment model.

** Option cost is defined as the difference between the OAS at market volatility and at zero volatility.

Exhibit 11: Analysis of Agency CMO

Issuer FNMA Type Agency REMIC Volatility Assumption Market implied

Deal Date January 2000 Prepay. Assumption* 153 PSA

Class	Size ($ mm)	Type	Coupon (%)	Maturity	Avg. Life	Price	Yield (%)	Spread to WAL (bps)	Zero-vol Spd (bps)	OAS** (bps)	Option Cost*** (bps)	Eff. Dur.	Eff. Conv.	St. Dev. of Avg. Life
A	82.5	Seq	7%	4/28	5.6	98-02	7.50	135	148	98	50	3.8	-0.6	1.70
B	65.5	Seq	7%	1/26	3.9	98-20	7.43	120	130	84	46	3.0	-0.6	1.14
C	10.1	Seq	7%	5/27	10.5	96-01	7.64	175	178	122	56	6.2	-0.4	3.57
D	6.8	Seq	7%	4/28	13.1	95-04	7.67	180	193	137	56	7.3	0.1	4.31
VA	12.5	AD Seq	7%	8/10	5.8	99-04	7.23	110	118	107	11	4.0	0.1	0.48
VB	10.9	AD Seq	7%	12/15	13.0	96-22	7.47	160	173	139	34	7.1	0.8	2.40
Z	11.6	Z-Seq	7%	2/30	19.7	89-24	7.69	185	216	168	48	17.7	7.3	4.01
Weighted avg life:					6.8					Weighted avg OC	43			

Analysis as of 4/4/00

* Yields and spreads are computed relative to a constant prepayment assumption.

** OASs and durations are calculated by a Monte Carlo simulation of rates which utilizes Prudential Securities Inc.'s Agency prepayment model.

*** Option cost is defined as the difference between the OAS at market volatility and at zero volatility.

Index

CPSIA information can be obtained
at www.ICGtesting.com
Printed in the USA
LVHW080252201220
674650LV00003B/11

9 781883 249960